DISCOVERY WALKS IN THE YORKSHIRE DALES

The Southern Dales

David Johnson

Published by Sigma Leisure – an imprint of
Sigma Press, 1 South Oak Lane, Wilmslow, Cheshire SK9 6AR, England.

British Library Cataloguing in Publication Data
A CIP record for this book is available from the British Library.

ISBN: 1-85058-468-0

Typesetting and Design by: Sigma Press, Wilmslow, Cheshire.

Cover design: The Agency, Wilmslow, Cheshire

Maps: Perrott Cartographics

Photographs and illustrations: The author, except where indicated

Printed by: MFP Design & Print

Preface

There can be few in this country today who would not be able to respond positively to a brainstorming session on the Yorkshire Dales. Yet, a mere ten years ago, on an enforced if temporary sojourn in southernmost Britain, I never ceased to be floored by what seemed to me a cataclysmic ignorance of the Dales. Mention of Yorkshire seemed to invoke only images of mills, coal mines, obdurate cricketers and perhaps, to Monty Python fans, the Third World. The hardened walking fraternity knew of the Three Peaks but could name few other fells or tops. Beyond that the Dales were usually confused with the North York Moors.

Not so these days. The success of the James Herriot stories, particularly in the form of visual images of the Dales, has firmly disposed of any lingering nescience among distant folk. As a response visitor numbers have soared over the last decade, the tourist infrastructure has mushroomed, the management of the countryside has seen itself transformed from a delightfully amateurish and enthusiastic corpus of individuals into a corporate entity, a necessary and benevolent Hydra.

An equal level of prodigiousness can be observed on the shelves of bookshops which bear the legend "Local Interest" or "Local Guidebooks". The writing of guides for the ambulant or motorised visitor has surely been one of the growth industries of our recession-bound times. A dazzling array of turn-left-past-the-second-holly-bush guides are available to tempt those whose passion is hours tramping across the fells and moors, or indeed for those who do not like to be separated too long from their mobile, metal cocoons.

There are the glossy coffee table editions on the next shelf: collections of evocative photographs of landscape, life and work ... and in there, too, are the more academic or, let's say, "serious" books on the Dales. What you will struggle to find, however, are books that marry the varying approaches. While a book like the one you are holding now can obviously never aim to be glossy, it can attempt to weld together the route finding narrative and the serious background detail.

I have been in the fortunate position of leading walking groups in the Dales, and beyond, for a good many years. Some have consisted of independent visitors to the National Park who have chosen to join a day's guided walk in the company of like-minded people, while others have been aimed at the more committed holiday makers who have opted for a week-long, structured walking-based course. Many have centred around the use of ancient paths and tracks as a means of delving into the landscape, contemporary as well as past. The primary aim of each of those walks has been to

discover as much as possible about the individual areas, to turn the land-scape inside out, to dig deep in a search for its inner secrets and charms.
Indeed, you could say they have been a kind of search by "those who like to travel intelligently" for the Holy Grail of trying to unearth "the reason behind what they are looking at", to use the words of that immortal and pioneering landscape historian, W.G.Hoskins, back in 1955.
Many have been the occasions when someone asked if I had ever thought of putting it all down on paper. The answer until now has always been "No, but maybe one day I might". Hence this book, and the companion volume on the Northern Dales, which invite you to embark on a series of journeys to discover the essence of the Dales. It may seem an arbitrary decision where to draw the line: where do the southern valleys become the northern valleys? For this book I have grouped together most of the dales whose rivers eventually work their way southwards before turning their backs on the fells to head east to the Humber or west to Morecambe Bay or the Irish Sea. Excluded from this volume are the valleys with rivers that choose to go east beyond the Pennine range before also turning inexorably southwards to the North Sea. For walks in this area you will have to wait for the companion volume. Each and every dale has its own individuality and charm, but the southern dales as a whole have a different character from their northern neighbours.

A BIG THANK-YOU TO ...

Inevitably, in compiling a book such as this, the efforts and inspirations of others have played a major part. It is, perhaps, invidious to single out certain people but I would like to record my heartfelt thanks to those who have been firm and true companions in wandering through time and space: Jean and her late husband Kurt, to whose memory I dedicate this collection, to David and Beryl, and to Pauline.
I am indebted to Judith Allinson for reading through the walks and the content, and for making invaluable comments. The book is certainly better for her efforts, though any errors of fact or interpretation remain mine.
I should also like to thank Karen Holmes for so efficiently and uncom-plainingly translating my illegible scrawl into typescript.
Thanks too, to Robin for his cartoon impression of you; and to the Access section of the National Park for checking the route maps to ensure I have not sent you astray.
For permission to reproduce illustrations I acknowledge and thank the following, who retain copyright of the originals: Dalesman Publishing Co. Ltd. for the geological sketch through Crummackdale; the Field Studies Council for the plan of the Prior Rakes sheephouse, the geological map and section of the Malham area, and the map of drumlin distribution; Dr John Varker, the Yorkshire Geological Society and the Ellenbank Press for the geological map and section of the Skyreholme area.

David Johnson

Contents

Introduction

Discovery Walk 1

Discovery Walk 2

Introduction

In this and the companion volume there are 24 Discovery Walks. My primary aim has been to make a selection that will whet your appetite for the whole of the Dales and, given that there are about two dozen different dales and numerous intervening ridges and fells, it would be impossible to do more than give a flavour. My hope is that this list of routes – a kind of dipping into the bran tub selection process – will stimulate you to make up your own walks in the areas I have omitted. You will notice I have excluded certain areas altogether: I am not taking you to the overcrowded honeypots of Malham, Ingleton or Bolton Abbey, nor am I sending you to join the pilgrim hordes on an ascent of the over-popular Three Peaks. It is, of course, impossible to avoid the masses all the time but these walks will give you, at times more or less, seclusion and an escape from the milling throng.

There is a common theme running through the book. You will largely be following ancient paths and tracks, utilising them as a means of under-standing and appreciating the landscape in depth as well as breadth, so the emphasis in the following chapters is on background detail and interpreta-tion. I am quite sure you already know that there is immense pleasure to be gained from making sense of what you can see around you.

There is another common element: flexibility. Most chapters have a basic walk but also offer you the option of extending or shortening the distance to fit in with your needs.

Distances . . . and other details

Walk	Location	Distance
1.	Ribblesdale	8.5 to 11.5km (5.3 to 7.2 miles)
2.	Austwick and Crummackdale	7 to 9.5km; (4.5 to 6 miles)
3.	Malham Tarn area	9km (5.6 miles)
4.	The Monk's Road, Arncliffe	8km (5 miles
5.	Bordley Parish	10km (6.2 miles)
6.	Above Grassington	8km (5 miles)
7.	Langstrothdale	8.5km (5.3 miles)
8.	Yarnbury	5.5 or 8.5km (3.4 or 5.3 miles)
9.	Appletreewick	8 .5 or 10.5km (5.3 or 6.6 miles)
10.	Ribblehead	10km (6.2 miles)
11.	Conistone and Kilnsey	7 to 11km (4.5 to 6.9 miles)
12.	Nidderdale	10 to 15km (6.2 to 9.4 miles)

I have started each chapter with some basic planning information such as public transport, local facilities, the relevant map number, grid references for start and finish, and an easy-reference guide to places on the walk.

On every walk, incidentally, you will be on rights of way, permissive paths or access land throughout. I do not believe in going astray so, if you stick to the route description, you should not come to grief or be faced with an irate farmer demanding to know where you think you are going.

There is a riot of detail waiting to be discovered in the Dales, if I may use the word "discover" in the vein of Livingstone "discovering" the Victoria Falls in Central Africa. There are some who feel the detail should remain secret. Thankfully in my opinion, there is a growing feeling amongst prehistorians that more sites should be made known to the interested public. What I have tried to do in this book is to put together a Selection Box of twelve walks that will aid you in your quest to uncover the detail, to explore that which lies beneath the obvious surface. The walks presented here are offered as cameos: not for a minute are they meant to cover the whole of the Southern Dales. That would be an impossible and infinite task for one book. I do not even claim that they are the best walks in the area; best is a subjective notion anyway. I would suggest, though, that this choice will give you more than a flavour of the Dales, past and present ... and they are twelve of my favourites. Furthermore, all have been most favourably received from groups that I have led over the years.

I have tried to present the facts – and sometimes ideas and theories – in a digestible way. The format of each Discovery Walk is basically the same. There are route details for each walk, which are more than adequate for you to find your way, though I am one of those who believes every walker, or group, should have an Ordnance Survey map in the pocket or map case. Each walk also has a sketch map to mark the route and the position of points of selected interest and access. All the chosen routes contain a varying number of such points, some more than others, and I have described and explained these as each walk unfolds. I have tried to make sense for you of the scenery from the perspective of geological and landscape processes; I have discussed in some depth the historical processes and influences from prehistoric to recent times because they are so prominently to be seen in the Dales-scape; and I have included notes on flowers, birdlife, current issues ... and whatever else crops up *en route*.

The walks are presented in no particular order of merit or priority. There is no increasing scale of detail or complexity but, to avoid possible repetition of particular points that occur on different routes, I have simply put in a note for you to refer to an earlier or later walk.

There follows an introductory section in which I have outlined the geological and historical frameworks in brief. To make sense of interpretative notes later in the book, it would be better to start by reading these frameworks first. In the conviction that it would be a useful exercise I have also briefly outlined matters of access and the role of the National Park.

I can but say that I hope you enjoy the twelve walks as much as I do; I

Discovery Walks
THE SOUTHERN DALES

0 Kilometres   10

0 Miles   5

- - - -   *Discovery Walks*

· · · · · ·   *National Park boundary*

hope they will add to your store of knowledge so you can leave the Dales understanding and appreciating the area to a greater depth. If both of these aspirations are realised, then this book will have succeeded, and I shall be a happy man!

The National Park

The Yorkshire Dales, one of Britain's ten fully designated National Parks, celebrated its fortieth anniversary in 1994 ... and how vastly different the park is now compared with 1954. I suppose that when you live in an area you tend not to notice the gradual, evolutionary changes but, when you stand back and consider what it was like ten, twenty or forty years ago (not that I can do that – quite), the changes seem immense.

There are some misconceptions in Britain about our National Parks because they are really neither parks nor national. The National Parks of Africa or North America, for example, have been set aside specifically for conservation and public enjoyment but the Dales, in contrast, have less than three per cent of the total area in public ownership: the vast majority is privately owned by landowners and farmers. The National Park most definitely was not set aside in 1954 as a museum or massive theme park where the public has open access to whatever form of recreation they might favour: the area within the Park boundaries is a living and working entity where some 20,000 people have their homes and carry out their daily routines.

So why is it a National Park? In its early days the Countryside Commission decided that this was a landscape with special qualities that needed to be granted a high measure of legal protection from possible future unsympathetic development or change, protection not only for the landscape itself but also for life and tradition. But that was forty years ago and our country has undergone changes that were inconceivable then, and our National Parks have not been immune to the immense pressures generated by increased levels of personal prosperity, personal mobility and leisure time.

A journey to the Dales in the 1950s had to be planned well in advance by Mr. and Mrs. Public but now anyone from virtually anywhere can jump into their car for a day out on the fells, even from distant parts of the country. It has been suggested that the Settle-Skipton area is one of the best areas for orienteers to live in because it is ideally placed for travelling to events in all parts of the country. That logic must also work in reverse, and the result is that the very landscapes we all treasure are in danger of being loved to death. Nine million visitor days are made to the Dales each year and, just from 1975 to 1991, there was a 44 per cent increase in road traffic within the Park. Thus, the task of the Park Authority is immeasurably harder now and its role has necessarily changed. In the words of the National Park Committee its

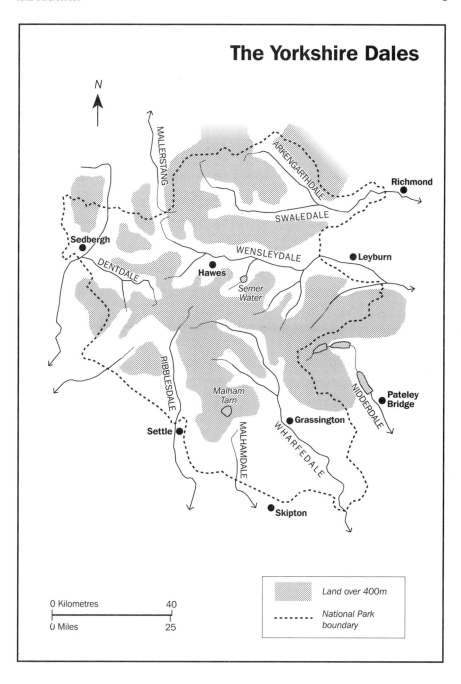

The Yorkshire Dales

N

MALLERSTANG

ARKENGARTHDALE

Richmond

SWALEDALE

Sedbergh

WENSLEYDALE

Leyburn

DENTDALE

Hawes

Semer
Water

RIBBLESDALE

Malham
Tarn

NIDDERDALE

Pateley
Bridge

Settle

Grassington

MALHAMDALE

WHARFEDALE

Skipton

0 Kilometres   40

0 Miles   25

Land over 400m

National Park
boundary

"primary statutory duty is to conserve the landscape character, scenic beauty, wildlife, cultural heritage and the peace and quiet of the area. It also has a duty to promote quiet informal outdoor recreation."

It also recognises better that the needs and interests of residents must be safeguarded and promoted. Alongside conservation we hear more and more of stewardship these days, and of the need to promote sustainable tourism by encouraging the thinking tourist and the Green tourist to help the Park and those of us fortunate enough to reside within its bounds to co-exist peacefully and amicably.

I am sure I will not be around in another forty years' time but I sometimes wonder whether our National Parks will indeed be able to sustain their current state of evolutionary change, or whether some of the more extreme solutions to snowballing visitor pressure will be enacted. I know you are a thinking and Green tourist: just encourage your friends likewise and always remember to respect the Park's " lifestyle, work and customs" and to "support local skills, services and produce" and follow the Yorkshire Dales Visitor Code.

The Yorkshire Dales Visitor Code

¤ Keep to public rights of way or access areas.

¤ Use gates and stiles to cross dry stone walls, hedges and fences.

¤ Leave all gates as you find them.

¤ Stay in single file through uncut hay or silage meadows.

¤ Leave wildlife and flowers alone for others to enjoy.

¤ Keep your dog under close control.

¤ Do not interfere with farm animals, machinery or work.

¤ Take your litter home.

¤ Do not start fires.

¤ Do not pollute rivers or lakes.

¤ Use public transport, whenever you can, or park thoughtfully.

¤ Respect the lifestyles, work and customs of the Dales and show consideration for other legitimate countryside users.

Keep these points in mind and you will receive a warm welcome in our "Treasured Landscape".

How the other hills were formed – geology and landscape evolution

From whatever standpoint we begin an exploration of the Dales, we cannot escape the importance of geology or the detail of the rocks beneath the surface nor the various forces that have operated on those rocks from within and without. The very landscape itself may have been subtly shaped and re-shaped by the never-ending attack of rain, wind and frost, or more dramatically carved up or plastered over by moving ice or meltwater, but the fells, moors and valleys are there in the first place because of geology. Any variations in how the landscape has been clothed with a cover of plants can only be a reflection of the underlying soil which in turn is derived from the breakdown of the rock beneath, the aptly named "parent material" in the language of the soil scientist. Of course, you may proclaim, climate must also be an important arbiter of plant growth. True, but is not climate – or at least weather – partly a response to landscape? We all know that the high places are wetter than the valleys, that the fell tops are invariably cooler than where you parked your car, that frosts and wind reflect height: they are all due to landscape, and to geology at the end of the day.

To take the geological argument further, the human response to nature's provision is as varied as the landscape. As you travel from one dale to another it is soon apparent that variation in geology has left an imprint on the local architecture. Buildings made of limestone have a different look and feel from those made of sandstone or slate. It can be claimed that settlements on a limestone base are more welcoming and less stern or brooding than those developed on dark gritstones.

The underlying geology determines land use also. Grits and sandstones do not allow the easy passage of water so the soil is often wet, or even waterlogged. The vegetation is coarse and will only support a low density of sheep which wander at will across their ancestral and remembered pastures. Limestones offer a quite different aspect: the soil is very thin and rather more basic but well-drained and supportive of pasture rich in grass and flowering species. No need here to scan the horizon for individual sheep forced by gastronomic paucity to forsake their gregarious nature. The limestone pastures high up the fells can support far more sheep as well as cattle and beef stock leaving the lower sweeter pastures for breakfast bowl fillers.

No, try as you might, you cannot escape from the all-encompassing embrace of geology.

The present "natural" landscape has evolved over the passage of geological time. To help you get a feel of geological time, here is a commonly used yardstick. Geologists say the Earth is something like 4600 million years old: try condensing that into just one of our years, so that the Earth began in the first seconds of the 1st January, and we stand now at midnight just as you are about to launch into Auld Lang Syne at the very end of that single year. Thus most of the rocks in the Dales were laid down back in late October or early November. The dinosaurs came and went in the last week of November and first few days of December; the first apes appeared early last week and our first humanoid ancestors walked the earth about twenty minutes ago. At the start of the sentence you are reading now, Mary was giving birth to

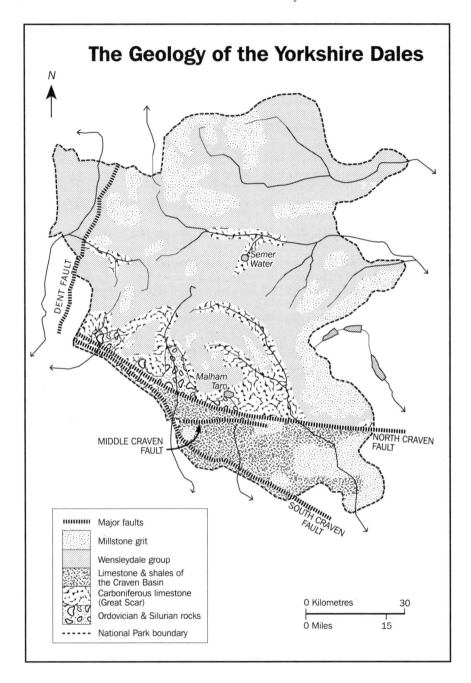

The Geology of the Yorkshire Dales

N

DENT FAULT

Semer Water

Malham Tarn

MIDDLE CRAVEN FAULT

NORTH CRAVEN FAULT

SOUTH CRAVEN FAULT

||||||||| Major faults

Millstone grit

Wensleydale group

Limestone & shales of the Craven Basin

Carboniferous limestone (Great Scar)

Ordovician & Silurian rocks

- - - - - National Park boundary

0 Kilometres   30

0 Miles   15

her famous son in a stable ... The mind boggles. Perhaps "a long, long time ago" is an easier bet.

Let us start at the beginning with a completely open mind. Between about 510 and 410 million years ago (m.y.) what is now the Dales was the bed of an ocean which geologists have called the proto-Atlantic or Iapetus Ocean that lay astride the equator. To the north and south of this ocean lay ancient continents and from these rivers carried great quantities of eroded material, called sediments, into the ocean. Great thicknesses of mud built up on the ocean floor and the weight of all these sediments compressed and solidified those below into rock. All this happened in the Ordovican and Silurian periods (see the following timescale). This was in "late October". At the end of the Silurian period (about 410 m.y.) a long drawn-out process reached its earth shattering crescendo: the plates (sections of solid earth's crust) carrying the old continents squeezed that old ocean bed as they collided, thrusting up a massive range of mountains where the Dales now lie. This is called by geologists the Caledonian mountain building phase.

Of course, all this did not happen overnight. The rate of movement of plates, and of the associated tectonic forces, is akin to the rate at which your finger nails grow. The various processes have not stopped either: plates will always be moving and new mountain ranges will always be thrust up (like the Alps and the Himalayas now) as others are removed by erosion.

No sooner had the new land surface, with mudstones and slates folded and contorted by the pressures, popped its head above the vanished ocean waves, than it began to be worn away, and throughout the following Devonian period (410 to 350 m.y.) the mountains were planed down to mere stumps. Also during this Devonian period a huge mass of volcanic rock, granite, forced upwards the stumps of the old mountains. This gave stability to what we lay people now call the Craven Uplands or what geologists prefer to call the Askrigg Block.

Then followed the Carboniferous period (350 to 290 m.y.) when "Britain" was very near the Equator and once again back under water, this time in a warm, clear tropical sea. More deposits were laid down on the sea bed south of the Askrigg Block in the Craven Lowlands. They were not muds this time but organic, algal remains which hardened to form limestones. Later on more incursions of the sea laid down more limestones, as well as sandstones and shaley mudstones, over the Block. It may seem hard to accept that during this period the sea level rose and fell several times, giving rise to a succession of deposits that can be seen in the landscape today. I will discuss these more in the Walks in this and the companion volume as and when they crop up.

It is the Carboniferous rocks – limestones, sandstones and shales – that make up most of the Dales. The older Ordivician and Silurian material occurs only at the surface in a few localities, as we shall see. No rocks remain from any period later than the Carboniferous.

This has been very much a whistle-stop tour of several hundred million years but I hope it has begun to put into perspective the complex geological processes that have affected and made the Dales. The table on the previous

THE GEOLOGICAL SUCCESSION IN
THE DALES

Million years ago	Geological Period	Main Geological Processes	Local Rock types
	Permian	- further folding and faulting - "Britain" now north of the equator - desert conditions in the "Dales"	none laid down
290			
	Carboniferous	- coastal swamps and delta cover much of the "Dales" - repeated changes of sea level: erosion and deposition alternate - ocean returns with warm and clear waters	Coal Measures, Millstone Grit Craven Uplands:the Wensleydale Group of limestones,sands and silts Craven Lowlands: Bowland Shales,muds and limestones Great Scar Limestone
350			
	Devonian	- granite pushed up into existing rocks - uplift of Caledonian Mountains, followed by rapid wearing down to stumps	none laid down (?)
410			
	Silurian	- deposition continues - the ocean closes up as tectonic plates converge	sandstones,siltstones and mudstones
440			
	Ordovician	- sediments pile up on the bed of the deep Iapetus Ocean - "Britain" lies south of the equator	siltstones,mudstones and muddy limestones
510			
	Cambrian	- no firm evidence of any activity	none laid down (?)

START HERE AND READ UPWARDS

page puts the main occurrences in chronological order, while an outline of surface geology is shown on the map. When you come across a bit of geology later in the book, refer back to this map and table.

The Historical Framework

In many parts of England there has been so much urban and industrial development, or intensive cultivation, that history has either been buried or destroyed. In the remote and less developed upland fringes, however, the legacy of the past is writ large in the landscape. It has survived the centuries: it has not been ploughed under or built upon. Venture to Salisbury Plain or Orkney and history proclaims itself amid manicured lawns, interpretative panels and informative guidebooks. Come to the Dales and you find the past is there aplenty, from prehistoric to early modern times, but you need to know what you are looking for. You need to take up sleuthing to make sense of what is on the ground. "Heaps of stone," a friend of mine once said. "It's all just heaps of stones." Maybe so, but then did Rembrandt, Renoir and Co. just slop blobs of paint on bits of canvas? If you have a mind for the past, it can be a fascinating voyage of discovery to recognise and identify different "heaps of stones" by their size, form and location, and especially to add the human dimension to those heaps. One of the most astonishing discoveries to be made is how little life and work seem to have changed through the centuries. In some respects a 2500-year-old pile of stone is little different from a 500-year-old pile but why should it be when the raw materials, the technology and ways of life had scant cause to change?

Join with me now on a whistle-stop tour through the past, this time in the historical time machine.

To begin this journey we must engage rapid rewind to the time before the last Ice Age had its final fling. It was warmer then and bands of nomadic hunter-gatherers visited the Dales in pursuit of migrating game, just as their post-Ice Age descendants would later do. As the glaciers retreated northwards and upwards, vegetation colonised the former frozen wastes allowing the herds of reindeer and elk to find a footing, providing food for the Old Stone Age (or Palaeolithic) people during the summer months. These temporary visitors left nothing behind other than the odd scrap of flint or bone which history has preserved by accident, hidden in the dark recesses of some limestone cavern.

It needed a change in climate for the better – global warming is nothing new – to herald a new way of life. Middle Stone Age (Mesolithic) people had a far more advanced culture but in these parts they were still only fleeting and nomadic migrants. However they began to make the first noticeable impact on their environment, burning the woodland cover to aid their hunting sorties, and perhaps they were thus, unintentionally and unknowingly, responsible for the creation of the first peat on the rain-sodden sandstone and gritstone moors.

This moistness was accompanied by warmth. In fact the period around 5000BC is considered to have been Britain's optimum (i.e. ideal) climate since the Ice Ages began. Their warm conditions provided the catalyst for another set of changes, this time on a dramatic scale. Those of us brought up on an early evening diet of "The Flintstones" may find it inconceivable that organised farming and associated forest clearance began back in the New Stone Age (Neolithic) period, but it is a fact. Because they lived settled lives and tilled their land, their lives became more structured and there is evidence of considerable sophistication. The Dales were marginal then as they are today so we have nothing to compare with the grand monuments or village sites of Orkney, but we know something of their lives from a smattering of clues hidden in the landscape, more of which later.

On no particular date did Wayne or Tracy Flintstone declare to their tradition-bound parents that they must forsake stone in favour of copper or bronze, rather a continuing process of evolutionary change saw the introduction of what we modern earthlings call the Bronze Age. It may well have taken generations for new ideas to take hold in our upland areas: resistance to change is nothing new, but invariably and inevitably change came about. In the Dales, though, flint tools remained in use long after the end of the Stone Age, possibly even into the Roman period. Inevitably landscape change accelerated, and camp fire discussions and the telling of folktales could well have focussed on land degradation and the pressing need for the conservation of soil and forest resources. These Bronze Age Dalesfolk have left us many more clues in the landscape in the form of settlement sites, ceremonial and burial sites, and material goods but, of the human element, we know next to nothing. We do not know what they looked like, what language they spoke, how they dressed, and we probably never will unlock these secrets of the past. Perhaps that is no bad thing as we seem to have an obsession these days with trying to find answers to every question. Let's leave some mysteries to tax our inventive capacities.

Historians are unsure whether these Bronze Age people were the progenitors of the Iron Age folk who followed, though it is possible that the latter were a fusion of Celtic incomers and native people. Whatever their origin may have been, we do know more about them, at least in the closing centuries of Iron Age culture, because of Roman writings. We know they were called the Brigantes and that they were Celts; we know the names of their major tribal leaders in what is known to historians as the Romano-British period; and we know something of their troubled political and military situation. Furthermore they have left us a profusion of settlement sites, defensive works and field systems. We can, in short, be much more positive about these folk than about their ancestors. Evidence of Brigantian occupation is clearest on the drier limestone pastures with an abundance of sites, indicating a density of population far in excess of today's, and a high degree of social organisation, perhaps especially so under the Roman yoke, when the Dales served as a guerilla stronghold.

It is perhaps ironic that we are more fully conversant with Brigantian days than we are of later centuries, the so-called Dark Ages. It is tantalising in the extreme to have so many gaps in our knowledge of the Germanic peoples who spread into the Dales between the Roman withdrawal and the Norman Conquest. We know that Celtic, British kingdoms existed beyond the Dales to east and west. If you have driven north up the A1 beyond Leeds, for example, you cannot fail to have noticed road signs indicating the exits to Sherburn in Elmet and Barwick in Elmet. Elmet was one such kingdom. Of the Dales at this time we have virtually no tangible evidence. Oh that Tantalus could reveal more to us concerning later influxes! The Angles (they of the Anglo-Saxon double act) spread up the Dales from the south-east in the seventh century; in the ninth the Danes infilled the gaps that the Anglian settlers had conveniently left; and after them came the Norsemen. They were also peaceful settlers who came in search of land to graze and till: they were not the pillagin', rapin', lootin' Hollywood stereotypes. From all these waves we know a great deal from place-name and archaeological evidence but, yet again, we are almost reduced to the realms of guesswork when we attempt to paint in the human picture.

The rest of the story is clearer as written records abound for the Norman and medieval periods and beyond. The registers of the great abbeys still exist, detailing many aspects of life and work, though of course there is precious little in concrete concerning the daily drudgery and toil of the long-suffering peasants. Who knows, maybe Blackadder's sidekick Baldrick is as true a representation as any we can conjure up from modern scholarship. Of more recent times, we have a mass of material to hand, of the great house re-building phases of the late seventeenth century, of the enclosing of fell and moor with miles of stone walling in the late eighteenth, and of the growth and decline of the lead and textile industries in the nineteenth.

*   *   *

The story of life in the Dales goes back more than a hundred centuries. Much of this story unfolds as you trace these Discovery Walks through the Dales.

Place-names

I gain my pleasures from walking in a number of ways, all of them fairly simple. I enjoy the physical act of walking, sometimes fast, sometimes at a dawdle. I enjoy the scenery and the views, even if I have seen them countless times already. I enjoy trying to make sense of the landscape and of all the diverse elements that add together to make the patchwork quilt that is the Dales. And, not least, I enjoy the hunt to untangle the meaning and origin of place names. This is my Rubik Cube and Trivial Pursuits wrapped up as one, but perhaps not such a simple game after all.

Some names are easy to disentangle. It is fairly obvious that Langcliffe means the long cliff, or that Settle is a place where people settled down long

THE HISTORICAL SUCCESSION IN
THE DALES

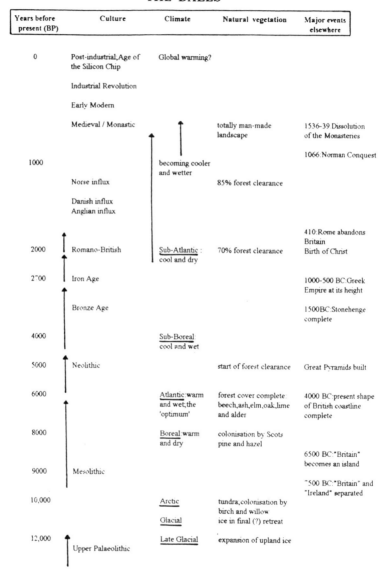

Years before present (BP)	Culture	Climate	Natural vegetation	Major events elsewhere
0	Post-industrial,Age of the Silicon Chip	Global warming?		
	Industrial Revolution			
	Early Modern			
	Medieval / Monastic		totally man-made landscape	1536-39:Dissolution of the Monasteries
1000		becoming cooler and wetter		1066:Norman Conquest
	Norse influx		85% forest clearance	
	Danish influx Anglian influx			
2000	Romano-British	Sub-Atlantic : cool and dry	70% forest clearance	410:Rome abandons Britain Birth of Christ
2700	Iron Age			1000-500 BC:Greek Empire at its height
	Bronze Age			1500BC:Stonehenge complete
4000		Sub-Boreal: cool and wet		
5000	Neolithic		start of forest clearance	Great Pyramids built
6000		Atlantic:warm and wet,the 'optimum'	forest cover complete: beech,ash,elm,oak,lime and alder	4000 BC:present shape of British coastline complete
8000		Boreal:warm and dry	colonisation by Scots pine and hazel	6500 BC:"Britain" becomes an island
9000	Mesolithic			7500 BC:"Britain" and "Ireland" separated
10,000		Arctic / Glacial	tundra,colonisation by birch and willow / ice in final (?) retreat	
12,000	Upper Palaeolithic	Late Glacial	expansion of upland ice	

ago. Others are easy to crack if you know what individual elements of the place name mean: wick, for example, was a dairy farm in the days of yore so Austwick was the east dairy farm, and Giggleswick was a dairy farm that belonged to a man with a name something like Gigel. Perhaps he could not stop laughing! If you know that a tun (or ton) was a farmstead, then it is easy to come up with Skipton having started as a sheep farmstead whereas Grassington was a grazing farmstead.

Other names are exceedingly perplexing. You could be forgiven for assuming that Cow Gill Cote in Bordley means the cottage near the ravine where the cows are kept. Sorry – it has nothing to do with cows, but is a corruption of a personal name, Kolli. Equally obvious, you might venture, is Goat Scar Lane rising above Stainforth but once again I am afraid you would be wrong. Down the centuries the original name of Gorse Scar has managed to become transmuted into Goat. It requires very little mental effort to see how such Chinese Whispers type changes can take place. If you ask anyone in my area what "that farm up there" is called, they will say Sherr'd (sounds like Sherred). Look on the map though and it is called Sherwood. Maybe in years to come the map will say Sherred. (I wonder what Robin Hood called his forest?) Not too far away is another farm called, and named on the map, Sannat Hall. On early maps it was Sandwith. Names can change, early map surveyors probably misheard a name given in local dialect, or maybe they just guessed at the spelling of a word that until then had not been written down.

Let me widely and wildly digress for a moment. In Central Africa there grows in profusion a stately tree which glories in the scientific name of *Khaya nyassica*. This was named by an early colonial official in what was then Nyasaland. Presumably he had demanded of some nearby local what the tree was called in those regions. What the official did not know was that *khaya* in the local language means "I do not know". So now we have a tree perpetuated as the I-don't-know-tree. Interesting!

Place names must reflect the language spoken, and the ethnic origins, of each particular area. If an area has been linguistically homogenous for millennia, you would expect the majority of place names to reflect that so it would come as no surprise to find so many Welsh place names in Wales. That might equally apply to England – or perhaps not because what is English anyway if not an etymological ratatouille with bits of this and bits of that? In the Dales English is a veritable hotchpotch. Many of the words in use today are not really English but more akin to the languages of Scandinavia, as the various waves of settlement that I described earlier have all left their mark in topographical terminology, in place names and in the local dictionary of life.

Very few local words have survived from the early Celtic period. Some of the rivers still bear British (i.e. Celtic) names: Wharfe, Aire Nidd, Cray, are all pre-English, as is Penyghent which stands proud to proclaim its Celtic ancestry. ("Why has that mountain got a Welsh name?" is an oft-heard cry

in these parts.) The Angles took up residence in the lowlands within the
Dales and you can trace the extent of their settlement in the early period by
place names. Anglian (i.e. early English) settlements of the early period
typically have names ending in ham or burn: Clapham, Coverham or
Bentham, but not Malham, and Winterburn and Otterburn. A later wave of
Anglian settlers spread their new roots around farmsteads or tuns (first
settled between 750 and 950) like Grassington, Skipton, Horton and Ingleton. Later still Anglian farmsteads often have ley in the name like Ilkley,
Keighley, Beamsley and Bordley. This is not to say, though, that all Anglian
place names end in ham, burn, ley or ton. Far from it.

   The next lot of off-comers were the Danes, who spread in from the Vale
of York and intermingled with the Anglians, fairly peacefully it would seem.
Places containing the element *booth* or *thorpe* are usually Danish, and *by* is
a typically Danish suffix also, though we must beware here, as some later
Anglian, and even Norse, names include *by*.

   Last, but by no means least, were the Norse who settled the higher and
remoter parts of the Dales. In certain areas there is aproliferation of Norse
place names and topographic names. In the old West Riding 13 per cent of place
names have a Norse origin but this rises to 37 per cent in the Ribblesdale-
Malham area, one of the main concentrations of so-called Viking settlement
in northern England. Many of the names for landscape features peppered
across Ordnance Survey maps are Norse, signifying the enormous importance of their linguistic influence and penetration. In modern Dales-speak
many words in common usage are distinctly Norse, and readily under-
standable by modern Norwegians; beck, gill, dale, scar, pike, force (or foss),
to mention but a few. Did these Norse words replace earlier English or Celtic
names, or did the Anglians not bother with the upland areas, fearing them
in much the same way as eighteenth century travellers and diarists scorned
the fells? Just something else we shall probably never know.

   At the end of each chapter I have listed the meanings and origins of the
place names en route, as they add to an understanding of the total landscape.
Some are infuriatingly missing, however. I would dearly like to know the
origin of Watlowes (Walk 3) or Crutchin Gill Rigg (Walk 9): the problem is
I simply have no idea; and the relevant volume of the English Place Name
Society can shed no light on the issue either.

   In the lists, the following abbreviations are used:

Brit	British i.e. Celtic
O. Dan	Old Danish
O.E.	Old English, i.e. Anglian
O.I.N.	Old Irish-Norse, i.e. Norse with an Irish flavour
O.N.	Old Norse
O.Fr.	Old French
M.E.	Middle English i.e. early Medieval
O. Welsh	Old Welsh
O. WSc.	Old West Scandinavian

Meanings of common topographical terms

bark	ON	hill
beck	ON	stream
ber	ON	hill
dale	ON	valley
fell	ON	hill
force/foss	ON/OWSc	waterfall
gayle	OWSc	ravine
gill	ON/OWSc	ravine
knott	OE	rocky hill top
keld	ON	spring
pike	ON	peak
rigg	ON	ridge
scar	ON	cliff
sike	OE/ON	small stream or ditch
tarn	ON	lake or pond

Access in The Dales

There are those – and emphatically I am not one of them – who would argue their "rights" to wander at will within the Dales, or any other upland area for that matter. Personally I believe there are enough points of access for walkers to leave the straight and narrow and head for the tops and nether regions, and I could never advocate deliberately going where I know I should not be. Whether the situation will change, if legislation being proposed and debated at the time of my writing this ever reaches the statute books, remains to be seen. Certainly there is one school of thought that advocated transferring trespass from the civil to the criminal law list. There again another school proposes increased access to open spaces: if this school wins the legal arguments, fine – the more the merrier, but legally so.

Here are a few figures. Within the National Park there were, when I started writing this book ....

¤ 1450km of public footpath (about 900 miles)

¤ 600km of public bridleway (over 360 miles)

· ¤ 18km of RUPPs and BOATs (around 5 miles)

We all know what a footpath is, and what our rights are on them – to pass unhindered from A to B on foot. Most of us know that a bridleway gives us the right to ride a horse or pedal cycle, though both should still give way to walkers. RUPPs are a legalistic anachronism. Once upon a time they were roads, in the days before the internal (or is it infernal?) combustion engine, but you would find it hard to get your shiny possessions along them now.

In fact we have only two sections of RUPP in the Dales, one above Maller-stang and a short length at Linton. What do the letters stand for? Road Used as a Public Path. A BOAT is a Byway Open to All Traffic, from foot sloggers to motorised "adventurers".

What about Green Lanes? They have no legal status: they may be a RUPP or a BOAT or simply an unsurfaced and unclassified County Road. If it is the latter you can, in theory, drive along it. The National Park Authority is, as I write, looking into the whole thorny issue of Green Lanes as confusion has merrily reigned, tempers have become frayed over what is or is not permissible, and many of them can only be described as a mess, a linear quagmire in winter when the ground never gets chance to dry out. So, ultimately, when the processes of consultation and enquiry have been finalised, and objections overcome, there will be re-classification "up" to County Road status "across" to BOAT status or "down" to bridleway status.

However, one point transcends all arguments and legal disputes: the vast majority of Public Rights Of Way (PROWs) in the Dales have ancient origins, sometimes back in prehistoric times. Most of the routes in this book are based on Old Roads, and there are very few corners of the Dales that I have not managed to explore and discover by path or track.

Apart from legal definitions, another change is afoot. The National Park is beginning to phase out the ubiquitous hardwood ladder stiles, on cost and ecological grounds. Some have already been replaced with stone stiles. If you come upon a stile that I have said is a ladder stile, and it is not, you now know why.

Be Prepared!

These days most people who go out walking seem to be adequately equipped and prepared for the worst. In fact I am sure I have seen more ill-shod and ill-clad groups in the high Lakeland fells than in the Dales. Perhaps the Lake District attracts more of the train spotter types of walker, keen to tick off "Wainwrights" or "authorised tops", whereas the Dales attracts the connoisseurs: probably not, but I should like to maintain this illusion in my mind.

None of the walks in this book takes you on to the mountain tops: indeed some of them are largely low-level routes. This does not mean you can venture forth improperly equipped, though, and basic mountain gear should always be carried as our weather can be notoriously fickle. In one dale it can be dry and bright while just over the watershed it is dull and miserable. We sometimes seem to experience three seasons in one day. A decent set of waterproofs, warm clothing, a sound pair of walking shoes or boots are essential. There is rough terrain on parts of all these walks and trainers are not to be recommended, particularly in wet conditions. It might also be useful to carry a compass, and to know how to use it, as a morale booster when the mist suddenly envelops you on some remote section of moor.

A map, too, is an indispensable item. The Dales are covered by three of the Outdoor Leisure series at a scale of 1:25,000 (2½ inches to the mile or 40mm to the km). To complete all the walks in this book you will need all three, but unfortunately they do not extend to the extremities of the Park. Nidderdale, for example, is omitted (Walk 12) so you will need the 1:25,000 Pathfinder map number 652. Better news is that almost all of the Dales is shown on the 1:50,000 Landranger map number 98 (Wensleydale and Wharfedale), though again not Nidderdale which appears on number 99 (Northallerton and Ripon). Parts of the Northern Dales are also not on the main maps, but that does not concern us here. Even better news is that the entire Park is depicted admirably on the Ordnance Survey's Touring Map and Guide number 6 (Yorkshire Dales) published in 1992 at a scale of 1:63,360 (1 inch to the mile or 16mm to the km). For gaining a general overview and for planning a walking holiday, this map is excellent.

I cannot stress too strongly that the sketch maps in this book are not meant to be maps to walk by. Take the appropriate O.S. map with you.

Take with you, too, a pair of binoculars and your trusted flower and bird guide and, if the weather is at all doubtful, a weather forecast. This can be obtained for the Dales from any National Park Centre or by telephone. As I write, the talking forecast can be obtained on 0891 500417.

A Note on the Divisions of Prehistory

We seem to use the terms Stone Age, Bronze Age and Iron Age with gay abandon, a "Three Age" system that has been in use since 1836. Further terms were introduced in 1865 to sub-divide the Stone Age: the Old Stone Age or Palaeolithic, taken to cover the period from 250,000 B.P. to the retreat of the glaciers around 10,000 B.P. in Britain; and the New Stone Age or Neolithic covering the period from perhaps 6000 to 4500 B.P. The intermediate period, the Middle Stone Age or Mesolithic, was added later still.

There is currently a move away from these typologies, as they are perceived to be too arbitrary and too rigid: change did not happen overnight. There is also a feeling that investigations into the past should be less narrowly focussed. Rather than basing interpretation solely on material finds and cultures, the prehistoric landscape, environment and land use should be given greater emphasis. After all, when a site is uncovered and surveyed, archaeologists have no way of ascertaining whether what they find represents everything that was there at the time of occupance ... or a mere fraction. This helps put the significance of material finds into perspective. It is very easy to jump to premature conclusions based on flimsy evidence.

Discovery Walk 1

Ribble Ways – North from Settle

Start and Finish: Settle Market Place for the full route (Grid reference SD819 637). For the short route, start in Langcliffe car park next to the primary school (Grid reference SD823 651).

Parking: There are three pay and display car parks in Settle, all within five minutes of the centre. Parking is difficult on Tuesdays, market day, unless you arrive early.

Public transport: Settle is well-served by public transport. Train services link the town with Skipton and Leeds and with Carlisle, with less frequent services from Lancaster to Giggleswick station. There are bus links from various directions: on the Lancaster-Skipton-Leeds-York route operated by Ribble (01524 424555); on the Ambleside – Kendal – Skipton – York route operated by Cumberland (01946 63222); from Clitheroe and Slaidburn operated by Hyndburn (01254 390816); from Skipton on the Pennine run (01756 749215); and from Ingleton, run by Bibby's (015242 41330). There is also the Dales Link summer service that connects Ingleton and Grassington via Clapham, Austwick, Settle, Malham area and Hetton (tel. 015242 41330).

Facilities: Settle has a very wide range of services for its size. Langcliffe has a good village shop which is also the post office and information centre; while Stainforth has the Craven Heifer offering morning coffee and bar meals.

Outline of the Walk: Settle – Langcliffe – Stainforth – Catrigg – Winskill – Attermire Scar – Settle.

Length: From 8.5 to 11.5km (5.3 to 7.2 miles) depending on where you start.

Ordnance Survey Map: Outdoor Leisure 10. Landranger 98.

Introduction

Today's walk starts in Settle, a small market town serving Ribblesdale and surrounding areas, and heads up the dale as far as Stainforth. There is a huge amount of detail to be seen or reflected upon. The now tranquil village of Langcliffe has a long and surprisingly varied industrial story to tell, while Stainforth owes more to the monks of Sawley Abbey. As you follow the route you will touch upon a series of historical cameos: Anglian farmers, Stone

Age cave dwellers, and nineteenth century railway builders, soldiers and miners have all left their mark on the landscape.

Natural forces have left their imprint, too, in the form of scars and massive fault systems and a hidden waterfall.

Much of the latter half of the walk lies within a Site of Special Scientific Interest (SSSI), so designated because of the limestone features, the cave archaeology and the flora.

This is not a route to try and squeeze into a half-day. There is too much to see. If time is limited you could start at Langcliffe and thus shorten the route. If so, start part way through the section "North from Settle" and follow the route from there.

To sample short sections you could begin at Stainforth and link together the Short Route and Long Route of "Onwards and Upwards". There again you could visit the Hoffman kiln as a separate exercise.

Settle

Start in the Market Place. Nowadays it is surrounded by shops and cafes with the Royal Oak Hotel to the right, the Town Hall on the left and, on Tuesdays, an array of market stalls filling every nook and cranny. Had you stood here in the nineteenth century or earlier, the prospect would have been vastly different. Market Place would have been filled with pens full of bleating sheep and squabbling geese. The basement shops of The Shambles would have been workshops, a hive of activity, along with a slaughterhouse and butchers shop at ground level. The cottages were single storied until 1898, and not there a century earlier. Where the present pillar stands was the market cross until 1863.

Ancient milestone in Settle

The whole scene would have been full of the hustle and bustle of the stock market, the coming and going or workers scurrying to their shift at the textile mills, teams of pack horses on their way hither and thither, and mail coaches rattling into the square to deposit their weary and bone-shaken occupants for a night at one of the inns.

And inns there were, to suit every taste. Look around the square: the electrical and sweet shops to the right were The White Horse inn; then there is The Royal Oak; in front, where now stands Ye Olde Naked Man cafe, was the Naked

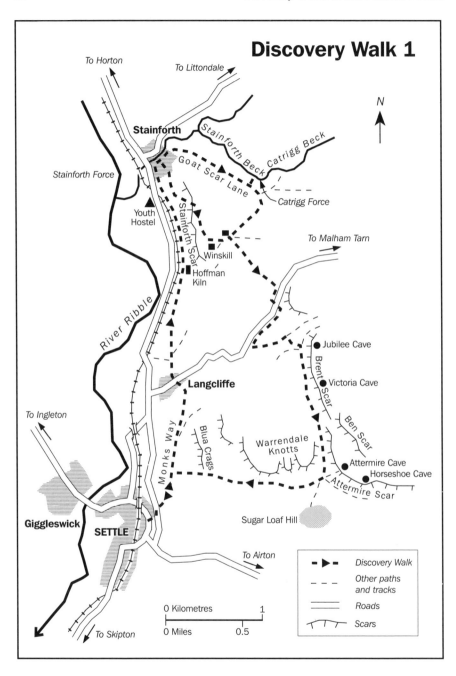

Man public house; the group of buildings that form the chemist and outdoor shop was The Crown. Turn around and look behind the Town Hall and, on the site of the Midland Bank, was The Black Bull. The newsagents and cafe on the other side of the town hall were the original Golden Lion inn, till it moved around the corner in 1753. Who said we are a nation of drinkers?

There are two buildings around Market Place with plaques proclaiming a past association with someone famous. See if you can find them. Clue: both now have financial associations.

Now, leave Market Place by going between the town hall and the Midland, straight ahead on High Street past The Talbot Arms, with its suggestion of an association with the old cattle droving trade (see Walk 10). The talbot was a breed of dog bred by the Talbot family of Bashall in Bowland, and was used by the drovers. Next to The Talbot is King William House, another former pub. **Bear left at the next corner, past The Folly,** begun in 1675 by a prosperous tanner called Richard Preston. It was not fully completed, lay derelict for many years, and looks somewhat out of place now. **The narrow road, called School Hill, leads steeply up from The Folly and you should follow this to the next junction below the Congregational chapel.**

The tall building on the junction – three or four storeys high, depending where you view it from – was built in the 1870s as flats, an early example of speculative building to maximise capital outlay.

Set into the right-hand wall at this junction is an old milestone. The lane you have just come up was the main road into Settle from Skipton in the days before the Keighley – Kendal turnpike was established and Settle was an important staging post on the coach road network. The road through Settle first appears in the records in the thirteenth century and was only superseded by the valley road (now the A65) in 1753. Note the mileages, all of which are less than the present distances. This is not necessarily because the old routes were more direct, though they may have been, but because until the eighteenth century some areas of the country still used "customary" miles. These were longer than statute miles, first introduced in 1593. Travellers even noted in their diaries how long were "Yorkshire miles" – part of the privilege of coming to the county! (I wonder, if Britain ever becomes fully metricated, will we have Yorkshire kilometres?)

When the turnpike trust met to discuss the creation of the new route, its members did so in the house of one Robert Johnson in Settle!

North From Settle

Turn left at the milestone, past the smithy and then right up Castle Hill to the T-junction at the top. Turn right again here to follow Constitution Hill as it bears round leftwards, levels off and becomes High Road. Just here a walled, stony track, called Banks Lane, heads off to the right alongside a wood and past a ruined barn within the wood. You are now on the Monk's

Way, a medieval monastic route, though of course neither the present surface nor the walls are medieval. The walled lane ascends quite steeply to open up onto the hillside just beyond a gate and second ruined building. Ignore the green track heading diagonally uphill but stay with the wall as continuous company for your left shoulder.

The views from this track, assuming you can see over the wall, are quite stunning providing you with a panorama from Pendle and Cleatop Park wood on the far left of the vista, through the sweep of the northern Bowland Fells with Settle and Giggleswick laid out before you. Giggleswick is dominated by the green copper dome of the public school's chapel while Settle from this vantage point seems to be under the shadow of the railway. Below you also are three former cotton mills, on the Langcliffe Road.

Shortly you will see a footpath sign, to Malham, where a ruined wall crosses your track. If you left your car in Langcliffe, this is where you should turn off to return to your car, having followed the route described in "Homeward Bound".

From the sign carry straight on and pass through the field gate where the track next forks: ignore the track to the right. Go through the gate and up between two walls over the ladder stile to the field beyond. Walk straight across the centre of this field, towards the top edge of the wood ahead, where there is a small gate to go through – and quite possibly a muddy mess, too. Follow the edge of the wood with its boundary wall that drops down, through yet another field gate, onto the road into Langcliffe.

Langcliffe

Langcliffe

If you were to drive on the main road up the valley past Langcliffe, you would never know it existed, other than as a row of houses. Turn off the road and a delightful surprise awaits you: a village green with rustic charm and solitude. Look in depth, though, and the picture contradicts first impressions. The form of the village owes much to an industrial past, with rows of former mill cottages, a row of back-to-back terraced houses (now desirable residences), an old workhouse, five former inns and ale-houses (The Naked Woman was one – see if you can spot the original datestone on the building that replaced the seventeenth century inn) and public buildings. There is an Anglican church, a Methodist chapel, two school buildings and a fine village institute. And then there is the Hall ...

What was the industrial base? There were two textile mills down on the Ribble, one of which was a huge undertaking; there were the paper mill and quarry operations north of the village; a candle-makers; and a tannery with tan pits where the Anglican church now stands. Apparently Langcliffe (like Settle) was an important centre for leather processing for a lengthy period.

A Recipe To Try At Home

You might like to have a go at tanning a hide when you get back home. If so, here are a couple of recipes.

1. A Medieval Method

Scrape the hide to remove the hair.
Soak and re-soak in lime and water to soften the outer layer of skin.
Scrape again.
Soak in a tub of either cold water and bird droppings or hot water and dog dung to further soften the skins and make them porous.
Soak in water and oak-bark several times.
Stretch, shave, and grease to make supple.

If you have done all this properly it will be time for your next annual holiday because the process could take up to a year!

2. A Later Method

Follow the same sequence but dispense with the bird droppings and dung. Instead substitute stale chamber lye called *sig*. This arrived in barrels and originated in London and other growing industrial cities. It is said the best quality was supplied from the working classes, because theirs was not tainted with gin or spirits, just wholesome ale. Have you guessed what chamber lye is yet?

Oh ... do not forget the tannin.

Who said rural life was idyllic?

Langcliffe to Stainforth

When you have had your fill of Langcliffe, **return to the car park and take the rough track between the Institute and the school, turning right at Hope Hill farm.** This is Pike Lane, which climbs to the top of the hill in the distance. It is another example of a medieval track – still traceable as such higher up – widened and walled during the Enclosure Movement (see "The Northern Dales"). If you keep your eyes to the right along the lane you will notice the collection of irregularly shaped fields rising up the hillside. These are of some antiquity and pre-date the Enclosure Movement.

Take the first ladder stile, signposted to Stainforth, and the next one just across the field. Beyond this second stile please stay in single file as the faint path snakes across a flower-rich hay meadow, presently sub-divided by a fence. Another ladder stile allows you to leave this large meadow with its terraces. Follow the crumbling wall ahead, go through the large gap by the far hawthorn tree and a short distance ahead yet another stile drops you onto a short section of lane down to a tar road by the railway bridge. Cross the road, shin up the steps and follow the path between the Settle – Carlisle railway and the high fence, into the council yard, where you should turn left.

On the other side of the main road is Langcliffe Paper Mill, originally a corn-grinding mill, like so many others in the Dales. The old, and no doubt derelict, mill was bought by a Kentishman called Robert Salmon for conversion to paper-making, but sold on to the Christies who owned Langcliffe's cotton mill, and sold again to John Roberts of Cumberland in 1880. Not a single tree passes its portals: the basic raw material is waste paper.

Ahead of you lies something now unique in Britain, and a gem of industrial archaeology, namely the Hoffman kiln. **If time is against you today, though, stay on the path which follows the ledge on the railway side of the kiln, cross the little footbridge at the end and climb the steps to cross the wall stile above.**

Straight ahead, by the railway, is the triple bottle kiln, really just three massive field kilns side by side. It is an impressive structure, from above and from below but, as yet, there is no public access.

Your route bears to the right from the stone stile, up the inclined plane. This was used to transfer stone, by tramway, from Murgatroyd's Quarry to the railway. You can see the remains of the gantry at the top. **At this point bear left, past the quarry entrance and over the step stile in the fence. Head across the next field, enlarged recently by the removal of a wall, across another stile and work round to the left of the small knoll ahead of you.** Depending on the time of year, you may be able to pick out the entrance to the railway tunnel under the road and grounds of the Youth Hostel. When the tunnel was being constructed the Midland Railway Company paid the owner, a West Yorkshire industrialist, to go away to avoid disturbance, or worse, from the blasting. The house, called Taitlands, was built by that

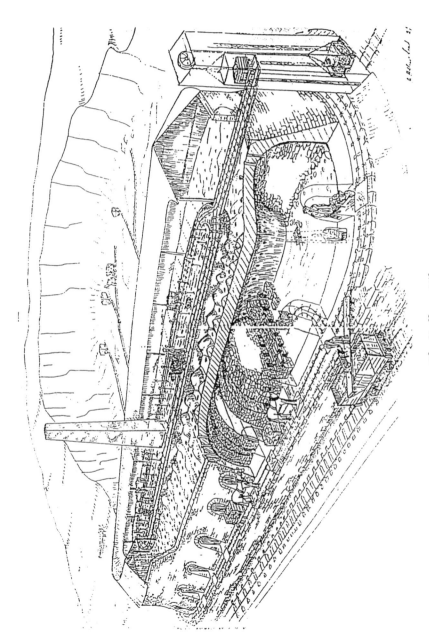

The Hoffman Kiln

family in 1831 around the core of an earlier farmhouse. It has the remains of a fine walled kitchen garden, in true Victorian style, a ha-ha and, in its pre-electricity days, it had its own gas supply run off carbide stored in a tank.

Just beyond the knoll a stile set into the wall gives access to the road. Turn right into the village of Stainforth.

The Hoffman Kiln

The Hoffman kiln is now unique in Britain. The few others that did exist have either crumbled or been removed. This one stands proud as a monument to a lost industrial process. It is difficult now to appreciate the scale of the undertaking as the surviving remains are only a part of what once existed.

There were two operations co-existing side by side. To the north of the whole site a small quarry was opened up in the early 1870s by Thomas Murgatroyd. An incline, with hand-pushed trams, led from the quarry to the triple bottle kiln by the side of the railway, the building of which made the whole undertaking possible. The amount of stone that could be won here was limited, however, and the quarry was exhausted and out of use long before the First World War.

Much more impressive were the workings on the main site, developed by the Craven Lime Company, also in the 1870s, and operational until 1939, though with a break during the General Strike a decade earlier and during the Depression of the 1930s. This operation was centred on the Hoffman kiln and on a later vertical tower kiln, long since demolished. The main quarry has largely been filled in over the years by refuse and it is impossible now to piece together every piece of the jigsaw.

Briefly, stone was worked in the quarry and carried by horse-tram to the Hoffman kiln. At the north end you can still see the tunnel leading from the quarry, complete with drinking trough nearby, and remains of a raised access half-way along the east side of the kiln. The tramway ran on the ledge that connects all the kiln entrances. Some stone, from the north end of the quarry, was brought down an inclined plane which still survives intact. The stone was taken on temporary rails from the tramway into whichever chambers of the kiln were being packed.

A continuous process of firing was undertaken. The stone was hand-stacked to roof height, leaving spaces for coal to be fed down roof chutes. When full, the entrance arches were sealed and the two chambers being worked in tandem were sealed off from the next, and fired. The next two would then be filled and fired, and on the job would go, taking weeks to complete a round.

When the stone was "cooked" it was hand-picked and barrowed out of the chambers, across planks, and onto railway wagons waiting alongside; there was one track to the west and a double track to the east.

Outside the kiln, the scene has totally changed. The whole area, presently occupied by the yard, consisted of railway sidings with shunters bringing in coal and arranging wagons full of lime or crushed stone for onward despatch. The squat structure attached to the south end of the kiln is on the site of a water-balance hoist used to lift coal wagons onto the top of the kiln. The remains of the curtain wall can be seen at intervals on the top but the rail track that circumnavigated within the curtain has gone, as have the roof structure and the massive chimney that towered over the whole complex. What do remain on top are the inspection hatches giving access to the central flue that ran the length of the kiln, the holes for shovelling the coal into the chambers and the metal rings, or dampers, used to regulate air flow.

Where did the material go? Most was sent to Bradford, Sheffield and Scotland. The purest lime was destined for chocolate makers, sugar refiners and leather tanners; the less pure as flux in iron and steel furnaces. Some crushed stone was destined to end up on railway tracks or roads.

Why did it close down? As with so many of our pioneering industrial processes, it was simply overtaken by technology.

For those of you who collect facts ...

number of chambers	22
number of flues	42
overall length	130 metres (420 feet)
overall width	29 metres (95 feet)
total length of chamber	244 metres (794 feet)
total volume of chamber	127 cubic metres (4500 cubic feet)

The Hoffman Kiln today

For budding chemists ...

The process used here is called calcining: the limestone rock is burned to produce quicklime. If water is added to quicklime, by slaking, and then dried, the end result is slaked lime.

As I write, the future of the kiln looks quite bright. In the summer of 1989 a full survey was carried out by Lancaster University Archaeological Unit and proposals were made for its future. Nothing happened until 1994 when the present owners, the local council, agreed to hand it over to the National Park Authority. In time, and as funds permit, the Park will undertake to do something, though it is too early to speculate what that might be. The matter is further complicated, however, by the genuine concerns of nature conservationists. The outer walls are an important plant habitat, a rare orchid and wild strawberry *(Fragaria vesca)* being but two of the biological gems. There are, in addition, five species of hawkweed (yellow, dandelion-like flowers, *Hieracium spp.*), one of which is very rare indeed. It is said these plants earned their name because hawks eat the flower heads to improve their vision! I wonder! Five species of bat have been recorded either within the Hoffman or triple bottle kiln (Daubenton's, Whiskered, Natterer's, Pipistrelle and Long-Eared). Personally I should like to see sensitive conservation and low-key visitor management.

Stainforth Major and Minor

There are two Stainforths and through history they have changed their names with bewildering regularity: to Domesday Man and Woman the manor was either Stainforde or Stranforde; to the monks of Sawley Abbey who owned the land and settlement it was at times Stainford Subtus Montem and at times Freer Stainford. Later on the main village is recorded as Stainforth under Bargh, and the First Edition of the Ordnance Survey map notes it as Great Stainforth. Similarly the off-shoot across the Ribble has changed from Knight Stainforth to Little Stainforth which aptly describes the hamlet, though not the impressive hall.

The village has a long history and appears extensively in the records, mainly because of its close associations with the abbey. It had also held a special place in the historic West Riding. As early as 1379, for which year the Poll Tax Returns still exist, Stainforth returned a value far in excess of Bradford's or Settle's and had a recorded population of around 200, close to today's total. Of householders listed all but one were described as free tenants, meaning they paid rent but held their land by hereditary right. The County Rate records of 1602 note that the village was now on a par for tax purposes with Bradford but far in excess of Sheffield, for example.

All in all the twin villages have a fascinating story to tell but perhaps this would need a book to itself. Sorry!

Onwards and Upwards

It is decision time now, folks. You can either opt for the full route or the short route and thereby lop less than 1km (half a mile) off the total. Either way, though, you have a stiff climb ahead of you.

Short Route

Leave the village at the south end. If you follow the short road directly opposite the pub and turn right at the end, and almost immediately left where the road swings to the right, you will see a stile fitted with a lamb gate behind the bungalow. Go between the walls into the main field and keep the post and wire fence to your left. Very shortly a kissing gate in the fence takes you into the wood to follow a mixture of path and rough hewn stone steps up Stainforth Scar. Locally these are known as Cat Steps and they are not natural. Some would say our long-forgotten ancestors built them, but those in the know ridicule that idea as it is perfectly obvious they are the handiwork of the Giant of Winskill.

This woodland is a delight in spring and early summer, its being species-rich in flowering plants.

At the very top climb out of the wood over the stile and cross the field, taking care not to fall off the edge. Again, if you have picked your time well, there should be a profusion of flowers: the purple of wild thyme *(Thymus praecox)*, the delicately patterned common eyebright *(Euphrasia officinalis)*, eggs and bacon or common birdsfoot trefoil *(Lotus corniculatus)* and primroses *(Primula vulgaris)*, to name but a prominent few.

The way continues across this and the next field by way of another stile to bring you out at Low Winskill, a former farm. Go through the yard and along the access track to the top where it joins the tarred lane at the entrance to High Winskill.

– At this point you meet up with the long route from Stainforth –

Long Route

Walk just past the Craven Heifer and turn right down the path alongside Stainforth Beck. Turn left when you reach the road which runs onto the village green and follow the road uphill past a renovated farmhouse with an original 1684 datestone. This stone displays a style common only to Upper Ribblesdale and Langstrothdale which suggests close contact between these two localities.

The view from just above here stretches round from Stackhouse Scar through the prominent edge of Smearsett Scar to Moughton with Ingleborough's flat top peeping above it. Across the valley the cluster of buildings that make up Little Stainforth can be seen.

Continue up the now stony Goat Scar Lane as it climbs upwards, and you might as well indulge in a close study of dry-stone walling techniques as the walls are so high. As you gain height the panorama begins to open up with views of Penyghent and Fountains Fell. The small building on the right may well have been originally built as a hogg house, hoggs being sheep subjected to their first winter and thus perhaps welcoming the shelter and the hay stored therein. The stone stile next to it is for farmer's access only. A little further on, near two sycamores, another interesting and easy to miss feature pops up. Look for the ribbed stonework across the track which looks like the top of a vault or a hump-backed bridge. Peer over the wall and you will see that is exactly what it is – a vaulted tunnel for stock to pass from one field to the other, this one being high enough for cattle. There is another one further up, if you can spot it. These were important since the lower fields gave access to water.

At the top of the lane it is decision time again. It is well worth a few minutes to cross over the stile to Catrigg Force, a narrow but impressive waterfall down which Cowside Beck plunges to become Stainforth Beck. It is very impressive after rain. **Retrace your steps to the lane, go through the gate onto the open pasture and head upslope on a cindery track to the stile in the top wall.** From this vantage point the Three Peaks display their full glory, as well as Fountains Fell and Silverdale down below beyond the prominent farm. In this field there is a scattering of rocks which do not seem to fit. They have a greenish hue rather than the grey-white of the native limestone, which is partly the way they weather but mainly due to colonisation by a lichen *(Rhizocarpon geographicum)*. Indeed these rocks do not belong here but were transported from the Helwith Bridge area over three kilometres to the north by the ice that once covered all but the fell tops: they are glacial erratics.

Once over the top stile, turn right off the main track and follow the walls to the entrance to High Winskill.

– The Long Route meets up with the Short Route here –

You can relax for the next stretch as you amble along the tarred lane below Winskill Stones to meet the Langcliffe – Arncliffe road. Part-way along the lane is Samson's Toe, a huge perched-block erratic sitting on a limestone pedestal, the height of this representing the general land surface at the time the block was dumped there (see Walk 2 for more detail). Between the junction and the cattle grid, which you cross, the remains of a slate water trough are set into the foot of the limestone face. You can well imagine how thirsty the pack ponies must have been having toiled up the long drag from Langcliffe.

Beyond the cattle grid there is a broad grassy track leading to a stile you want, but this track is not a right of way. To stay legal follow the road downhill for about 500 metres, just before a three-way wall junction on the right-hand side of the road. Double back sharp left here and follow the long wall north-east to the ladder stile, and over into the open access area. On one side of the stile there is a modern man's version of a drinking trough: on the other side is a much more aesthetic stone trough ... but imagine the effort required to get it here in the first place, and to hew it from solid rock. Men were men in those days! If you are fortunate, the Lakeland fells should be visible now on the horizon away to the west. **Follow the permissive path but soon leave it to follow the crag round to a ladder stile in the wall above.**

Directly over the wall you can see the twin entrances of Jubilee Cave, and the deep ruts worn on the old packhorse track by the passage of countless hooves.

Hidden Secrets

Of the two dozen or so caves in the vicinity, four are worthy of mention for the wealth of archaeological detail they have revealed. Material remains have been preserved over the millennia, protected by cave deposits and safe from the vagaries of changing climates. All have been extensively excavated and documented and, seeing their dank and musty and often hostile innards now, it is difficult to appreciate how welcoming they must have seemed to our distant forebears.

Jubilee Cave has yielded Neolithic ware, dated to 1800 BC as well as Romano-British pottery.

Attermire Cave has yielded artefacts from the Neolithic, Bronze, Romano-British and medieval periods as well as a Roman coin hoard and Anglian material ... and a human skeleton.

Horseshoe Cave surrendered a wealth of Romano-British material including pottery, brooches, coins and a dismantled "chariot".

Victoria Cave has provided artefacts and material from a warmer period before the onset of the last Ice Age to post-Roman times. As the Victorian excavators dug deep into the cave-earth they uncovered bones of animals associated with other climes, namely hippopotamus, straight-tusked elephant, rhinoceros and hyena, dating way back 120,000 years. At a higher layer the cave-earth had preserved remains of animals of arctic climes: reindeer, bear and lynx, not to mention horse and red deer, dated to between 12,000 and 10,000 BC.

It is interesting to speculate why so many intact bones have been found in these caves, rather than shattered or splintered fragments. Were the predators scared off their cache and forced to abandon their supper, only to forget it, or were the predators themselves demolished by a higher being before having the chance to tuck in?

Signs of human occupation were also uncovered: in the earliest layers were antler tools, possibly used for fishing in the lake that lay at the south

Victoria Cave

end of Attermire Scar. These have been dated to Upper Palaeolithic times during warmer interglacial spells. Neolithic flint and barbed antler harpoons have been dated to the immediate post-glacial phase and, near the top of the cave-earths, a veritable horde of jewellery and coins came to light, all dated to between 200 and 500 AD. Maybe a family or clan group took refuge here in the years of turmoil leading up to and following the Roman withdrawal ... and the cave was really only found by chance in 1838.

Within the near future, as I write, a full archaeological survey is to be carried out in Victoria Cave, by Lancaster University, prior to consolidation work following a recent roof slippage.

I have at times taken shelter in Victoria Cave and have explored all four but I have always been reluctant to linger in their eerie recesses. I find it hard to accept that as late as the late eighteenth century people took refuge in these caves. They must have been desperate.

From the stile opposite Jubilee Cave, turn to the south along the track but, before it reaches the gate, look for a stile over the wall to its left, signposted to Stockdale Lane. Please take heed of the warning signs from the National Park: part of the roof of Victoria Cave slipped a couple of years ago.

Your path maintains a stumbling course between the wall and Brent Scar, crossing another wall on the way, runs out of wall and continues as an obvious track in the same general direction. When it starts to drop down

a boulder-strewn slope you are presented with a new vista. Ignore the ladder stile on the right but follow the wall to the gateway at the bottom, at the foot of Attermire Scar.

Attermire Scar

A Geological Interlude

Look to the right and the left and you will see a major escarpment stretching as far as you can see. Look ahead now. The vegetation changes from bright green to yellows and browns, reflecting different rock types. This escarpment is in fact the Middle Craven Fault (MCF), the boundary between the stable Askrigg Block to the north and the Craven Basin to the south. There is not just one fault: between the MCF and the South Craven Fault is a whole shatter belt with a multitude of smaller cross-faults, in the geological past an extremely unstable zone prone to earth movements, uplift and down-throw. Some of these faults can be identified in the MCF where erosive forces have exploited the lines of weakness and carved out gullies, separating the limestone layers into fault blocks.

Owing to the complexity of geological and tectonic processes, what may seem to the casual observer to be merely limestone is in fact a number of very different limestones, including some which began life as coral reefs on the edge of a tropical sea.

If you look far to the east, up towards Stockdale, you can mentally draw the line of the MCF: to the north is the bright green and grey-white of the limestones; to the south the browns of Rye Loaf Hill are based on younger

Millstone Grit, laid down in later delta conditions. The line is particularly clear here as there has been less cross-faulting.

Down below you is a very wet and flat area – a former lake bed – which has defied earlier attempts to drain it. This lies on Upper Bowland Shales, mud-stones formed in very different conditions from either the limestones or the gritstone. The dominant rushes (species of *Juncus*) testify to the reluctance of the shales to allow the penetration of water.

Different again, in geolspeak, is the conical Sugar Loaf Hill to the right of the marsh. This is made up of various mud-stones and shales, not surprisingly called Sugar Loaf Shales, capped with Sugar Loaf Limestone. I have never seen a sugar loaf but I have been assured they were this shape.

Wherever faulting has occurred, there are likely to be mineral veins: the mineral solutions were able to flow along the pressure cracks within the rocks, later to solidify. On Ben Scar above Attermire Scar, to your left and behind, the Settle Mining Company dug one major cut and sank four shafts after 1868. The main minerals they sought were galena (lead) and chalcopyrite (copper) but secondary ores also occur such as malachite and azurite (both coppers), smithsonite (zinc) and gangue minerals, mainly calcite, baryte, quartz and pyrite.

Homeward Bound

Pass through the gateway and trudge off into the blue keeping the Roman-straight wall on your left. Almost immediately you will stumble across a pile of scrap metal. This is, or was, a Woods Target built in 1860 to be used by Settle Volunteers, a unit formed a year earlier by Morrison of Malham Tarn House. **Carry straight on, ignore the stile on the left, hop over the stile ahead and, at the next cross wall, take the broad grass track, the middle of the three.** Bivi Cave, the obvious cave on the right, is only three metres long! There are twelve caves altogether in Warrendale Knotts. **Carry on along the track,** part of an old road from Settle to Malham Tarn and beyond, **past a ruined lime kiln,** quite a contrast to the Hoffman kiln. **Ahead lies a gate with an attendant squeeze stile, and the track then drops away diagonally** with the view you had at the start of the walk opening up again. **When the wall on your right shoots away to the north, continue ahead to pick up a ruined wall coming in on the left.** Near the bottom you will see clearly the line of the old road but **the right of way dictates that you stay with the wall to meet the Monk's Way.**

If you started from Settle, turn left and retrace your steps: if you started from Langcliffe, turn right and turn back to the section "North from Settle".

Place-name meanings

Attermire	ON	*Authulf's* (pers.name) marsh
Catrigg	ON	the ridge with (wild?) cats
Giggleswick	ON	*Gikel's* (pers.name) dairy farm
Goat Scar	OE/ON	the gorse-covered scar
Langcliffe	OE	the long cliff
Pike Lane	OE	the lane going to the hill top
Ribble	OE	boundary (?)
Settle	OE	dwelling place
Silverdale	OE/ON	the silvery-coloured valley
Smearsett	ON	the shieling where butter was made
Stackhouse	ON	the settlement with hay ricks/stacks
Stainforth	OE	the stony ford
Stockdale	OE/ON	the valley with an outlying cattle farm
Warrendale Knotts	ON	the knobbly hills near the rabbit-filled valley
Winskill	ON	the windswept shieling

Discovery Walk 2

Austwick and Crummackdale: a somewhat erratic meander

Start and Finish: Austwick village green (Grid reference SD768 684).

Parking: There is no car park in Austwick, so park sensitively on the road. There is limited parking in Crummackdale for motorists choosing that part of the walk.

Public transport: Austwick lies on the bus route from Settle to Ingleton, operated by Bibby (tel. 015242 41330). Austwick also lies on the Dales Link route (see Walk 1).

Facilities: Only in Austwick: The Game Cock serves morning coffee and lunches. There is a good village store cum post office.

Outline of the Walk: Austwick – Jop Ridding – Wharfe – Crummackdale – Norber – Austwick.

Length: 9.5km (6 miles) for the full route; 7km (4½ miles) for the shortened route.

Ordnance Survey Map: Outdoor Leisure 2. Landranger 98.

Introduction

Austwick and Crummackdale lie off the main tourist track and benefit from a lack of congestion. Perhaps it is because Austwick has no car park, and the dale no through road, that this area is safe from honeypot status.

The dale is a honeypot in one sense, though: it has long been a mecca for students of geology, such is the complexity of the rocks here. Norber, too, is a favoured spot for its incredible array of boulders, large and small, that were dumped by passing ice sheets, but looking as if dropped from the sky.

The National Park has a greater concentration of protected areas, SSSIs, than the rest of the county put together. On today's walk you will encounter two, designated for different reasons. The Oxenber and Wharfe Woods SSSI has importance for flowers and wooded limestone pavement, while Crummackdale is bounded by the enormous Ingleborough SSSI, designated to conserve vast stretches of limestone pavement.

You need a full day for the whole route, though it would not be a long day

Discovery Walk 2

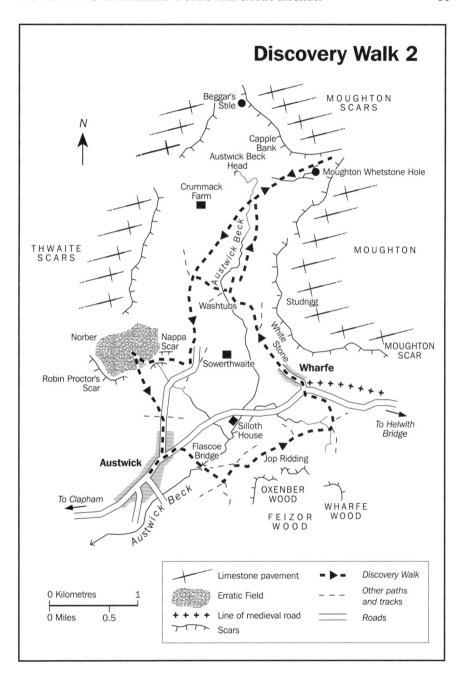

N

Beggar's Stile

MOUGHTON SCARS

Capple Bank

Austwick Beck Head

Moughton Whetstone Hole

Crummack Farm

Austwick Beck

THWAITE SCARS

MOUGHTON

Washtubs

Studrigg

Norber

Nappa Scar

Sowerthwaite

White Stone

MOUGHTON SCAR

Wharfe

Robin Proctor's Scar

+ + + + + + + +

To Helwith Bridge

Silloth House

Flascoe Bridge

Jop Ridding

Austwick

To Clapham

Beck

OXENBER WOOD

WHARFE WOOD

FEIZOR WOOD

Austwick Beck

Symbol	Description	Symbol	Description
Limestone pavement		Discovery Walk
Erratic Field		Other paths and tracks
+ + + + Line of medieval road		Roads
Scars		

0 Kilometres 1

0 Miles 0.5

unless you choose to explore some of Moughton's pavements. For those with less time at hand you have the option to shorten the route.

One option is to miss out the bulk of Crummackdale. For this first read "From Austwick to Oxenber Wood" and follow the main route through to the early part of the "Crummackdale" section to Washtubs. Pick up the route again in the section headed "Down Dale" and follow it to the end.

From Austwick to Oxenber Wood

Like many of the villages in the Dales, Austwick can trace its roots back to the Dark Ages when it was founded as the "east dairy farm", presumably east of Clapham. The village remained subservient to Clapham until 1879 when it was separated off as a parish in its own right. Today Austwick is a pleasant village, away from the hustle and bustle of main roads, centred around its village green.

The walk starts from the village green. Head east along the road past The Game Cock and the primary school. On the other side of the road, shortly before the school, is the three-storied Norcliffe House. This was built in the early nineteenth century by members of the Independent Order of Rechabites, a benefit society that strictly forbade alcohol. The building consisted of two households with the top floor designated as a meeting room.

Continue on the road, out of the village, until you reach a bridleway leading off to the right by the first barn. Turn down the bridleway which soon brings you to Austwick Beck with its ancient clapper bridge and ford. Amazingly one of the slabs of Flascoe Bridge was smashed by vandals in 1992, but the villagers soon rallied round to repair it.

Carry on up the narrowing lane, ignoring the stile on the left but taking note of the lichen-encrusted thorns. You may well enjoy the company of an inquisitive robin who guards his linear territory well from his home in the ivy, and of a rather garrulous wren who seems to take exception to all-comers.

Buff,
Streaked

Buff,
← Streaked

White
hint on
Rump

At the four-way junction bear left onto Wood Lane and follow it to the viewpoint at the next junction. Straight across the valley lies the entrance to Crummackdale, between Robin Proctor's Scar to the left and Moughton Scar to the right. The dale itself is hidden from view

Wren (average size: 10cm)

by a rock rib on which sits Sowerthwaite Farm. In the field immediately below you are early medieval cultivation terraces (called lynchets) whose form and pattern will be seen more clearly near the end of the walk.

Turn right at this junction, off Wood Lane, and up the short length of walled track to a field gate. Beyond the gate keep the wall on your immediate left. Rising up on your right to Oxenber Wood is an exceedingly pock-marked landscape, the result of a long period of quarrying. Stay with the wall beyond the next gate, as the main track heads upslope next to an ancient holloway, or sunken track, heading over to Feizor. It is no longer a right of way.

In the spring these banks are carpeted with bluebells *(Hyacinthoides non-scripta)*, one of the sure indicators of ancient woodland cover, most of which has now gone from these lower slopes.

Oxenber Wood SSSI

The three woods on the limestone tops above you are part of the Oxenber Wood Site of Special Scientific Interest (SSSI), designated way back in 1955. The woods contain outstanding examples of wooded limestone pavements, open glade grassland and pockets of marsh, all of which have been subjected to controlled grazing. Please note that entry is strictly by permit only.

Some of the pavement has been designated as being of national importance in view of the flora within the grykes (cracks between the limestone blocks). On the northern slopes, those you can see from the walk, the dominant tree species are birch, hazel, rowan and holly, with ash and hawthorn on the less acidic soils. The ground flora is rich indeed: dog's mercury *(Mercurialis perennis)*, wild thyme *(Thymus praecox)*, and blue moor-grass *(Sesleria caerulea)* are ubiquitous on the more alkaline limestone soils. On the more acidic slopes tufted hair-grass *(Deschampsia cespitosa)* and mat-grass *(Nardus stricta)* are the common grasses, providing a welcoming habitat for flowering plants that include wood anemone *(Anemone nemorosa)* and heath bedstraw *(Galium saxatile)*.

Above Jop Ridding, at the foot of the main slope, ground conditions are wetter and the soils more acidic so here the plant community differs. Various rushes *(Juncus spp)* and sedges *(Carex spp)* replace the grasses with such botanical beauties as bog asphodel *(Narthecium ossifragum)*, marsh valerian *(Valeriana dioica)* and marsh arrowgrass *(Triglochin palustris)*.

Now you know why access is by permit only.

Onward to Wharfe

Down below in the valley bottom you will see a white-painted house where the road crosses Austwick Beck. Now a residence called Silloth House, it used to be the site of a water-powered mill where flagstones from Dry Rigg Quarry were cut and polished using a water-powered saw invented in the late eighteenth century. These flagstones were in great demand in the southern dales in the building of houses and cow-byres. This former activity is preserved in the names of Mill Bridge and Dam House Bridge, the site of the mill dam.

Carry straight on along the wall, past a decomposing barn and over two ladder stiles to pass in front of Jop Ridding Farm, whose owners are doing their bit to put trees back into the Dales-scape. **Your route now follows the farm access track to where it crosses a small stream by a young copse.**

Leave the track here by climbing the stone stepping stile on the left to a ladder stile across the field. A small footbridge takes you across another stream, both of which are head-waters of Wharfe Gill Sike. These two sikes are soon in for a shock as they crash and plunge down into the recesses of the gill. **Beyond the footbridge another ladder stile leads you into a larger field in which the path is not apparent on the ground. Cross it diagonally, heading just right of a prominent rocky knoll, making for a lonesome telegraph post. Another footbridge here confirms your position and just beyond a stone stile allows you to join the road. Turn left here but bear right at the first major bend, along the unmade lane into Wharfe.**

There is a maze of lanes ahead, so take careful note. From the tarred road follow the lane making sure to bear right again at the very first junction, past a gate (on the right) where a lost medieval road from Helwith Bridge enters Wharfe. Go past the house and then immediately bear right again by a barn left of the track. Carry on past the front door of the next cottage (tread lightly through their front garden), then to the right of a minute cottage above a wider track. Contour to the right on White Stone Lane which soon joins the main, stony track from the village.

Crummackdale

Carry straight on by two adjoining barns, ignoring the stiles that permit entry to White Stone Access area. Further along, just before an isolated field barn, you will see that part of the crag has been fenced off. Part of the Access agreement involved a scheme to render stock-proof an area of relict woodland to encourage regeneration of trees and ground flora.

The ground falls away on your left to a secluded valley and in wet conditions you can hear the thundering of the water higher up this valley where Austwick Beck cascades over a falls before disappearing into the depths. The wooded area in which all this occurs is, like so many little gems in the Dales, denied to us.

The lane begins to lose height slightly on the approach to a track junction. Take the left fork but only for a short distance to Austwick Beck. The beck is bridged by an ancient clapper bridge constructed of great slabs of local flagstone laid on stone piers. Just downstream of the clapper bridge there is a single-slab bridge and I would defy anyone to think of moving that slab. Even the thought of trying to lift it makes me shudder.

Until the early decades of this century, local farmers used to bring their sheep here to be scrubbed in the days before chemical dips and tanks. They would plunge into the beck and man-handle the sheep one by one to remove ticks, lice and whatever else had established squatters' rights in the fleeces. Appropriately this now delightful spot is known as Washtubs.

Washtubs

For the short route, cross the clapper bridge and follow White Stone Lane onwards to its junction with Crummack Lane, and rejoin the long route later on. For the full course, however, re-trace your steps back from the beck to the track junction and turn left up Moughton Lane, as it gently ascends beneath Studrigg. This track is yet another example of an Occupation Road (see "The Northern Dales") that bears a long ancestry.

At the top of the initial rise on the track, pause to take in the view. You will see that the very top layer of rocks is quite different from the bulk of the lower slopes. In fact the two sets of rocks were formed in different geological periods. As you progress up the dale you cross and re-cross a succession of rock types, and these changes are, to a certain extent, reflected in the walls that bound the lane. The original wall builders were opportunists, taking the stone that lay to hand to craft their linear masterpieces. At first the walls consist of dark Austwick sandstones, many of which provide a favourable habitat for the lichen *Rhizocarpon geographicum* which tinges the rock green.

Further up the track, beyond the first cross-gate, thin flagstones begin to appear in the walls, and an increasing quantity of grey-white limestone. As you approach the next gate thin, flaky shales come to the fore which, with the benefit of hindsight, were clearly of no use for walling. Beyond the gate the right-hand wall has completely weathered away in places. Here today, gone tomorrow.

Between the two gates take careful note of the hillslope away to the right on Studrigg. The top layer of rocks is formed of limestone laid more or less horizontally: the lower layers consist of the older rocks whose beds slope at an angle of 40-45 degrees. You can see the junction of the two very clearly just before the point where the wall leaves the scree, where the topmost crags are most pronounced. The junction between them is an obvious break, what geologists call an unconformity: a whole geological period is missing and horizontal rocks cannot logically sit directly on top of tilted rocks.

The unconformity at Studrigg

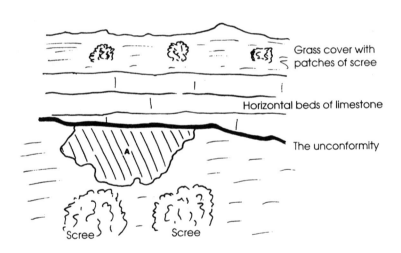

A - Steeply dipping Silurian rocks

The cross-section depicts the structure of Crummackdale's rocks and shows the overall folding pattern. The oldest rocks have been exposed by erosion, the tops of the two anticlines have completely gone and the syncline now appears as the highest outcrops within the valley. This is what most geologists call inverse relief. The following diagrams also illustrate these features.

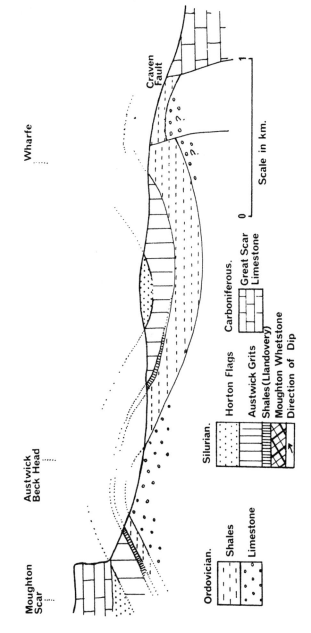

A Sketch Section along Crummackdale, (approx. North to South).

Moughton Scar

Austwick Beck Head

Wharfe

Craven Fault

Scale in km.

0   1

Ordovician.
Shales
Limestone

Silurian.
Horton Flags
Austwick Grits
Shales (Llandovery)
Moughton Whetstone
Direction of Dip

Carboniferous.
Great Scar Limestone

(Reproduced with permission from: D. Crutchley "Geology of the Three Peaks", published by Dalesman.)

THE ROCK SEQUENCE IN CRUMMACKDALE

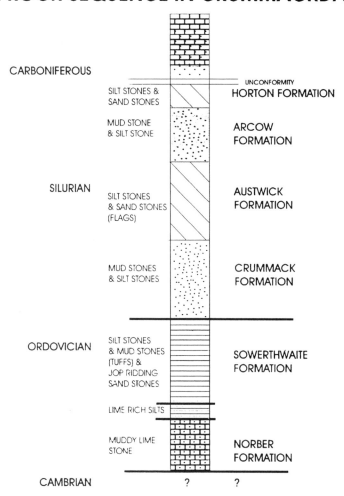

CARBONIFEROUS

UNCONFORMITY

SILT STONES & SAND STONES	HORTON FORMATION
MUD STONE & SILT STONE	ARCOW FORMATION

SILURIAN

SILT STONES & SAND STONES (FLAGS)	AUSTWICK FORMATION
MUD STONES & SILT STONES	CRUMMACK FORMATION

ORDOVICIAN

SILT STONES & MUD STONES (TUFFS) & JOP RIDDING SAND STONES	SOWERTHWAITE FORMATION
LIME RICH SILTS	
MUDDY LIME STONE	NORBER FORMATION

CAMBRIAN   ?   ?

A Villainous Past

Stay on the lane as it approaches the beck and meets a footpath from the left at a ladder stile. If you look to the head of the dale, where the limestone seems to hem the valley in, you may be able to pick out a nick on the skyline. This is Beggar's Stile, which leads to the upper part of the dale, so what your eyes think is the valley head is nothing of the sort. Beyond Beggar's Stile the dale becomes a huge, rocky amphitheatre, hemmed in on all sides by limestone pavements. This amphitheatre is known as Thieves Moss.

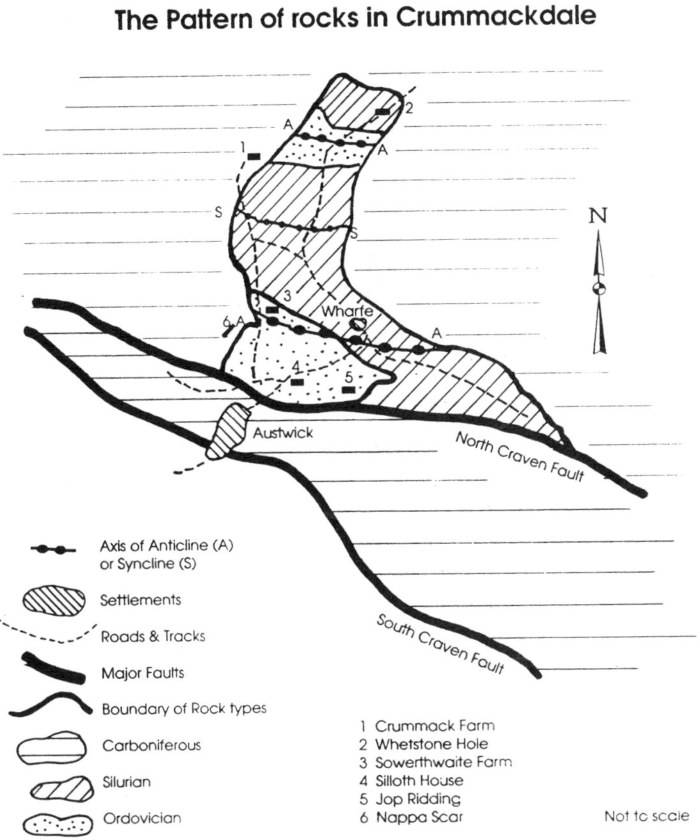

The Pattern of rocks in Crummackdale
N
A
A
S
S
A
A
1
2
3
4
5
6
Wharfe
Austwick
North Craven Fault
South Craven Fault
Axis of Anticline (A) or Syncline (S)
Settlements
Roads & Tracks
Major Faults
Boundary of Rock types
Carboniferous
Silurian
Ordovician
1 Crummack Farm
2 Whetstone Hole
3 Sowerthwaite Farm
4 Silloth House
5 Jop Ridding
6 Nappa Scar
Not to scale

Beggars and thieves? Running along the edge of the plateau beyond the head of the dale is the old coach road that linked Lancaster and Newcastle, on an open stretch that has no sign of habitation for more than eight kilometres. If any stretch of road was fertile hunting ground for highwaymen, thieves and beggars, then this must have been it.

To the Head of the Dale

You will be returning to the stile later but carry on up the dale for the present where the scars above begin to close in on you. There is a site worth inspecting at the head of the valley, so it is well worth the diversion. The names around here are a little confusing. Everything to your left is called Moughton and everything to your right is also called Moughton as far back as Wharfe and Helwith Bridge. You need to be in a hot air balloon to fully

Capple Bank

appreciate the Moughtons: it is almost an infinity of limestone pavement, stretching unbroken into the distance. Much of it was formerly cloaked with juniper bushes, some of which you can see on the skyline, but they seem to be shrinking in area. No one is really sure why.

The edge on your left, Capple Bank, is home to one of our most majestic birds, the peregrine falcon. Now here is a real ornithological success story. In 1994, in the Park, twelve known and closely monitored nest sites success-fully reared 29 chicks, more than double the total for the previous year. I have sat here for hours entranced by the aerial display of mother and father feeding fledgling junior on the wing, or amused by the persistent and piercing shrieking of chicks on the nest as they demand to be fed.

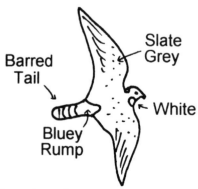

Barred Tail

Slate Grey

White

Bluey Rump

Peregrine Falcon (average size: 43cm)

However, you do not have spare hours at hand. It is time to move on. **As the track begins to climb,** ribs of rock break its surface, thin beds at first but soon thicker beds are interspersed. Bear in mind that you are stepping over the truncated, upturned ends of the beds which dip very steeply beneath your feet. **Soon the final gate is reached,** beyond which the lane be-comes an open green swathe climbing through the bracken. To the left, by the wall, lie the remains of an old shooting hut, a relic of a bygone grouse shooting era. **A short step ahead from the gate is a spring,** Moughton Whetstone Hole, the whole point of the diversion to the head of the dale, and another place to linger awhile.

Moughton Whetstone

Scattered around in the bed of the beck, between the spring and the wall, are fragments of rock with thin purple-red and green bands. Wet the fragments to make the colours stand out clearly. These bands are called liesegang rings and they were formed, probably in the Devonian period, before the limestone was laid down. The coloration is due to weathering of oxides within the sandstones.

The whetstones occur in situ on Capple Bank. They were quarried from there and brought to the spring en route to the growing industrial enterprises of the West Riding. Whetstone is a quarryman's rather than a geologist's term: before the days of Carborundum, whetstone was used for sharpening metals. There you have it – another lost industry.

Down Dale

Re-trace your steps back along the lane as far as the ladder stile, noting the long-range view to the south-west across the Wenning Valley to Burn Moor on the horizon, as well as Austwick Beck Head (to the west) which is one of the major sources of the River Wenning. **Cross the stile and the footbridge over the beck.** Note the water mint *(Mentha aquatica)*, with purplish leaves, growing in the beck. Have a smell! On several occasions I have seen a grey heron patrolling this stretch of beck in its endless search for a full stomach, and I have never failed to see a dipper here. Keep your eyes peeled for this beautiful little bird. It is slightly smaller than a blackbird but has very distinctive colouring, with a white breast and chestnut belly. It has the ability to walk on the bed of the stream looking for its favourite invertebrates, and finds sufficient food to overwinter in the Dales. If you do not catch a glimpse of one skimming along the beck, you may see one in its characteristic pose, bobbing up and down on a rock.

Stay with the wall on your right to a second stile, after which you should keep the wall to your left, as the way drops down from the highest point on this path, though it is in fact the lowest point of the skyline. Note how the thin and flaky siltstones between the more massive sandstone beds are being more rapidly weathered away.

At the foot of the slope is another ladder stile and you should follow the faint line of the path over this and the ensuing three ladder stiles to join Crummack Lane at its junction with White Stone Lane, where the short route rejoins. You have also crossed a small sike, covered in summer with a mass of white common watercress *(Nasturtium officinale)* which is actually not common at all. It is, of course, edible if you enjoy rabbit food. The small blue flower growing in the water is brooklime *(Veronica beccabunga)*: it too can go on your salad.

Follow Crummack Lane southwards, past the entrance to Sowerthwaite Farm, to yet another ladder stile on the right. The view from the lane, particularly at its highest point, illuminates much of the geology of the area, and displays the entire rock succession in the Dales from the very oldest Ordovician rocks beneath you now, through the Silurian and into the Carboniferous limestones on Moughton and on the broken ridge that runs from Smearsett Scar to Oxenber Wood. The Wensleydale Group capped with Millstone Grit form Fountains Fell in the distance. Between the prominent proboscis of Moughton Nab and Smearsett is the line of the North Craven Fault, while the South Craven Fault marks the right-hand edge of the wooded Oxenber. Beyond this lies the Craven Basin. Away to your right, across the Wenning are the grits of the Bowland Block. No wonder that Crummackdale is a favourite haunt for geologists.

Back to the route: climb over the stile (on the right) and follow the wall along as it contours to Nappa Scar.

Nappa Scar

Nappa Unconformity

The geological term unconformity is given to a situation when there is time gap in the rocks. As you stand on the shelf above the dark grey Ordovician rocks (over 440 million years old) raise your hand and touch the horizontal beds of Carboniferous limestone (340 million years old). You are spanning a gap of over 100 million years! The Silurian and Devonian are missing from the record. Between the two sets of rocks is a layer of rounded boulders and pebbles which lay on the ocean floor here in the Carboniferous. They have long since been cemented together to form a type of rock called conglomerate, Nature's own concrete.

A Norber Erratic

Back to the Start

Beyond Nappa there is a new stone stile which allows access to Norber where you can wander at will amongst the enormous glacial erratics that litter the hillside. Higher up, away to the right are the famous perched-block erratics, whose massive Silurian boulders now balance precariously on limestone plinths. See if you can find the famous tripod stone. This whole collection of rocks certainly puts one in awe of the unstoppable power of moving ice.

Leave Norber by heading south-south-eastwards to the bottom enclosing wall, to the left of a clump of trees, passing by a scar where wild strawberries *(Fragaria vesca)* have found a safe foothold. **The walls funnel into a step-over stile by a small gate, beyond which you cross the large field to exit over the final ladder stile of the day. Turn left on Thwaite Lane,** part of a medieval route from Fountains Abbey to Lancaster and the Lake District. **At**

the cross-roads turn right down the tarred road towards Austwick. The first building you pass is the former Dear Bought farm.

A Tragic Story

Dear Bought was given this name as the result of a disagreement between two brothers. When their father died, one of the brothers inherited the whole lot, leaving the other dispossessed, but he kicked up a fuss. The bickering went on for so long that the lucky brother agreed to a wager. If his dispossessed brother could hand mow a huge meadow within one day and have it completed by nightfall, he could have the farm – and be damned.

The brother took on the challenge and began his seemingly impossible task at first light. He drove himself hard all day and far into the evening, determined to prove himself. Indeed he did, completing the job just before the night fell. He strode back to the house to claim his prize, had a drink of water ... and dropped dead. There could be a moral here!

Shortly afterwards you will pass by the entrance to Austwick Hall which has medieval origins and has been held by several illustrious families: the Darcys first, later on the Yorkes, and from 1573 to 1846 the Ingilby family. You cannot see it from the road so no need to dally. **Continue down the road and turn right at the bottom, back into the village.**

Place-name meanings

Austwick	OE	the east dairy farm (i.e. east of Clapham)
Bowland	OE	the curving valley
Capple Bank	ON	the bank where horses graze
Clapham	OE	the homestead by the noisy stream
Crummack	Brit	the crooked valley (or hill?)
Feizor	ON	*Fiach's (or Fech's)* (pers. names) shieling
Flascoe	ON	the marshy wood
Helwith	ON	the ford where flagstones are found
Hunterstye	OE	the hunter's stile
Moughton Nab	OE/ON	the hill with heaps of stones
Nappa (Scar)	OE (ON)	the hill top looking like an inverted bowl
Norber	OE	the northern hill
Oxenber	OE	the hill where oxen graze
Smearsett	ON	the summer shieling where butter was made
Sowerthwaite	OE/ON	the clearing where the grass is sour
Studrigg	OE/ON	the ridge where there is a herd of horses
Thwaite	ON	the clearing in the forest
Wenning	OE	the dark river
Wharfe	ON	the nook (between two streams)

Discovery Walk 3

Malham Tarn and Malham Lings: a classic landscape trail

Start and Finish: Street Gate, 1km south-east of Malham Tarn (Grid reference SD905 656).

Parking: There is ample off-road parking at Street Gate. Motorists could park at Water Sinks if doing only parts of the walk.

Public transport: A Sunday service operates in the summer, run by Pride of the Dales (tel. 01756 753123). The bus stops at the south of the tarn on its route linking Grassington, Malham, Settle and Littondale. See also the Dales Link service (see Walk 1).

Facilities: There is normally a mobile ice-cream van at Water Sinks during the summer and some winter weekends.

Outline of the Walk: Street Gate – Malham Tarn – Dean Moor – Comb Scar – Malham Lings – New Close – Seaty Hill – Street Gate.

Length: The full route is 9km (5.6 miles), but it can be split into four loops, each of about 3km (less than 2 miles).

Ordnance Survey Map: Outdoor Leisure 10. Landranger 98.

Introduction

This walk passes through some splendid limestone scenery which has been shaped by internal forces creating the North Craven Fault, and by the erosive power of ice. I will discuss the detailed limestone and glacial features as the route progresses. Geography students come to Malham from all over the country to study such features because of their outstanding quality, so you will be in good company.

The area also possesses a wealth of archaeological features hidden in the pastures, onwards from Bronze Age times over 3000 years ago. It takes a tutored eye to pick them out and make sense of them, and I hope you will be able to develop some of these skills today.

Botanical diversity, too, is outstanding and I will point out some special flowers and ferns that grow on limestone, in what is part of the Malham-Arncliffe SSSI.

It is partly for these reasons that most of today's walk lies within an Open Access Area, with only Great Close and Ha Mire being excluded, as shown on the route map. This open access policy has been made possible under the Countryside Stewardship scheme. In return for guaranteeing public access and sympathetic land management, farmers are entitled to grants.

The route can be split up into a series of loops as desired:

Loop 1 – start with the section "Best Foot Forward" then jump to "Kames and Kettle Holes" and follow the main route through to the end of "Comb Scar to Water Sinks", then return to the road.

Loop 2 – also start with "Best Foot Forward" and "Kames and Kettle Holes" but then jump straight to "Blood or Water?" and follow the route through to the end of "A Historic Landscape", again to return by road.

Loop 3 – follow the road south from Street Gate and pick up the route at the start of "New Close" and follow it to the end.

Best Foot Forward

Forsake the pilgrim hordes snaking up to the giddy heights of Malham Cove, or into the dark recesses of Gordale Scar, and explore the lesser known aspects of Malham.

At the start, at Street Gate, you could head off in any one of five directions and in each case you would be following a road that has been in continuous use since the Middle Ages and, no doubt, for long before then. The track that comes through the gate from the east, Mastiles Lane, and heads off to the west, now tarred, was a major artery in the monastic period from 1150 to the early sixteenth century.

On this walk you have a choice of two directions. **On a short route you can follow the tarred road from Street Gate westwards, soon passing the second crossroads,** where another track leads to Malham Tarn. Almost exactly 100 metres past this crossroads is a slab of sandstone to the right of your road. The slab has a square-cut hole in it. In medieval times there were no walls in this landscape, and the tracks across the moors could be difficult to follow, especially in murky conditions. To give the traveller a morale booster, marker crosses were set up at intervals. Several of them survive in situ along Mastiles Lane and elsewhere in the Dales. This sandstone slab was the base into which a cross or post was set. There is another further along.

Carry on along the road ignoring the Pennine Way crossing, until you reach the car park and rejoin the full route.

The alternative is to head north from Street Gate on the gravelled track which heads off to Middle House Farm, which can be seen in the distance. Everything up there is limestone – the heights of Parson's Pulpit (538 metres)

Discovery Walk 3

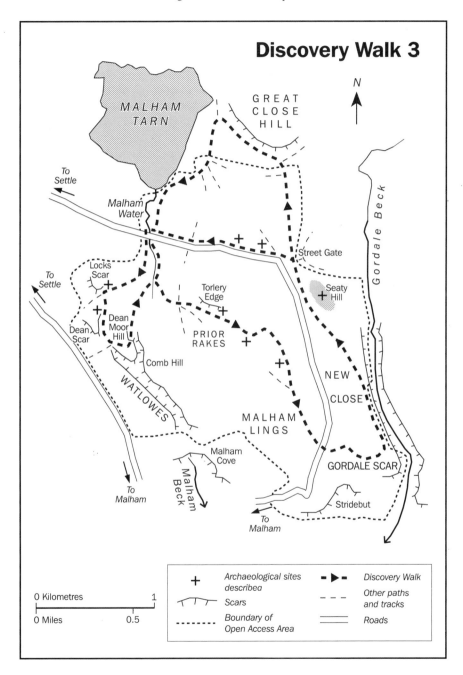

MALHAM
TARN

GREAT
CLOSE
HILL

N

To
Settle

Malham
Water

To
Settle

Locks
Scar

Street Gate

Torlery
Edge

Seaty
Hill

Gordale Beck

Dean
Scar

Dean
Moor
Hill

PRIOR
RAKES

Comb Hill

W A T L O W E S

NEW

CLOSE

MALHAM
LINGS

Malham
Cove

GORDALE SCAR

To
Malham

Malham
Beck

Stridebut

To
Malham

+ Archaeological sites described	▪▶▪ Discovery Walk
⊤⊤⊤ Scars	- - - Other paths and tracks
••••••• Boundary of Open Access Area	═══ Roads

0 Kilometres 1

0 Miles 0.5

and High Mark (515 metres) to the east, and to the west the rounded form of Great Close Hill, with an Iron Age burial mound forming a pimple on top. **The track drops down into Great Close Mire,** with small watery remnants reminding us that there once lay another lake here, in the immediate post-glacial period. **Cross the cattle grid and turn left on the rough track that swings between the plantation and the foot of the hill.** This is a permissive track. Further round Great Close Scar becomes more pronounced and has an old stone wall along the top, presumably to stop cattle from committing a bovine version of hara-kiri.

A Lesson in Geomorphology

Whenever geological maps depict limestone they use a brick-like symbol. This is because the rock is split by horizontal breaks called bedding planes, and vertical cracks called joints.

The limestone formed when this area lay under a warm and clear tropical sea. During settled periods lime deposits from sea creatures (algae) accumulated on the sea floor as layers, or beds. When the sea became "cloudy" – maybe because of an earthquake or owing to silt being brought in by rivers – algae died off. They could not survive in the darker water. This silt formed a thin layer on top of the limestone bed, forming the bedding plane. The process was repeated many times.

In the Carboniferous period the vertical cracks, if present, were closed tight yet, if you look at any exposed limestone face today, the cracks are wide open. You can see this very clearly on Great Close Scar. The question is why?

There are three geomorphological processes that have acted on the scars. Firstly, imagine by how much the whole land surface must have been depressed under the weight of the glaciers and ice sheets. Remove that weight and the surface would slowly spring back, thus starting to open up the cracks. This process is called pressure release or dilation.

Secondly, in the period immediately after the melting of the ice, when temperatures were far more extreme than nowadays, frost action further opened up the cracks. Water in the cracks would freeze and expand, then thaw, then freeze and further expand, thereby weakening the rock. This is called frost shattering.

Thirdly, natural carbonic acid in rainwater and soil water reacts chemically with limestone. Water settling in the cracks slowly dissolves the rock away in a process called dissolution and it is, of course, a process still occurring wherever limestone outcrops.

By Malham Tarn

Your track joins the main East Drive alongside the Tarn so you should turn left across Ha Mire, formerly part of a larger lake, and through the gate where you will find a small box containing National Trust leaflets. The individual trees have walls encircling them as a protective measure against grazing animals, by the way. In early summer look out, along the side of the path, for the delicate pink bird's-eye primrose *(Primula farinosa)*, the unofficial emblem of the Dales. On the drier ground nearer to the gate, mountain pansy *(Viola lutea)* has found a niche. With flowers of yellow or violet, or a mixture of both, it must rank as one of the best loved flowers,

Leave the drive at the gate and take the grass path alongside the south edge of the predominantly larch wood, and down to the water's edge. At the head of the tarn stands Tarn House, nestling in the woods at the foot of Highfolds Scar. Across the tarn, on the skyline to the west, look for a V-shaped nick, where the telegraph poles are. This marks the line of the North Craven Fault. **Follow the shore-line to the outfall at Tarn Foot** where Malham Water drains away over an artificially raised slipway. **A path takes you, parallel to the stream, to the unsightly and unofficial car park where the short route rejoins. Turn right on the road, through the gate and over the stream.**

If "Dee" is there with his van you can relax with an ice-cream while you read on.

Highfolds and Great Close Scar

Kames and Kettle Holes

The area between the tarn and the higher ground to the south is very hummocky with irregularly shaped and sized mounds with shallow, often wet, depressions between them. The mounds are called kames and the hollows are kettle holes. Just across the stream, half way between tarn and road, one kame has been cut into by the stream, exposing its innards. This kind of terrain is the result of deposition onto melting ice.

As the last ice sheet was finally melting, much of the melt-water escaped down channels such as Watlowes and Gordale Scar, but eventually some of the ice became trapped and marooned in the basin that is now the tarn and the area around it. The stagnant ice melted unevenly, and was slowly covered by material brought in as melt-water flowed down off the hills. Because the material was deposited by water, it is well-sorted and lacking the rocks and boulders you would find in ice deposits. As time went on, all the stagnant ice in the basin melted away, leaving the material – up to 15 metres thick – behind. Because the ice had been uneven, so the layers of material were uneven, and the resulting land surface was itself bound to be uneven – hence the kames and kettle holes.

A Fault and a Fault-line

Between Malham Water and Street Gate the road you are now on lies directly on top of the North Craven Fault. It is the Craven equivalent of walking along California's infamous San Andreas Fault. Everything south of the road is limestone, the same rocks that appear north of the tarn above the scars. Between Highfolds Scar and Great Close Scar and the road the rock is Silurian siltstone (of the Horton Formation – see Walk 2). I have seen it written in a guidebook that Highfolds is the North Craven Fault. It is not. What has happened in the 280 million years since the fault was created by tectonic forces (forcing the north upwards relative to the south) is that processes of erosion have been attacking the weakened and shattered rock along the fault, wearing back the limestone layers from the fault to Highfolds Scar. Thus the road sits on the fault while Highfolds and Great Close Scar are the present fault-line. Movement on any fault takes the form of countless earthquakes as pressure builds up and is released in a series of jerks, over a period of hundreds of thousands of years. There is no sudden drop.

Dean Moor

Go through the kissing gate in the fence and take the bridleway uphill, parallel to but away from the fence. It is signposted to Langscar Gate. When you reach the top, catch your breath, enjoy the 360 degree panorama, get your map out and fix your long-distance bearings.

The grassland here is liberally sprinkled with blue common dog violet *(Viola riviniana)* and bright yellow tormentil *(Potentilla erecta)*. This latter seems to grow everywhere on slightly acidic soils, and appears to flower for ever. In the past it was one of the stalwarts of Nature's herbal remedy cupboard. An infusion (drink) made from the roots was guaranteed to cure your diarrhoea and colic, your cystitis and your sore throat. Quite a package! In addition much of the limestone Dales is liberally covered in summer with the purple of the aromatic wild thyme *(Thymus praecox)*, and the tiny white heath bedstraw *(Galium saxatile)*, present in profusion wherever there is a plastering of acidic glacial drift.

Press on but leave the track before the top. Head to the right, to the small limestone outcrop with a prominent, if small, overhang. Clamber up above the overhang. Below you is an Iron Age homestead. Look carefully and pick out the remains of small hut circles directly below, and enclosure walls sealing the grassed area between this and the adjacent outcrop. If there happens to be a west wind blowing, you will realise how sheltered the site is. Now transfer to the other outcrop – Locks Scar – and look below the cliff. There are more enclosure walls, sufficient shelter for trees to gain a foothold, and a permanent water supply.

Drop back round on to the bridleway but take the green path that heads south from here. Do not follow the bridleway over to the gate in the far wall. You are making for an obvious gap between the gently shelving limestone plateau ahead right and the small knoll on the left. When you are nearer to the gap, leave the path and make for the massive isolated boulder to the right of the path.

Bronze Age hut circle, Dean Scar

This boulder is a rock garden in itself, and it illustrates how soil is formed. By the end of the last glaciation all soil and plants (and much rock) had been scraped away by the ice. Only bare rock and gravel remained. The first organisms to colonise this bare ground were lichens, and there are a number of species here, variously coloured, growing outwards at no more than 1 millimetre per year. Lichens subsist by extracting minerals from within the rock and from rain and dust as they grow. Ever so slowly they change the micro-habitat on the rock and so allow mosses to gain a foothold. They, in turn, bring about the "optimum" conditions for the other types of flora you can see in the crevices of this rock. In other words they help to break down the rock surface into a thin layer of soil, by chemical action. Perhaps the cactus-like biting stonecrop *(Sedum acre)* is the prettiest sitting tenant here.

Walk on towards the foot of the scar and look for an almost round stone enclosure with wall footings made of limestone slabs. Compare the size, structure and building quality of this enclosure with the Iron Age homestead seen earlier. Mankind is supposed to progress as time advances, yet this structure is almost certainly the remains of a Middle Bronze Age hut, possibly a thousand years older than the other site.

Leave the enclosure and pass around and below Dean Scar, through the natural open doorway between it and the knoll. Two of my favourite flowers maintain a precarious existence on the face of this scar. There is the attractive yellow of the common rock-rose *(Helianthemum nummularium)* and the rich purple-crimson of the bloody cranesbill *(Geranium sanguineum)*.

Watlowes

Drop downslope and follow the wall beyond its dog leg into the head of a narrowing chasm. Ignore the ladder stile and the twin step-over stiles and stick to the higher path that contours round the edge of Dean Moor Hill.

As you begin to contour round you are presented with a magnificent view along the full length of Watlowes Dry Valley, with a long-distance prospect of the fells to the north of Skipton.

Watlowes and Comb Scar

These are both dry valleys, that is they do not have a stream flowing through them. In fact they are meltwater channels. Glaciologists (they who study glaciers and glacial processes) believe the melting of the ice sheets lasted about two thousand years. Water in the ground would have been frozen solid preventing surface water from sinking into the cracks, and the incredible volume of water flowing beneath and issuing from the ice, flowing roughly south-eastwards, carved for itself deep valleys.

Watlowes is the very deep valley that starts where two much smaller valleys converge: the one you have followed just now, and the one you are about to enter.

There are two reasons for the difference in scale between Watlowes and Comb Scar. Watlowes would have channelled water from a much wider area than Comb Scar valley. In fact Comb Scar has been left "hanging" where it enters Watlowes. The other factor is that a fault runs down Watlowes: the meltwater exploited this line of weakness. If you know what you are looking for, you can locate hardened and mineralised crystals of rock, superheated and transformed by the pressure of movements down the fault. Watlowes ends in the precipitous 80 metre drop that is Malham Cove. In those two thousand years it would have been a waterfall to rival Niagara or Victoria Falls.

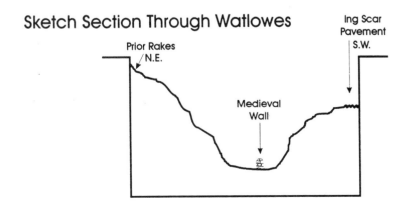

Sketch Section Through Watlowes

As you stand above the head of Watlowes you will see that the valley is asymmetrical in cross-section: the south (right) side has a steeper wall than the north (left) side. Why should this be so? The north wall receives direct sunlight for much longer than the south wall. In the post-glacial millennia the difference in temperatures by day and at night would have been far greater on the south facing side, and this would have caused frost shattering there, eroding it back more rapidly than on the shaded side.

A final point about Watlowes: the stone wall that runs all the way down the middle was built as early as 1300, to separate sheep runs belonging to Fountains Abbey and Bolton Priory. If only those stones could speak ....

Comb Scar to Water Sinks

Stay with this path, whose initial ease of walking soon degenerates into a stumble over chunks of rock, as it passes above the dry waterfall of Comb Scar and into Comb dry valley.

Comb Hill is another of those spots where I have sat entranced by local inhabitants. Hereabouts is a large warren now home to a clan of what must be feral ferrets, though I must confess to having difficulty distinguishing the various members of the *Mustelidae* family. I first came upon one by chance as it dived underground. I sat down and waited, and one by one heads popped up from hole after hole, their inquisitiveness and wariness being obvious. When they realised I was friend not foe the more adventurous came out to romp around in the sun.

You soon pass some tiny sheep-folds by the path which bends round to the right and loses its distinctive path-like form. In dry weather it is a pleasant walk: in the wet it can be a gruesome slither, so cling to the wall for succour. When the way flattens out the walking is immeasurably easier. After 500 metres, just before the wall bends slightly to the left, you will pass by an obvious rock-filled hole – this is the farthest point that Malham Water reaches in prolonged wet spells before seeping below ground. Beyond that, either side of the wall where the ladder stile is, the stream finds its usual way into the bowels of the earth.

If you are returning to the road, carry straight on from Water Sinks.

Blood or Water?

It is amazing. Water flows out of the tarn, disappears below ground and reappears as a spring at Airehead beyond Malham village. Another stream disappears south-west of the tarn, at Smelt Mill Sinks, and resurges at the foot of Malham Cove. As the cross-section shows, somewhere along the line there is slight mixing of the water. Here are some figures: of the water that reappears below the Cove, 60 per cent has come from Smelt Mill Sinks and three per cent from the tarn. The remaining 37 per cent has percolated through the joints in the rocks above the Cove. This limestone is in fact the

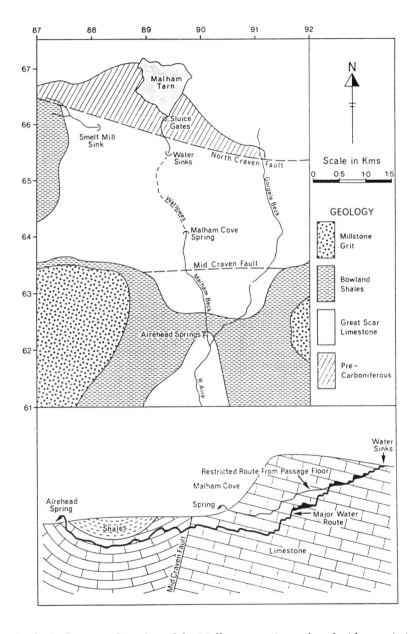

Geological map and section of the Malham area *(reproduced with permission from D.I. Smith and T.C. Atkinson "Underground Flow in Cavernous Limestone", published by the Field Studies Council)*

most permeable rock in Britain apart from Cheshire's rock salt. Ninety-seven per cent of tarn water, and 40 per cent of Smelt Mill Sinks water gushes out at Airehead.

How can anyone be so sure of these figures? A number of years ago millions of spores, mainly dyed red, were poured down Malham Water Sinks and Smelt Mill Sinks and the water issuing at the other ends was monitored.

No caver has as yet succeeded in following any of these passages. In fact, no one knows what passages or caverns may be down there. What everyone does know is that there is underground flow here, as in any similar limestone area. It is like some enormous hydrological catharsis, purging clean the earth's innards.

A Historic Landscape

Climb over the stile and follow the path as it gently climbs. In a few minutes you will come to a three-way path junction near a water-filled depression. The path to the right is called Trougate further on, and it has early medieval origins, and may even date back two thousand years to the Iron Age. Nowadays it is part of the Pennine Way. Ignore all three paths: **instead cut across left to the wall and follow it south-eastwards, keeping it close by.** You are now in the thick of an area where visible archaeological remains are scattered about as closely as trees in a forest. I intend to take you to a small selection, giving a cross-section through time, but keep in mind that what you see is a tiny portion of the whole.

Trougate

The Malham Project

Extensive archaeological field surveying and excavation were carried out under the direct supervision of the late Dr Arthur Raistrick throughout the 1950s. This was pioneering work. It was he who recognised the importance of the whole limestone area for the sheer amount and variety of prehistoric detail that has survived the centuries.

In the intervening forty years technology has arrived on the archaeological scene. It is no longer necessary to dig to see what lies buried. Aerial photography is much more efficient at initial site identification than any amount of field walking, while geophysical techniques can focus the archaeologist on the precise sites that offer the greatest potential for excavation.

Geophysics involves the use of instruments to measure differences in electrical resistance below the surface. If changes in resistance are detected, it means the soil has been disturbed at depth, and the patterns of disturbance can be plotted on a computer.

In addition, ideas change as more evidence becomes available and it is often necessary to re-interpret earlier findings and conclusions, on occasions quite profoundly. Archaeology should never be viewed as a static subject, even though it is often dealing with the distant past.

For these reasons, the Malham Project was launched in 1994, managed by Bradford University, co-funded by the National Park Authority. The primary aim was to extend knowledge of the historic landscape in the area loosely known as Malham Moor, by collating Raistrick's work and by further field studies. It was also the intention to identify those important sites that are undoubtedly at risk from visitor pressure and animals (rabbits and stock), and to come up with a conservation strategy. Work concentrated on New Close at first, though hopefully work will extend to Malham Lings and elsewhere in due course.

Together with the Dales Project (see "The Northern Dales") it represents an exciting development in local prehistoric studies.

An Iron Age Site

About 250 metres along the wall from the Pennine Way stile, nestling below Torlery Edge, is a linear grouping of hut circles which have been dated by artefacts to the Iron Age. Clearly this was a more substantial settlement than the one on Locks Scar (See Walk 6 for a discussion of Iron Age life and work.) One of the huts has what appears to be a stone door jamb still upright.

A Norse Site

Carry on along the wall towards Abbot Hills but only until it changes direction slightly. Leave the wall, fix your compass just east of south and make for the low rise ahead, and walk for 100 metres or so. On the lower grassy area there is an obvious rectangular enclosure about seven by three metres in size. Fifty metres beyond it is another one, this one lacking the dividing wall. Both are the remains of Norse (i.e. "Viking") farmsteads. Whether both houses were occupied at the same time is yet another of history's secrets.

Malham Lings

Cut back to the wall and continue alongside it until you reach a pond and a large circular depression. This is too perfectly round and basin-shaped to be natural. Rather it is a dew pond, used in "olden days" to hold water for stock. Water would not normally stay on a limestone surface, so in the dew pond a puddled clay lining prevented seepage below ground. A feature such as this is impossible to date.

From here head off south-south-eastwards on the faint path that runs parallel to the traces of an ancient wall. You are entering a broad way between two areas of limestone pavement. To your right is a huge area of pavement stretching from Prior Rakes to Broad Scars, all part of an area known as Malham Lings.

I could spend a day on the pavements, seeking out traces of lost settlement sites and field systems, and peering down the grykes between the limestone slabs or clints. There are botanical delights galore. Some are relics of a past woodland cover, including dog's mercury *(Mercurialis perennis)* with its

Broad Scar limestone pavement

almost apologetic and tiny green flowers in March; herb Robert *(Geranium robertianum)* with its pinkish flowers; and lesser meadow-rue *(Thalictrum minus)* with delicate hanging flowers unable to decide whether they want to be yellow, green or purple-blue; and I have found the odd specimen of common twayblade *(Listera ovata)*, an orchid with greeny-yellow flowers on a spike towering above its twin leaves. There are also some rather special ferns hiding down in the grykes. The only ones I can definitely identify are hartstongue *(Phyllitis scolopendrium)* and green spleenwort *(Asplenium viride)*. Elsewhere on the Lings, summer brings a fine display of yellow to purple mountain pansies *(Viola lutea)*.

A Monastic Sheephouse

As you pass between the two areas of pavement – the path is small but clear – the path leads directly into a series of rectangular earthworks marked on the 1:25,000 map as "settlements". This is the remains of a sheephouse.

Have a look at the plan and reconstruction before you walk round the site to relate the ground features to the drawings, and thus identify the details.

There is place name evidence in the area – Prior Rakes and Abbot Hills – to hint at monastic ownership in the past. There is also ample documentary evidence that the abbot of Fountains Abbey near Ripon leased the Lings, Rakes and New Close to Bolton Priory as sheep grazings. The written records make frequent mention of a sheephouse on Malham Moor, including repairs to it in 1290. Excavation of this site and another hut site against the scar have turned up medieval artefacts including pottery. Case proven: this is a monastic sheephouse, in use from at least 1290 to the Dissolution of the monastery in 1539.

The large building housed an over-wintering flock of perhaps fifty ewes, and possibly also lambing ewes. It was timber-built, with a roof of thatch or ling (heather), the timbers resting on a low and very thick stone wall. The small yard or paddock, attached to the sheephouse, would have served as a place to milk and shear the sheep. Possibly the attached lean-to, if that is

what it was, could have stored the fleeces and the other products awaiting dispatch, namely meat, butter and cheese. The larger enclosure would have been used like modern in-bye fields. The small building in the south-west corner was the shepherd's hut. At one time a shepherd and four foldmen lived here, so the other hut site by the scar may well have been used by the latter. This last is supposition, but then so is much archaeological interpretation.

Monastic cross base

It may be of value, before you leave the site, for you to review the settlements encountered today – to clarify in your mind the differences of style and size and the similarities in basic construction. You have seen the two Iron Age sites, a Bronze Age hut circle, two Norse farmhouses and now a medieval complex.

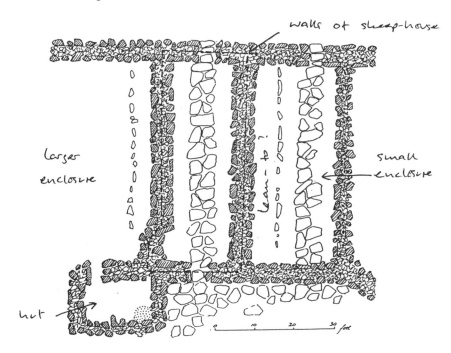

Sheephouse, Prior Rakes.

Possible restoration of Sheephouse.

Reproduced with permission from "Archaeology of Malham Moor" by A. Raistrick, published by the Field Studies Council.

As you proceed, look to the right and there are other small enclosures, huddled against the scar, and a number of larger ones that cross your path, both before and after **it merges with another from the right. The way is clear now and the track soon brings you to a ladder stile next to a field gate. If you are anxious to return, turn left and follow the road back to Street Gate. If not, cross the road and look for a concrete step-stile just to the left in the opposite wall.** You are now entering an area known as New Close, a Countryside Stewardship Access area with permissive routes across.

New Close

The whole area between the road and Gordale Beck, between Mastiles Lane and Stridebut Edge, is as festooned with ancient walls and hut circles as Malham Lings. I am not pointing out any more particular sites but you might like to use the rest of the route as an exercise in identifying traces of the past.

From the concrete stile look away to the east. You will see a field gate standing prominently in the wall at the top of New Close Knotts. This is your next target but you cannot walk directly to it as there is another stone wall in the way, hidden from sight in a dry valley. **So head diagonally left from the stile, towards the head of the dry valley, and look for another concrete stile in the intervening wall. It lies just to the left of a short section of fencing down in a dip. Make for the post and wire fence ahead** – newly built to allow plant regeneration free from stock – **and follow it round to the right. On the top of New Close Knotts it meets a wall which you follow southwards to a third concrete stile just before the gate you could see from the road.**

A faint path snakes across the Knotts, in an east-north-east direction, and descends into the valley of Gordale Beck above Gordale Scar. When you meet the main path from the Scar, turn left and over the stone stepping stile. The path is now obvious: at first it hugs a post and wire fence but then leads away to the north-west when Great Close Hill comes into view. The public footpath eventually climbs over the wall onto the road but you can stay in the field, contouring between the boundary wall and Seaty Hill, right at the northern apex of New Close Pasture, on a permissive path.

The top of Seaty Hill is ringed by a ditch and bank which enclose a mound. This has been excavated and was found to be an Early Bronze Age burial mound, over 3,000 years old. Around the mound, archaeologists also unearthed thirteen Iron Age burials, in one of which a musical pipe was found, made from the leg bone of a sheep. Obviously this site had symbolic significance over many centuries. If you choose to explore the surface, do so with a respectful air.

At the end of the pasture climb over the last concrete stile back to your starting point.

Place-name meanings

Comb Hill	ON	the crest of the hill
Dean Moor	-	the Deans were the first tenants after the Dissolution of Fountains Abbey
Gordale	ON	the dirty valley
Great Close	OE	the great enclosure
Langscar	OE/ON	the long scar
Locks Scar	OE/ON	the enclosure by the scar
Malham	ON	(maybe) the stony or sandy place. It is *not* a *ham* ending.
(Malham) Cove	ON	the recess
(Malham) Lings	OE	the heather- covered area
Mastiles Lane	OE	the lane through the marsh with a stile
New Close Knotts	OE	the new enclosure within the rocky hills
Prior Rakes	OE	the sheep runs belonging to the priory
Street Gate	OE	the gate on the road. (In ON gate also means road so...?)
Trougate	OE	the road through the narrow valley

Discovery Walk 4

In Monastic Footsteps: following the Monk's Road to Arncliffe

Start: Water Houses at the north-west entrance to Malham Tarn (Grid reference SD885 675).

Finish: Arncliffe village in Littondale (Grid reference SD 932 718).

Parking: There is roadside parking on the Settle to Arncliffe road near the entrance to Malham Tarn Estate, and in Arncliffe village. The National Trust does not permit vehicular access to the Estate except on business.

Public transport: A very infrequent Sunday service operates one way in summer, from Malham to Arncliffe, and from Grassington to Settle via the Tarn. There is also the Dales Link service (see Walk 1). Contact Pride of the Dales (tel. 01756 753123).

Facilities: Only in Arncliffe where there is a tea shop and the Falcon Inn.

Outline of the Walk: This is a linear route, starting north-west of the Tarn, following a monastic route for most of the way. Malham Tarn – Middle House – Dew Bottoms – Clowder – Yew Cogar Scar – Arncliffe.

Length: 8km (5 miles).

Ordnance Survey Map: Outdoor Leisure 10. Landranger 98.

Introduction

This Discovery Walk provides you with the opportunity, not just to walk through Malham Tarn Estate, but to appreciate why it is an internationally renowned SSSI and a National Nature Reserve. You will learn something of its birdlife, both on the tarn and in the woods, and of its rich flora.

The walk also guides you across the Monk's Road to Arncliffe in Litton-dale, a route which has been in existence for at least six hundred years, and one which passes through some truly spectacular limestone scenery. As you trace the route you will be entering the lives of people from distant times:

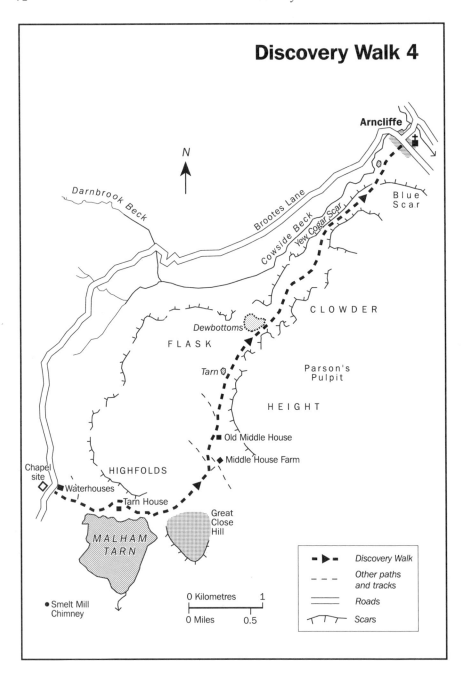

Discovery Walk 4

N

Arncliffe

Darnbrook Beck

Brootes Lane

Cowside Beck

Yew Cogar Scar

Blue Scar

CLOWDER

Dewbottoms

FLASK

Tarn

Parson's Pulpit

HEIGHT

Old Middle House

Middle House Farm

Chapel site

HIGHFOLDS

Waterhouses

Tarn House

Great Close Hill

MALHAM TARN

Smelt Mill Chimney

▪ ▶ ▪	Discovery Walk
– – –	Other paths and tracks
═══	Roads
⊤⊤⊤	Scars

0 Kilometres   1

0 Miles   0.5

Bronze Age farmers, Norsemen, medieval shepherds, and the inhabitants of Tarn House in its days of glory.

The entire walk, from start to finish, lies within the Malham – Arncliffe SSSI, a very special area. You could complete it in half a day but a full day would give you more than enough time to enjoy the area to the full.

Chapel Fell

Start by the roadside near the entrance to the Tarn Estate. The hill next to the road is called Chapel Fell and is another open access area, so designated under the Countryside Stewardship scheme. Dotted over it are a number of hut circles, dated to the Iron Age and Romano-British period. The most exciting site lies a few metres from the sheep-folds in the corner by the road.

Clearly discernible on the ground are the foundations of a rectangular building, seven by fourteen metres. Under the turf the whole floor is cobbled and at the eastern end there is a raised, paved dais. This was a chapel, thought to have been built by Fountains Abbey in the twelfth century for use by local shepherds and visiting monks and lay brothers. It was probably demolished, or at least stripped, at the Dissolution of the monasteries.

Malham Tarn Estate

Thousands of visitors tramp around the Tarn every year, many of them seemingly expecting some kind of theme park hidden away in the woods. In a way it is a theme park, but very definitely Nature's own.

Malham Tarn and Tarn House

The National Trust owns over 1700 hectares between Fountains Fell and Malham. Of these 136, around the Tarn, were designated as a National Nature Reserve in 1992. That in itself is an honour but even higher status was accorded later when the Reserve was granted recognition as a Ramsar site, a wetland of international importance.

What makes the area so special? It is England's highest lime-rich lake. The tarn is relatively poor in nutrients but lime rich whereas other lime rich lakes in Britain are also nutrient rich because fertilisers from adjacent farmland drain in. Here, though, the tarn is fed by springs which come from land where very little fertiliser is added.

The Tarn has a distinct flora and microfauna. There are nineteen plants around the Tarn which are rare in Britain; there are many rare insects, including one species of flightless caddis fly that occurs nowhere else in Britain. It is one of the best examples in the country of a semi-natural wetland. Last but not least is the birdlife.

Because the area west of the Tarn and the north shore are so important for nature conservation, access is strictly by permit only. This also applies to fishing on the tarn.

Let's go back to the beginning. As I described in Walk 3 the basin that holds the Tarn was carved out in the geological past, and glacial melt-water deposited material at the southern end so that water was trapped as a lake. This lake was originally much greater than now: Tarn Moss and Tarn Fen west of the Tarn, and Ha Mire to the east were then under water.

The Tarn is slowly drying up. In geological time it represents no more than a blip. Small streams feed the lake from the surrounding hills and this spring water contains a high proportion of dissolved limestone. This is precipitated by a chemical reaction and deposited on the bed of the lake, and onto special algae called stonewort which grow all over the rocks on the bed. The dissolved limestone, when re-deposited, is in the form of lime rich mud called marl. As this builds up it is slowly but irreversibly reducing the depth of water. At no point today is the water more than five metres deep.

It was even shallower until 1791 when a weir was constructed at the outflow to increase both depth and surface area to improve the fishery. Incidentally the Tarn had been stocked with native brown trout, but also contains perch which prey on young trout, and it has been an important fishery since monastic times.

A Walk through the Estate

Leave the road and turn down the tarred driveway past Waterhouses which now consists of the National Trust Office and Home Farm. The office building housed an estate manager's house in Morrison's time and the home farm. What is now the farm house was then the elementary school that served Malham Moor from 1872 to around 1940.

Malham Tarn Estate

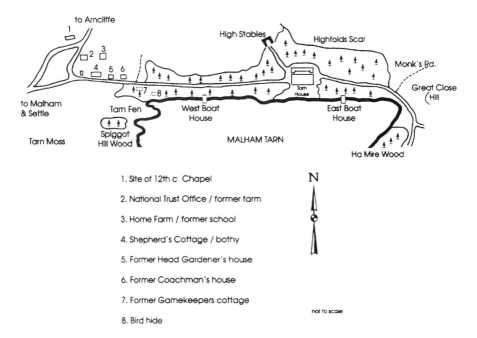

1. Site of 12th c Chapel
2. National Trust Office / former farm
3. Home Farm / former school
4. Shepherd's Cottage / bothy
5. Former Head Gardener's house
6. Former Coachman's house
7. Former Gamekeepers cottage
8. Bird hide

N

not to scale

Carry on along the lane past the junction with Pot Hole Lane (by the post box), which used to be the main entrance to the estate. **You then come to a gate across the road** with a fine seventeenth century cottage beside it. Notice the stone mullioned windows with the hood moulding running above them, the main moulding having returned ends, and the kneelers at the bottom ends of the roof gable. In Morrison's time (see later) this house had two functions: the west end, near the porch, was the shepherd's cottage, while the eastern end was a bothy for workmen up from Settle or wherever.

Carry on through the gate and past two more cottages: the first was the head gardener's house and the second was the coachman's (and later chauffeur's house). **You then pass where the Pennine Way heads off north, and a fourth cottage** – Sandhill Cottage – on the right, formerly the residence of the gamekeeper, who was married to the cook.

The drive leads through a mixed broad leaved and coniferous wood whose floor is carpeted with the green dog's mercury *(Mercurialis perennis)*; the pungent Ramsons, or wild garlic *(Allium ursinum)* with its tall white flowers; and the similar-leaved enchanter's nightshade *(Circaea lutetiauna)* with minute white flowers. Growing along the roadside, in places, and reaching a flowering crescendo in June with more than a hint of aniseed, is sweet cicely *(Myrrhis odorata)*. Dog's mercury, incidentally, is poisonous to us and to stock, though stock never seem to be tempted by it.

The drive climbs now, passing a public bird hide, and through a cutting blasted through solid limestone. It is said Morrison had this cut because his car could not cope with the gradient. **Pass round to the left of Tarn House** and the block, now laboratories and bedrooms, that used to be a coach house. The glass structure on the left was a greenhouse heated by the boiler room below.

On the other side of the House, East Drive continues from the car park to the far edge of the wood. Beyond the cattle grid and gate leave the drive and turn uphill. If you were looking up towards Highfolds scars and screes as you walked, you will have noticed large swathes of "something" growing all over them. It is not natural but was an ornamental planting of Victorian days that has completely run out of control. It is cotoneaster and it is high on the Trust's hit list.

A Bird Watcher's Dream

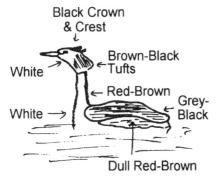

Great Crested Grebe (average size: 45-50cm)

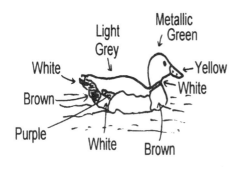

Mallard (average size: 60cm)

There is the opportunity for a spot of bird watching in the public hide, if time permits. Between Easter and the end of June a coot often nests immediately in front of the hide, and a great crested grebe has nested there on occasion.

The Tarn Estate is an important habitat for birdlife. A survey published in 1991 recorded a grand total of 179 species. Of these 91 had bred here at some time since the Second World War, including 72 which still breed regularly. These figures, I would stress, are for the whole Estate rather than just the tarn. Despite these impressive numbers the Tarn is not regarded as necessarily having national importance for birdlife.

Common winter sightings include coot by the hundred, mallard, great crested grebe, little grebe. Less numerous visitors can often be seen: tufted duck, teal, pochard and goldeneye are all on my tick-list. In the woods you should see – or hear – a range of tits and finches, tree-creepers, redstarts, warblers, flycatchers, nuthatches, woodpeckers, owls by night, and prowling raptors. A determined bird count should reach sixty species with little trouble. I think the greatest recent live sighting, in 1994, was of an osprey, presumably stopping off while heading south for the winter. Sensible chap! Perhaps the most amazing recent dead find was of a tawny owl. This had been ringed and it proved to be the oldest recorded wild tawny in the country, being 21 years old when it died. Interestingly it was found dead not far from where it had been ringed in its first year of life.

A Plant or Two

What of flowering plants on the Fen? There are far too many to list but here are a few to make you wish you had a permit. There are carpets of yellow bog asphodel *(Narthecium ossifragum)* and globeflower *(Trollius europaeus)*. In the sixteenth to seventeenth centuries bog asphodel was valued in industrial Lancashire as a hair dye (yellow hair – did they go in for hair streaking even then?) Sheep are not so keen on it, however, because it can give them a bone disease called cruppany.

There are also scores of white grass-of-Parnassus *(Parnassia palustris)* and bogbean *(Menyanthes trifoliata)*; the beautiful pink bird's-eye primrose *(Primula farinosa)*, the emblem of the Dales ... and ... Heaven on Earth. Actually 360 species of higher plants grow on the Tarn Estate.

An Eccentric Millionaire ... and Others

There may well have been a farm house, where Tarn House now stands, in the late sixteenth or early seventeenth century and the remains of this may form the cellars of the current house. This farm was bought and rebuilt as a hunting lodge by Thomas Lister, first Baron Ribblesdale, of Gisburn near Clitheroe. Around 1780, he set about constructing a rather fine and very symmetrical lodge in Georgian style. It was he who began the immense task of planting an ornamental woodland.

For most of the time the lodge was left in the care of the agent-in-residence, though perhaps care is too precise a description. He could never curb the excesses of the butler, who was too generous to himself with his lordship's wine, nor those of the gardener who would give away m'lud's vegetables to whoever happened to pass by.

In 1852 the estate was sold to the Morrison family who had made a fortune out of industry and dealings in South America. The very next year they added the stable block, which is what you actually walk round on the drive. In 1857 Walter Morrison was given the estate by his father. He was just 21. He undertook a programme of continuous extensions and alterations, including a tower above the present main entrance to the "big house", which reached well above the general roof height.

Walter remained a bachelor till the end, he never needed to work, though he twice served as an MP, and he was a Justice of the Peace. He divided his time between here and his other two properties in the South. He had – and still has hereabouts – a reputation as a generous benefactor. He sponsored the restoration of Kirkby Malham church and the building of the copper-domed chapel at Giggleswick School. He also funded a school on the Tarn Estate, and was a generous, and sometimes anonymous, benefactor elsewhere.

Yet he lived frugally and would choose to walk from the stations in Settle or Bell Busk, rather than use his carriage. This frugality, however, was set aside when he entertained guests, and he certainly had some notable visitors. Thomas Hughes, author of "Tom Brown's Schooldays", Charles Darwin (possibly), J.S.Mill, John Ruskin (on a painting holiday) and Charles Kingsley, all stayed here awhile. There are some references to local spots in Kingsley's "Water Babies" which are identifiable if you know the area well enough.

Walter died in 1921 and a nephew inherited the estate but chose to sell it six years later. It changed hands again soon after and – like many grand houses that had outlived their usefulness – was bequeathed to the National Trust just after the Second World War. In 1948 the house was leased to the Council for the Promotion of Field Studies, now the Field Studies Council. It still operates as a Field Centre, offering school children and adults of all ages a wide variety of courses, including one that uses old roads as a means of discovering the landscape. What a coincidence!

Malham Tarn to Old Middle House

There is no need to dog-leg past the finger-post as you head uphill from the grid. Cut the corner off to reach the old, engineered track that used to carry straight on westwards before wall and wood were created. You are now on the Monk's Road, an ancient packhorse route from Littondale that was but one link in a whole network of medieval roads. You will be following it all the way to Arncliffe so please adopt a reverent and contemplative mien before you proceed.

Anyway ... continue upslope over the north shoulder of Great Close Hill, then down the other side into Great Close Pasture. At the bottom there is a step-over stile in the fence, and then a path cuts diagonally uphill, leading left of Middle House Farm but straight towards a prominent gash in Scab Hill. Your path leads round to a ladder stile by a gate in the wall and joins a bridleway. Beyond the stile follow the clear farm track over Low Midge Hills, but fork right at the top of the first rise, and turn towards the clump of trees, your immediate objective.

The view from here is quite something. To the south, across the broad

Aire gap, the skyline is dominated by Pendle Hill while the moors of the Forest of Trawden stretch eastwards from there towards Keighley and Haworth. Over to the north-west lies Fountains Fell. On your immediate right are a large number of field enclosures, of irregular size and shape.

Walk on to the clump of trees, between Old Middle House and Back Pasture Hill. The house is worth a thought or two.

Enclosures at Middle House

Cattle Fairs

The enclosure that includes Middle House farm extends to nearly 300 hectares. At that size, despite its being surrounded by one continuous boundary wall, it can hardly be called a field. A field it is though, according to the dictionary definition. It is so vast you need good visibility to see from one end to the other. The various internal fences are recent, but the walls are shown on a pre-Enclosure estate map, dated 1760.

This is Great Close and it had a most important function from the late seventeenth century to the early to mid-nineteenth centuries. It was the major focus of the cattle droving trade, which I have discussed elsewhere (see Walk 10).

The herds of cattle were brought here through the summer months from Scotland and fattened in the huge pasture prior to the next cattle fair. In the late eighteenth century it was not uncommon to see up to 5000 head here at any given time. Farmers from all around would converge to replenish their stock, and meat traders from the burgeoning cities also bought cattle to be herded off for slaughter. It was business with a capital B.

The trade and the fairs developed as a response to increasing demand for red meat, a trend that began in the seventeenth century. Ultimately the practice was killed off by later developments. The enclosing of open land and commons, the containing of roads between walls and the consequent loss of "free" grazing, made droving that much harder. The final death knell, however, was sounded by the coming of the railways: cattle could be shunted across country in hours rather than weeks.

As we contemplate the scene today with scarcely a sound to break the silence, it is hard to imagine the scene during a cattle fair. The bellowing of cattle, the bleating of sheep, the whinnying of horses, the coarse language of drovers and dealers, the caterwauling and bickering of drunken protagonists fresh from Great Close's own licenced grog-shop ... it must have been a sight to behold.

Old Middle House

It does not look much, as you pass by its rear wall but, like many old houses, it has a tale to tell.

There has been a settlement hereabouts for over two thousand years, and certainly continuously so for around half of that time span. There was a Norse farmstead here, and the site was taken over by Fountains Abbey and occupied throughout the monastic period by their tenants. In the Poll Tax

Old Middle House, restored

returns of 1379, for example, Adam de Medlehewe and his wife were assessed at 4d per annum. In the 1450s John Brown paid a yearly rent of twenty shillings for the farm, but he also received payment from Fountains Abbey for tending their flocks. At the Dissolution his descendant, Richard, still paid the same amount (take note, Chancellor!).

The Brown family held onto the tenancy after the abbey fell and another John, who died in 1555, left a will which has survived. By the early seventeenth century, however, the tenancy was in the hands of the Knowles family. Henry rebuilt the house in the 1620s and his family also held Capon Hall and one of the Trenhouse farms, so they were clearly yeomen of some substance. The parish registers for Kirkby Malham for 1655 record Oliver Cromwell's attendance at a wedding of a Knowles (possibly so, because one of Cromwell's chief henchmen, Lambert, hailed from Calton near Airton). There is some doubt about this though, as Cromwell is recorded as having been in London at the same time. Take your pick.

In the following century the name of the tenant is again known. In the 1851 census returns one Charles Metcalfe resided here with his wife, three children, three farm workers and a maid, so he was clearly a man of substance.

As for the stones and mortar ... the irregular field enclosures are sixteenth century; the pigeon cote (mysteriously burnt in autumn 1994) is seventeenth. In the days before red meat became available pigeons were a prized possession – and a badge of status – for yeoman farmers, not only for their meat but also for their eggs and guano.

The house, as I said, was rebuilt in the 1620s. The porch was added in the late seventeenth, and the stone bearing Henry Knowles' initials was transferred from the main wall of the house – unless there was a later H. Knowles, Esquire. The west wing of the house was added prior to this, making it a three-bay house, and the eastern byre in the nineteenth. The windows are as they were in the past, unglazed. Ruskin painted the house in about 1875, when he was staying with Morrison, and it has apparently changed little in the meantime. Except in one respect: it lay empty and derelict for many years and the frontage had collapsed so, in 1988 and 1989, the National Trust carried out major renovation work to stabilise and preserve the shell.

To the Parish Boundary

Just beyond the house the track passes by a bright green flush, indicating the spring that was one of the sources of water for the house when inhabited. **Shortly beyond a ruined wall a finger post marks the parting of the ways: you want the bridleway to Arncliffe, so ignore the left turn. Carry on through Out Pasture heading towards the limestone pavement of Flask.** Nestling against the wall at the foot of Flask is a small, unnamed tarn, which owes its existence to a veneer of glacial drift plastered over the limestone. If your luck is in you could spot redshank here, not to mention black-headed gulls, oystercatchers and lapwings. **Climb over the wall at the stile.**

In the distance, the skyline is dominated by the bulk of Old Cote Moor Top, separating Littondale from the uppermost length of Wharfedale. Down below, to the left (north-west) are the fields and barns of remote Darnbrook farm. Note also the attempts at afforestation: the higher trees are really struggling to overcome adverse climatic and soil conditions, not to mention rabbits. This 1000 hectare hill farm came on the market in the summer of 1995 and was purchased by the National Trust, thus reuniting it with the Malham Tarn estate for the first time since Morrison's days. Yet another large chunk of the limestone Dales is assured of protection from unsympathetic development.

Up on your right are a series of limestone pavements, all marked on the Ordnance Survey 1:25,000 map. On the longest stretch, in the pasture you are in now, there are the remains of ancient walls which originally enclosed fields. Why make fields on limestone pavements would be a logical question. They did not, is the answer. In prehistoric times soil and turf would have covered the clints. It was the very fact of disturbing the thin and fragile soils for cultivation that paved the way for wind and water to remove all trace of soil. Similar situations have been identified elsewhere in the southern Dales, for example in Crummackdale and Bordley.

The path dips down into a grassy dry valley, cut through by the next wall you need to cross, again by a ladder stile. Look carefully to the right. Parallel to the path are the footings of an ancient wall. Further up the dry valley is another wall and, if you sweep your eye along the edge of both sets of pavement, either side of the Enclosure Wall, you will see the whole dry valley was enclosed by a boundary. Such hollows as this, offering shelter and deeper soils, were crucial for early settlers. When you come across hollow-fields you can normally assume there will be settlement signs nearby. Keep your eyes skinned now.

Having climbed over the stile in the dry valley, continue ahead until the ground drops away slightly, almost exactly half way through this pasture. Immediately before this descent the path runs alongside another ancient wall footing. This is Dew Bottoms.

Dew Bottoms

If you climb up the slope to the right of the path, you will gain a clearer overview of this important site. The sketch plan will also help to make sense of the site as you explore it.

There are a number of large enclosures, the largest of which is next to the path. Note that it is now mainly reduced to pavement: years of use and the centuries since have taken their toll. If you set off at right angles to the path across this first field, you will find two smaller fields or paddocks beyond it, with a further two away at the north-east corner. All are bounded by the

Dew Bottoms

N

0 M 15
0 Feet 50

⊕ Hut sites
⌐ Boundary walls
_-_ Footpath

remains of low stone walls which would either have been higher when in use or may have had a palisade on top.

There are many smaller enclosures in addition. For example four circular huts can be seen, and at least six rectangular enclosures which could have been stores or animal shelters. The whole site has been excavated but nothing of substance was found. It is, frustratingly, impossible to date and could have been occupied at any time from the Neolithic to the Iron Age. The only certainties are that it is prehistoric, and it would have housed an extended family group at subsistence level.

Just south of the settlement, beyond the limestone knoll, lie the remains of an early lead mine with mainly shallow workings but also one shaft. It is a tiny mine but has earned its place in the history books: in 1678 gunpowder was used here in the mining operations, and that was the first recorded use of blasting in the Southern Dales.

The Last Lap

From Dew Bottoms continue along the path, noting another hollow-field at the lowest point in this pasture, sandwiched between two low knolls. **A short distance ahead is another wall and ladder stile.**

Perhaps you can solve a puzzle or three that have me beaten. This wall marks the parish boundary between Malham Moor and Arncliffe. In Malham Moor the route is designated as a bridleway: in Arncliffe it is a mere footpath. Why does it suddenly change when there is no logical reason to so do? Why is it not a bridleway now in Arncliffe considering it was a packhorse route for centuries? And how do horse riders, who may wish to come this far from Middle House, man-handle their steeds over the two previous stiles? None of it makes sense. Just one more thing to worry about!

By the left foot of this stile, on the Arncliffe side, note the rock with a cylindrical hole through it. Is it a natural hole, or was it hewn out to take a marker or boundary post on the Monk's Road? Food for thought.

Beyond the stile the path contours along a limestone shelf and you have the first real views into the chasm that holds Cowside Beck, below Yew Cogar Scar. **The way then descends to a lower shelf,** representing another bedding plane in the limestone. **Carry on, over a ruined wall and past the workmanship of the Society for Erecting Piles of Stones.** On the distant skyline now, by the way, Great Whernside maintains a brooding presence.

Drop down through another dry valley and look for the path – unclear just here – through a section of spiky rocks and on to the fifth ladder stile of the day. (I once had the pleasure of escorting a party of thirty or so adults on this walk – each stile took up five minutes!)

The path drops again and passes several wet flushes where water seeps out from between the layers of rock, so the ground flora is very different from what you would expect on dry limestone. **Eventually you come upon another ladder stile tucked into the wall corner.** Before you tick this stile off, have a look down into the valley.

There is a good geography lesson here, illustrating river and slope processes. The beck is winding, or meandering, from side to side and its energy is concentrated on the outside of the bends. The result of this is clear enough to see. Secondly, soil on the slopes creeps downslope, maybe too slow to register at rates we can comprehend, but nevertheless inexorably so, because of gravity and lubrication from water in the soil. In certain circumstances the end result is a series of tiny steps, as you can see down there. These are called terracettes. They have not been made by sheep.

So, over the stile and walk along left of the fence to yet another ladder stile, the seventh. Arncliffe village is now in view. **Pick your way carefully downslope and over the next ladder stile.** I can go no further than here, unless it is pouring, without sitting down and savouring the view. It is one of those I can never tire of.

Arncliffe from the south

A Grand View Indeed

Obviously one feature you can see is Arncliffe, whose plan stands out clearly. Buildings surround the village green and there is only restricted entry into it: the way you will be entering; over the bridge from Brootes Lane; by the road from the east; and over Skirfare Bridge from Litton, entering the green along a narrow, high-walled lane.

Across Cowside Beck valley the road climbs steeply up past Brootes Barn. Either side of the road there is a series of grooves etched into the ground, all roughly parallel to the lane, though higher up one of the grooves describes a wide zigzag. You will notice that the Enclosure walls cut across them indicating that the grooves came first. What you are looking at is a series of holloways. In the days of packhorse trains the ponies would quickly wear the surface down, turning it into a slippery morass in wet weather. The packhorse drivers would then pick a new way up the hill. Over the centuries these ways have been cut ever deeper into the surface by hooves and by the flow of rain water.

Down below, just before the first building of the village, there is an oval enclosure with thick grassy banks around it. Look carefully and you will see a dry ditch running into it from the beck. This was the mill pond for Arncliffe's cotton (and later silk) mill, now a residence, that is half-hidden in the trees where the beck disappears from view.

Like so many mills in the Dales, it began life as a manorial corn mill but was converted to cotton, probably in 1793. It was extensively rebuilt in the nineteenth century, but eventually closed down, its being too remote. The business was transferred to Colne in Lancashire.

Beyond Brootes Barn many of the fields on the lower valley slopes are long and narrow. In some cases low banks can be made out. You are looking here at a late medieval field system that has become fossilised in the present day landscape. This is but one of the many reasons why Littondale was recently (1994) granted Conservation Area status with a scheme to grant aid farmers to repair and conserve traditional stone barns and walls. By the end of that year, five barns had been grant-aided, a drop in the ocean but a start. The dale is also one of the country's Environmentally Sensitive Areas (see "The Northern Dales").

Up dale you can see a good example of a glaciated U-shaped valley whose floor is very flat. As the glacier here was retreating, a temporary lake ponded up behind dumps of moraine down valley. Deposits on the lake bed, being water-sorted, are fine and level.

The main villages in Littondale are built where side valleys join the main valley. Boulders and other material were swept out of these side valleys and dumped, raising the level of the main valley floor here. The villages have developed on these slightly higher and drier sites above flood level. The village of Litton that you can see up the valley is one such site.

Directly across the dale, straight over Arncliffe village, near a shooting cabin, you may be able to pick out the scant remains of the eighteenth century Black Rock lead mine. South-east from there, further along the hillside, the prominent gash and still unvegetated spoil heaps are the remains of the older Coldstreak lead mine. The mineral rights in this area were owned and exploited by Lord Ribblesdale. He initially sent his ore to be smelted at Kilnsey, but later transferred it to the smelt mill he built south of the Tarn, a mill that operated from 1816 to 1860.

Arncliffe

And so to the end of today's walk. **Leave the viewpoint and tread carefully as the path descends steeply to a drunken ladder stile below. Cross the last field to a small gate in the wall. Turn left on the walled lane-cum-stream, past the row of former mill cottages, then the telephone exchange. The lane ends at the corner of the village green next to the Falcon Inn.**

Arncliffe was the setting for early episodes of the television series, Emmerdale Farm, a name derived from Amerdale, an alternative name for Littondale.

Finally, if you are "in to" churches, I would recommend you have a look at St Oswald's down by the riverside before you depart.

Place-name meanings

Arncliffe	OE	the cliff with eagles or (some say) the settlement below the cliff
Brootes Lane	ON	the lane in (or to) a clearing
Clowder	OE	a large area of rocks
Darnbrook	OE	the hidden stream
Dew Bottoms	OE	the low,wet area
Flask	ODan	the swamp
Fountains Fell	-	so named because it belonged to the abbey
Great Close	OE	the great enclosure
Great Whernside	OE	the large hill where grinding stones were won
Height	OE	the high up place
Litton	OE	the farmstead below the slope
Low Midge Hills	OE	the low hills near the muddy hole
Middle House	ON	the house near the middle hill
Old Cote	OE	the secondary farmstead outside the village
Skirfare	ON	the sparkling river
Tennant Gill	–	from a local family name, former tenants of the abbey
Yew Cogar Scar	ON	the scar with yew trees: Cogar?

Discovery Walk 5

A Circuit around Bordley

Start and Finish: By Bordley Gate at the top of Malham Moor Lane (Grid reference SD952 653), reached from Threshfield by taking Skirethorns Lane from the B6160. It is 5km (around 3 miles) from the filling station to the starting point.

Parking: There is ample roadside parking shortly before the gate across the road. Avoid parking on the road or pastures beyond the gate.

Public transport: None at all!

Facilities: None, except for a telephone kiosk at Lainger!

Outline of the Walk: Lantern Holes – Bordley Town – Mastiles Lane – Cow Gill Cote – Bordley Hall – Lainger – Threshfield Moor – Heights – Malham Moor Lane.

Length: The full route is 10km (just over 6 miles) but it can be split up into a series of short loops, as suggested in the text.

Ordnance Survey Map: Outdoor Leisure 10. Landranger 98.

Introduction

Almost all of today's walk lies within the parish of Bordley which, like Malham Moor, possesses neither village nor church. It is an upland parish with a smattering of remote farms, at the head of the Winterburn valley. It is well off the beaten track, as far as most walkers are concerned. Apart from the short section along Mastiles Lane, I doubt you will see anybody today other than farmers.

This present day tranquillity hides a very different past when Bordley Town really was a sizeable settlement, though never a town as we under-stand the word now. An indication of this past importance is suggested by the number of bridleways and footpaths that converge either on Bordley Town or on Bordley Hall. Sheltered places such as this were favoured sites for settlement in medieval times, below the marginal fells and moors but above the main wooded and marshy valley bottoms.

If you are walking one or more of the loops, rather than the full route, read on here. You must go through Bordley Town regardless, so read "Best Foot Forward" and "Bordley Town" for all loops.

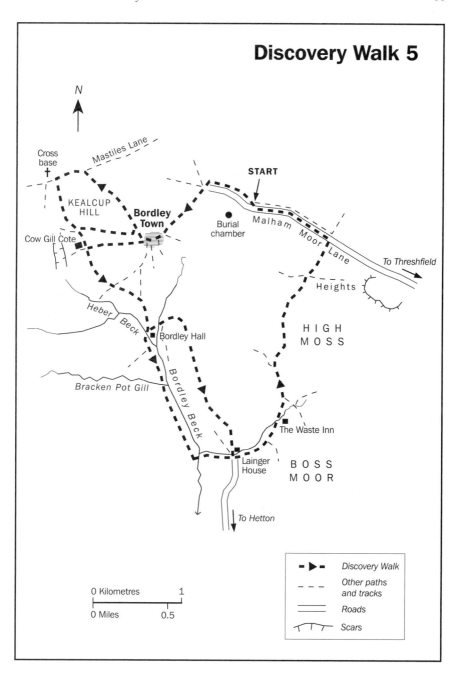

Discovery Walk 5

N

Cross base †

Mastiles Lane

KEALCUP HILL

Bordley Town

Cow Gill Cote

START

Burial chamber

Malham Moor Lane

To Threshfield

Heights

H I G H
M O S S

Heber Beck

Bordley Hall

Bordley Beck

Bracken Pot Gill

The Waste Inn

Lainger House

B O S S
M O O R

To Hetton

0 Kilometres 1

0 Miles 0.5

■▶■ Discovery Walk

‑ ‑ ‑ Other paths and tracks

Roads

Scars

Loop 1 – follow the short route of "Kealcup" and then pick up the route further on with "Cow Gill Cote".

Loop 2 – after "Bordley Town" follow the full route of "Kealcup", then "A Medieval Motorway" and "Southwards Now", then return to Bordley Town from Cow Gill Cote.

You could also cut the full route short by returning from Lainger to Bordley Town, if you have the 1:25,000 map with you.

Best Foot Forward

Walk along Malham Moor Lane through the gate, which is the parish boundary between Threshfield and Bordley. Before you leave the gate set your bearings: if you look west to the horizon you will see a hill. That is just south of Malham Tarn. If you follow the full route today you will be describing a circle so by fixing in your mind that Malham Tarn is in that direction, you will not become disorientated.

Follow the road down into the dry valley, through the gate, to a major cross-roads of tracks that have seen continuous use since the monastic period. **You should turn left on the main track, through another gate, and gradually uphill.** At the crest there is a long-range view down the length of the Winterburn valley (it is not called a dale, as such) to Winterburn Reservoir. **As the track descends again** look to the right beyond the small copse near the bottom of that dry valley. Pick out the bank that encloses much of Tommy Low Pasture – more of this later.

The track passes through another gate and down to the farms that are Bordley Town.

Bordley Town

Two farm houses make up Bordley Town today, remote and isolated from the main dales. It never was a town in the way we understand the term today, but it was an important settlement for several centuries. One local census, carried out in the seventeenth century, counted one hundred people living in the area, many of whom would have lived around the village.

Like so many Dales villages Bordley began as an Anglian settlement established by a man called Brorda. It is unusual as an early English settlement in being so high up: generally speaking the Angles stuck to the main valleys. Brorda was either a late comer to the area, and had to look higher up, or perhaps broke away from another settlement when population pressure began to be felt.

Later on Bordley was an important grange for Fountains Abbey, subsidiary to their centre of operations at Kilnsey. It would have consisted of a cluster of houses for lay brothers and farm labourers, farm buildings, crop fields, stock pens and enclosures, with outlying sheep runs and a sheep-houses in the surrounding hills.

One indication of its past importance as I suggested earlier, is the large number of tracks that radiate out from Bordley.

The monastic records relate that much of Bordley was tenanted by the Proctor family during the fifteenth century, and they maintained their tenancy after the Dissolution of the abbey in 1539.

Later on the Wade family took possession of Bordley (more of them in Walk 11). On the large barn to the left of the path within Bordley Town there is a datestone "CW 1664" that would originally have adorned a house. CW was Cuthbert Wade.

Kealcup

Walk past the frontage of Bordley House Farm and round to the left of the wooden fencing. Follow the track between the fence and wall to a gate at the top corner by the large tree. At this point you have a choice of routes.

Short Route

A clear farm track heads westwards from the gate up the flanks of Kealcup Hill. Very shortly you come to the point where the stone wall abuts onto the track, opposite a small quarry. This is cut into a type of glacial deposit called 'till', and it very clearly displays why glacial till is often called boulder clay. **Climb over the stone stile set into the wall and pass by the barn just ahead.** If the door is open you can peer in to see the wooden boskins separating the stalls. Above the small door is an early and very simple datestone 1635 RP:HW. This must have been taken from a house, probably in Bordley Town. There is no possibility of a field barn having such a datestone, and this particular barn post-dates the seventeenth century anyway.

Continue past the barn and through the gap in the ruined wall ahead. Beyond that there is a field gate in a fence. Note the ancient wall footings, made of massive boulders, parallel to the fence. **Just ahead lies Cow Gill Cote where you rejoin the full route.**

The Full Route

From the gate, leading out of Bordley Town, turn uphill to follow the wall on your right. Look down into the dry valley as you climb up to the beech wood of Kealcup Plantation, seemingly doomed through lack of stock control and regeneration. In the dip you can see close up the earth bank that forms a large enclosure, obviously pre-dating the walls. At the southern end, near the small wood in the dry valley, there is a smaller banked enclosure. The larger one is actually shown on the 1:25,000 Ordnance Survey Map.

It is an old feature – there is some dispute as to how old – and erosion over the years has worn down the bank. Imagine it being slightly higher, topped with some kind of paling or brushwood fence, or maybe a hedge. This type of enclosure is called a cool and its purpose was simply to hold stock, sheep or cattle. It could date from the monastic period, as a sheep fold: there is documentary evidence of cools elsewhere in the area. Alternatively it could have been a fattening enclosure dating from the late sixteenth or the seventeenth century, connected with the cattle fairs held on Boss Moor (of which more later).

From the plantation the track leads across a large pasture, north-westwards away from the wall. Make for the gate in the wall at the north end of the pasture. As your way flattens out Fountains Fell comes into view in the distance in the north-west. Stretching from there away to the east is the limestone upland of High Mark.

Notice the small conical depressions all over this pasture. They are called shakeholes. The limestone here is covered with a layer of glacial till. As the limestone is eroded by chemical processes, the till slumps to fill the spaces below. Normally this subsidence is an imperceptible process, but not always. A huge new shakehole appeared overnight (in 1993) at the head of Littondale, much to the consternation of the local farmer.

When you eventually reach the gate you find yourself on a green lane. This is the famous Mastiles Lane. Turn left along it for about 400 metres to a gate across the lane, and then turn left again to follow a track alongside the wall.

A Medieval Motorway

Further along Mastiles Lane, nearer Malham Tarn, there is a Roman marching camp. The Lane, today's right of way, cuts right through the camp. There was a known Roman road running up Wharfedale. It would, therefore, not be too fanciful to suggest that Mastiles Lane may have Roman origins as a road, connecting the two.

During the monastic period (1150 to 1539 here) Mastiles Lane was a major artery connecting Fountains Abbey near Ripon with Kilnsey (their corporate headquarters for the Dales) and all places west. Fountains held large estates in Lakeland's Borrowdale and had port facilities at Lancaster, so Mastiles was the medieval equivalent of the M62: the main connection from east to west across the Pennines.

In those times it was not walled: the walls come much later in the Enclosure Movement. Instead it would have been an open trackway, spreading ever outwards as parts became too boggy. The way was marked every so often by large crosses or marker posts, and the stone bases of four of these have survived in situ.

I once made a point of seeing how much of the main artery can be

How shakeholes are formed

1   ← —— Land surface

← —— Glacial till

← —— Limestone beds

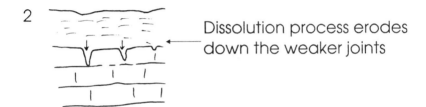

2   Dissolution process erodes down the weaker joints

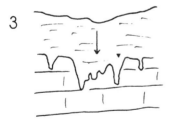

3   The surface begins to subside

4   Eventually the till collapses in to form the shakehole

identified now. The route is clear, without interruption, from the abbey, right through the Dales as far west as Ingleton. Beyond that I do not know what course it took, though it probably crossed the Lune at Kirkby Lonsdale. Of the entire traceable route, some is now modern road, some is by-way, bridleway or footpath, and some is private track.

The most controversial section of the whole route is Mastiles Lane. A glance at the Ordnance Survey map gives a clue: much of the Lane was still officially classified as a County Road until recently. Indeed, at the western end, at Street Gate, there is a road sign pointing to Grassington. In Bordley parish the lane had dual status, also being a bridleway. In 1988 the National Park undertook a detailed site survey of thirty-six of the Park's 100 green lanes. The survey of Mastiles illustrated that 25 per cent of its total length of eight kilometres was "seriously damaged". A further 26 per cent was "adequate at present", the rest "in good order". Since 1988, there has been a mushrooming in the use of off-road vehicles and trail bikes. Mastiles is rapidly deteriorating and something drastic has to be done. I suppose there are only two options: stop vehicular use completely, except for farmers, or accept the inevitable and re-designate the whole lot as a road.

In 1994 an official enquiry was convened to try and settle the issue once and for all. In early 1995 a Modification Order was confirmed: Mastiles Lane was re-designated as a Byway open to all traffic (BOAT), but the whole matter went to appeal and in October the order was rejected on appeal. Back to square one!

Mastiles Lane

Southwards Now

Just beyond the wall you are following there is a pronounced valley with a stream running into it from the north of Mastiles Lane. This is called Cow Gill. In normal weather conditions the stream disappears underground about 100 metres past the major bend in its course, not to reappear again for a full kilometre to the south. I wandered this way once, in a prolonged spell of rain and snow, and the whole valley bottom here was a lake from one side to another, and the stream was a raging torrent beyond that. The subterranean passage could simply take no more water.

Note the fine dew pond on the inside of the major bend.

Continue southwards on the green track to a concrete stile next to a gate on the track. If you wish to, you can return to Bordley Town and your car by taking the other farm track that turns east from this gate to follow the wall around Kealcup Hill into Bordley Town. Otherwise climb over the stile and proceed to Cow Gill Cote, a long-abandoned farm. Just before the stile you crossed the North Craven Fault but there is no indication on the ground of any change because limestone is on both sides plastered with till.

Cow Gill Cote

Just as place name evidence confirms that Bordley was settled by Brorda, so it also establishes that Kolli gave his name to this former farm. He was a Norseman, basically a pastoralist who, like his kinsmen, preferred outlying places. He came to settle here sometime in the tenth or early eleventh century and no doubt his descendants continued to farm this area until the land was taken over by Fountains Abbey. It could be that they stayed on as tenants, or they may have been dispossessed and forced to leave. There was nothing new about the infamous Highland clearances centuries later.

The present building is seventeenth century, though the barn is more recent. At the rear a fine mullioned window survives. Two more original windows upstairs at the front have lost their centre mullions. The house has a simple two-bay plan, meaning there are just two rooms on each floor. It conforms to a common seventeenth century plan, being Direct-Entry: the front door (the one on the right) leads directly into a room. The left-hand bay is slightly wider to take the rear stairway, the lower steps of which have survived.

Plan of a two-bay direct-entry house

F Room | Room F

D - Door

F - Fireplace

Originally the downstairs room in the right-hand bay was the living-room cum kitchen where daily life and rest centred. The other was the parlour – the master's bedroom. Upstairs rooms served a variety of purposes. The children, servants and anybody else slept up there, and all the stores were kept there.

It cannot have been a prosperous family. The external walls of the house are quite crudely put together with undressed limestone pieces. Contrast this with Lainger House later on. Both are of the same century. Cow Gill was finally abandoned as a house well before the end of the nineteenth century.

Down Bordley Beck

The path leaves the old farmhouse by heading between the twin walls at the front, over a stone stile (with a lamb gate) in the bottom wall, and then straight down the large field beyond. The path is not clear on the ground unless you have a vivid imagination. As you amble along, the long-range view ahead may occupy your mind. The view is clear right down the Winterburn valley, between the mass of Rylstone Fell and the knobbly tops of Flasby Fell, to the moors around Lower Airedale.

Go through the gate at the bottom (south-east) corner of the field into the next field. Stick to the left-hand wall now, ignoring the stone stile (unless you wish to return to the car: a path from this stile follows the walls through three fields to Bordley Town). When you reach the first wall junction leave the wall and head off right through the remains of a gateway in the ruined wall and across the third field down into the dip where there is another gate. Go through this and straight down the next field.

If you look due east, when you are in the third field, you will note a distinct change in vegetation colour to the left of the highest wood, Bark Plantation. The North Craven Fault runs up through the gully by the wall: to the north is limestone while the tops south of the fault consist of Bowland Shales, much more impermeable and thus wetter and more acidic underfoot.

Go through the gate at the bottom of the fourth field and through another gate in the right-hand corner of the last field, just before Bordley Hall. The present farmhouse, built in 1749, is perhaps not what one might expect a hall to be. Nevertheless there used to be a substantial structure here, and a chapel.

A Choice of Routes

If conditions today are particularly wet, I would advise turning left here behind the Bordley Hall complex and following the access road that climbs up the bank above Wood Gill Plantation, all the way to Lainger House. This way involves more climbing but is no longer and is certainly drier. Both paths that follow the beck become very wet and muddy in rainy spells ...

... otherwise ... **turn right now, through the gate at the corner and down to the footbridge over Heber Beck.** If that bit is horrendous, take the road!

Follow the crude track, ignoring the signposts, **alongside the wall** (on the right of the wall, not to its left as the Ordnance Survey map shows).

One hundred metres beyond the first signpost you cross the Middle Craven Fault. You have left behind the limestone and the faulted shatter belt between the two main faults, and are entering an area of Bowland Shales then Millstone Grit.

When you run out of wall, climb over the ladder stile and ford Bracken Pot Gill and head to the right of the lowest telegraph pole. Continue down the valley, staying at first on the lower slopes, through one gate and over a ladder stile to reach another ladder stile in the corner of the last field, by the confluence of Bordley Beck and Lainger Beck. Turn left on the gravelled road and climb up to the cross-road at Lainger House. Lainger Beck marks the parish boundary between Bordley and Threshfield.

Places to Rest Awhile

Lainger lies at the cross-roads of important medieval roads, connecting Mastiles Lane via Bordley, Threshfield and Grassington, Hetton and the south, Malham and the west. One of the possible meanings of the place-name Lainger is "a place to rest awhile" in both Old English (i.e. Anglian) and Old Norse. Originally it could have served as a traveller's halt, offering shelter and succour. The arched bridge, now out of use, may well pre-date the present house which stands on the site of much earlier buildings.

The present house dates from 1673. It is a fine and early example of what is known as the "Lobby-Entry" style of vernacular planning. The main door opened into a lobby between the two main living rooms. The extension at the rear, the off-shut, is later. The house also sports an impressive two-storey porch with decorative mouldings and a well-weathered, carved stone face.

Plan of a two-bay lobby-entry house

f - Fireplace

l - Lobby

p - Porch

d - Door

The route leads up the beckside from the cross-roads on an old green lane. This is a track with no official status, neither path or bridleway nor county road. Officially it is not a right of way, but the farmer seems to accept access by foot. Should access be denied in the future, the alternative would be to follow the road south to the old quarries, then double back along the bridleway across Boss Moor, as shown on the Ordnance Survey map. You can deduce from the wall alongside that you are well and truly on Millstone Grit here.

Where the gradient eases you come to a fork and a gate. The right fork leads onto the open land of Boss Moor. **You, however, should carry on up the main track through the gate and up to a rapidly disappearing barn.**

Now, when is a barn not a barn? Was this a barn? The answer to the latter is both yes and no. Yes in its later days, but prior to that it served a far more useful function. This was "The Waste" inn (though some say it is not!). Boss Moor was the venue for annual cattle fairs like Great Close at Malham Tarn. From the seventeenth century Boss Moor was subsidiary to the Great Close fairs though in the early nineteenth century Boss Moor seems to have become the more important with the other being relegated to use for fattening cattle after their long journey on the hoof. (See Walk 10 for a discussion of the droving trade.) Around the ruin are the remains of several other buildings, now half hidden piles of rubble.

If you ford the stream and look over the wall by the ruin you will see an entry into the banking. This was the inn's ice-house (simply the place where ice blocks were stored). It is well-preserved internally, and well-constructed. The roof is vaulted and the floor flagged. The south wall has a recess, and two huge flagstones still stand vertically in place, having been internal dividers. Last time I looked in there was also a putrifying sheep!

The series of smallish enclosures either side of the lane could have been used during the cattle fairs or to hold pack animals overnight.

Lainger

From Lane Head to Heights

The ruin is no longer called The Waste: now it is Lane Head, accurate enough though hardly romantic. **From the ford carry on up the lane, now officially a bridleway, to the gate and the T-junction.** If you were to turn right here, more ancient roads would take you in various directions, **but you turn left.**

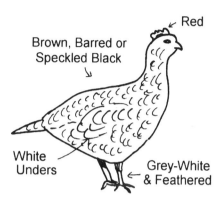

Red

Brown, Barred or Speckled Black

White Unders

Grey-White & Feathered

Red Grouse (average size: 36cm)

The heather moorland ahead, part of Threshfield Moor, is prime grouse habitat. You should see at least one covey of red grouse as you proceed. Away to the north-east the isolated building is a shooting cabin, beyond the line of grouse butts. I have more to say about grouse shooting in "The Northern Dales".

The distant views, away to the south-east, are down Wharfedale. The odd, bright green and conically shaped hill is Elbolton, south of Grassington while beyond that, with the knobbly top, lies the mass of Barden Fell. To the south-west the view is equally expansive: Pendle Hill and the Bowland Fells dominate the skyline, while Winterburn Reservoir lies in the valley below.

The land either side of the lane could not be more different: heather moor to the right with field grasses to the left. This does not reflect different rock types but shows the extent to which mankind can alter the landscape by draining and "improving" the land for agriculture.

Shortly before the lane turns sharply to the right, exactly where a footpath cuts off to the left, you re-cross the Middle Craven Fault. In this vicinity the gritstones overlie the fault so you are not getting back onto the limestones just yet.

The enclosed track – another Occupation Road – **ends at a gate, the parish boundary, and things take a turn for the worse as you cross High Moss.** Navigation is no problem (except in thick clag!) as **a line of blue marker-posts sets the route,** but this is real Millstone Grit moorland with bogs and mires awaiting those who tread unwarily. The agony does not last long, though it has a sting in the tail. **Just beyond a new fence the track crosses a stream. It is only tiny but is surrounded by bog. Pick your way through it carefully.** I tried jumping it once, showing off to an elderly group, but misjudged and ended up with egg on my face as well as mud.

However, Nature makes amends almost immediately as you are back on dry limestone on the approach to the area generally called Height or Heights and re-cross the North Craven Fault. It would be quite in order now to clean your boots.

Heights

The track leads through a gate into a walled green lane and along to a signpost and stone stile at a path cross-roads. To your right there is a large depression, offering shelter and more fertile soil. Anyone would recognise that this spot could be a sensible place to settle and it should follow that Heights has a long history of occupancy. At the far, east, end of the depression is Cave Scar with the twin entrances of Heights Cave showing up at this distance as black patches. It is only about ten metres long but excavation uncovered Mesolithic and Bronze Age items. On the limestone plateau to the west of your track, beyond the lime kiln, there is an Iron Age settlement with associated field systems. Recent work, under the auspices of Bradford University, has revealed a large number of pre-Roman artefacts, including flint tools and arrow heads. Evidence of unsavoury goings on was discovered in the form of a human skull that had been deliberately severed from its body at the time of death. Did it belong to a captured opponent?

On the knoll behind Heights Cave, where there is strictly no access please, are more Iron Age hut circles.

In this general area there is also a Norse village but I am not at liberty to disclose its location. It is called Hubbacove and it is one of the very few Norse villages in the Dales that has not continued in use to modern times. Perhaps it was too remote. If you happen to have visited the Norse village at Brough of Birsay on Orkney you will know what I am talking about, though ours is much smaller and less impressive, Nevertheless, it is a recognisable village with nine or ten long-houses, plus out-buildings and streets.

Iron Age enclosure at Heights

The path to the west passes through the middle of a fourteenth century house site, where the fields are incredibly narrow. This site is named and referred to in Fountains Abbey records. Finally, again at the eastern end, stands Height House, a farmhouse with a long history, though not presently inhabitable.

It is ironic perhaps that a site such as this, deemed an ideal location for more than 6,000 years, is now considered too remote. Have we got our priorities right these days?

Your way continues along the bridleway, alongside the barn with its unusual twin, arched doorways and equally unusual external stairway to the hay loft. **Leave Heights through the gate and follow the clear green track, marked again with posts, to Malham Moor Lane. Turn left and trudge the 800 metres back to the start.** As you go note the two distinct humps in the road below which are tunnels to allow cattle and sheep access from one side to the other.

One final thought ... if you have ever wanted to try your hand at dry-stone walling, you must have noticed the infinite possibilities in Bordley!

Place-name meanings

Bark	OE/ON	hill
Bordley	OE	*Brorda's* (pers.name) clearing
Boss Moor	-	named after the Bosse family (17th.c.)
Cool	ON	the hill where cows are / stock pen
Cow Gill Cote	ON	*Kolli's* (pers.name) outlying cottage near a ravine
Heber Beck	ON	the stream on the hill
Heights	OE	the high up place
High Mark	OE	the high boundary marker
Hubbacove	ON	the recess in the hill or the recess where *Hubba* (pers. name) settled. (There was a strong Viking leader called Hubba who conquered much of northern "England" – was this him?)
Kealcup	OE	the hill top where cabbages are grown
Lainger	OE/ON	the place to rest awhile or
	ME	the long, triangular piece of land
Lantern Holes	ON	the hollow where lambs graze among the thorn bushes
Mastiles Lane	OE	the lane through the marsh with a stile
Threshfield	OE	the threshing field
Winterburn	OE	the stream that flows freely in winter

Discovery Walk 6

In Search of Ancient Folk – Grassington Old Pasture

Start and Finish: In front of Grassington Town Hall (Grid reference SE004 642) at the top of Main Street.

Parking: There is a large car park (pay and display) at Colvend, the National Park Centre, at the bottom end of the village.

Public transport: Grassington is served by buses from Skipton that run up dale as far as Buckden. Contact Keighley and District, tel. 01535 603284. There is also a Sunday service operated by Pride of the Dales, tel. 01756 753123. In addition Harrogate and District operate a Dalesbus service, in conjunction with Keighley, from Harrogate via Leeds and Bradford to Grassington and on to Hawes, Keld and Ingleton or to Leyburn. Both services only operate in summer (tel. 01423 566061). See also the Dales Link service (Walk 1).

Facilities: Grassington has a wide range of shops, eating places, pubs as well as banks, a museum and the tourist information centre.

Outline of the Walk: Grassington – High Close – Bare House – Dales Way – Lea Green – The Cove – Grassington.

Length: 8km (5 miles).

Ordnance Survey Map: Outdoor Leisure 10. Landranger 98.

Introduction

There are few areas in the whole country where the ground you tread upon is so full of archaeological detail. Salisbury Plain is one of them: Grassington Old Pasture is another. Here, though, do not expect impressive monuments. You need to use your eyes to sift out what is there. You also need to use your imagination to reconstruct the past, as there are no English Heritage style display boards. There is, to the north of Grassington, a mass of settlement sites and field systems, as well as signs of early mining, possibly dating from Roman times.

The walk is on limestone throughout so the walking is relatively easy, and

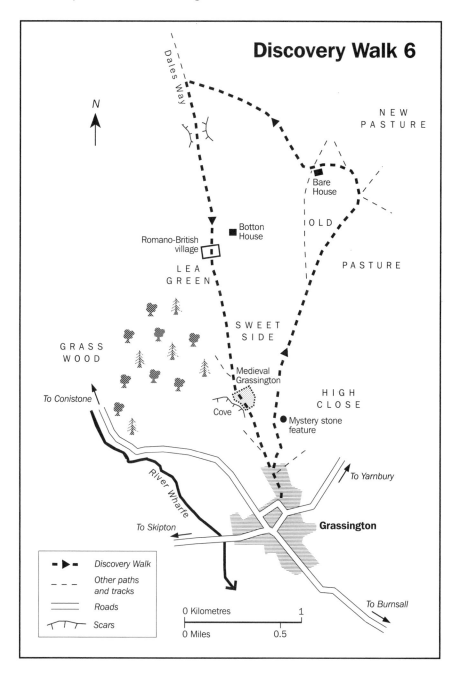

Discovery Walk 6

N

NEW PASTURE

Dales Way

Bare House

OLD

Botton House

Romano-British village

LEA GREEN

PASTURE

SWEET SIDE

GRASS WOOD

Medieval Grassington

HIGH CLOSE

To Conistone

Cove

Mystery stone feature

River Wharfe

To Yarnbury

To Skipton

Grassington

To Burnsall

- ►- Discovery Walk

- - - Other paths and tracks

—— Roads

⊤⌒⊤⌒⊤ Scars

0 Kilometres   1

0 Miles   0.5

it could be comfortably completed in half a day. There is, therefore, no need to suggest shorter loops for Walk 6.

Grassington

Grassington can trace its origins back in the mists of prehistory, though the earliest settlement was higher up, where you will be walking later on. The present town dates from the Middle Ages but it remained a small rural village until the development of lead mining in the seventeenth century. As this industry grew, especially from when the Dukes of Devonshire inherited the mineral rights, so did the need for labour and for a host of ancillary tradesmen to serve both mines and workforce.

Later on the textile industry came to the fore but, like lead, this has long since disappeared from the scene.

It is now tourism that supports the town. Grassington is one of the honeypots of the Dales, a place of pilgrimage for droves of visitors. These large numbers can at times be a reason to avoid the town: to fully appreciate its charms you really need a less busy day. While you are here I would recommend a visit to the Upper Wharfedale Museum on the east side of the square. Also, a booklet is available locally, entitled "One Hundred Things to See on a Walk through Grassington".

Through High Close

With your back to the Town Hall steps, take the right fork, Chapel Street, past the hardware shop, built in 1851 as the town's police station, the Methodist Chapel and, further on, a row of small, former miners' cottages. Turn right now up Bank Lane. This soon turns into an unmade walled track. Just after a small stable block the way could be confusing. Ignore the first two field gates on the left. Instead take the step-stile next to the gate that blocks the main lane.

Continue gently through the very narrow field as the path climbs. Where the field begins to open out more, at the sign post, have a look over the wall where it is not too high. You will see a stone structure: more than semi-circular, with stone slabs stood on end. What is it? It is still a complete mystery to me.

Everything to the right of the wall you are following is called High Close, not marked as such on Ordnance Survey maps. To appreciate High Close fully, you need to hail a passing hot-air balloon. It is absolutely peppered with ancient field systems – some rectangular, some narrow and drawn-out. These systems continue westwards across the area called Sweet Side, shown vividly on the 1:25,000 Ordnance Survey map as a mass of dashed lines.

The walls that stand high – the present field boundaries – date from two hundred years ago when High Close was enclosed by an Act or Parliament (see "The Northern Dales") All the other banks and wall footings are ten times older, maybe even more. Some sites have been tentatively dated, by methods of construction, to either the Iron Age or the Romano-British period, with at least one Bronze Age burial mound in amongst the rest. Now here is a thought. If the fields are Romano-British, then the burial mound was as ancient to the Romans as they now are to us.

The path continues to climb, crossing a number of ancient boundaries, to a squeeze stile at the north end of this unusually long field. Carry on through the next field, cutting the corner, to the ladder stile that you can see. Beyond this, to the left of the path on the second ruined wall, are the remains of a dew pond, built to hold water for cattle and sheep. This one may be datable because nearby are the ruins of a seventeenth century house and an old lime kiln. It is possible that the dew pond is contemporary with the house.

This field, and the next, are still packed with ancient field systems and just before the next ladder stile your path crosses a clearly defined ancient track.

Just over the next wall, to the right, are the foundations of two shepherds' huts, of indeterminable age. This field is much wider than the previous one, though equally long. Bear left, uphill, to the next ladder stile by the wall junction. You can see it from the previous stile. A few metres from the wall junction you cross some old lead workings and leave behind the old field systems.

The paths now fork – the main one goes straight up the next field – but you bear right, through the nick and past the dog-leg in the right-hand wall. There are four more fields on this path. Between the present one and the second is a gap stile with a lamb gate, then a ladder stile in the next wall, a stone stile at the far side of the third field, and the wall after is ruinous. At this point bear slightly left, past old lead workings and two huge limestone erratics to the final ladder stile of this stretch.

You might think you are now on open moor but it is all enclosed though. This last wall separates Grassington Old Pasture, to the south, and Grassington New Pasture to the north. Neither is named by the Ordnance Survey. (Who decides what to include?)

Less than 100 metres from that last stile there is a green lane. It is called Lime Kiln Lane. Turn left along the lane but only for a minute or two. The lane continues northwards: your way is left through the gate by the signpost to Conistone. The track is clear now, following the wall past High Barn and round to the deserted farmhouse that is Bare House.

Bare House

... or Barras in local-speak. The present building dates from the mid-seventeenth century but the farm existed before that. An inventory of 1603 lists it as a house with "garden and hemp plot". The house as you see it was built

on a modified two-bay Lobby-Entry plan (see Walk 5). The original door into
the lobby was blocked up when the third (left-hand) bay and porch were
added. The original door is next to the porch but was very effectively
disguised. Bare House was abandoned around 1960, just another to add to
the long list of forsaken homesteads on Old Pasture.

Looking up Littondale from Barras

From Bare House to Botton House

Your route follows a path north-westwards from Bare House, level at first.
As you proceed you are looking right across Upper Wharfedale and straight
up Littondale, beyond the television mast on Wassa Hill. To the left of the
mast the buttress of Kilnsey Crag is just visible.

**The path soon begins to descend to a clump of trees, past a spring and
tank.** This was the water source for Barras, quite a trudge before the days of
pumps and pipes. **Go alongside the trees, through two gateways and then
gently downslope again across a boulder-strewn patch,** below a well-preserved field kiln, used for "sweetening" the acid soils to improve the pasture.

**Near the foot of the slope there is a triple obstacle: a ladder stile then a
step-over stile and a gate. In the next field the right of way proceeds
north-westwards to meet the Dales Way path on which you turn south to
a ladder stile in the same wall you crossed earlier.**

As you follow the Dales Way, a long-distance route linking Ilkley with
Bowness on the shores of Windermere, look back upslope where you have

just come from. Can you identify more ancient field boundaries? **The path passes a massive lime kiln in a mini-gorge between two limestone pavement-covered knolls. Continue on the clear path, over a ladder stile and through a gate with further pavement. The path hugs the western side of this field to exit at yet another ladder stile.**

On the far side of this wall is a huge field covering an area known as Lea Green. Before you climb over, however, look over to the east side of the previous field, to its south-eastern corner. There is a ruin built into the boundary wall. This was Botton House, and the building you can see has been ascribed to the fifteenth century. It is tall and narrow and very crudely built of limestone rubble. The steep angle of the surviving gable end points to its having been thatched. There are signs of two windows, both blocked up. In a document drawn up in the first decade of the seventeenth century, Botton House was described as "an ancient mansion house".

Into Lea Green

Like High Close, Lea Green is smothered in prehistoric and medieval remains, some of which the path cuts right through.

A few metres beyond the previous stile, to the right of the path, there is a burial mound tentatively dated to the Early Bronze Age. **Then you cross what looks like a an old walled lane,** fanning out to your left to join the Enclosure Wall. This old "lane" leads to a dew pond and permanent spring but it is not actually very old and was not a lane either. The pond and funnelling walls were constructed in 1822.

The path climbs slightly onto a rise and slices a settlement in two. This is a very clearly defined village site and you can readily delimit the various huts – here mainly rectangular – and enclosures which were gardens or stock folds. The site has been excavated to reveal occupation in the last centuries of the Iron Age and throughout the Romano-British period. On the western side there is a much larger rectangular house site with a well-defined enclosure adjoining. This is too big to have been Romano-British and could well be early medieval, possibly Norse.

There are further enclosures beyond the next limestone pavement, undated. Their outline is depicted on the 1:25,000 Ordnance Survey map. More pavement comes next, one area with a spreading sycamore that has found a safe niche in a gryke.

Limestone Pavement

A prominent feature of most walks in this collection is limestone pavement. I have tried to show the processes that operate to create limestone pavements in the sketch diagram.

No other part of Britain can boast such extensive pavements. Indeed more than a half of all pavement in the country lies within the Dales.

Development of a limestone pavement

Selected stages

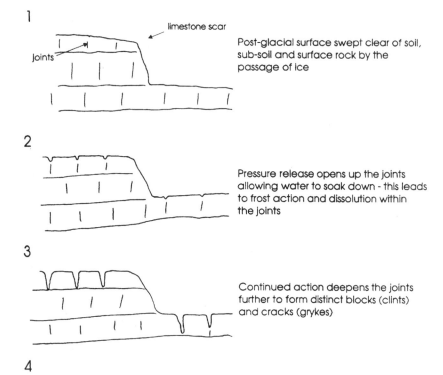

1

limestone scar

Joints

Post-glacial surface swept clear of soil, sub-soil and surface rock by the passage of ice

2

Pressure release opens up the joints allowing water to soak down - this leads to frost action and dissolution within the joints

3

Continued action deepens the joints further to form distinct blocks (clints) and cracks (grykes)

4

A

C

D B

Clints may separate into loose blocks (A); grykes deepen to 1 metre or more (B);wind and rain action cause fretting on the exposed scar face (C); dissolution causes shallow channels or runnels on top of the clints (D)

Traditionally they have been viewed as a convenient quarry for wall and house building stone. Now, however, they are under threat as never before, and our obsession with garden rockery stone is having damaging results in the Dales. This is despite theoretical protection from the Wildlife and Countryside Act 1981. A survey prior to the Act found that only three per cent of British pavements were intact.

In the past this may have been due to the wrong signals being passed down from "above". Incredibly, 1000 tonnes of limestone pavement were removed from the flanks of Ingleborough for the 1951 Festival of Britain in London! Increasingly in the 1990s the National Park has been exercising its right under the Act to impose Limestone Pavement Orders to afford them full legal protection: they must not be disturbed in any way other than within the bounds of normal land management. Most recently a national publicity campaign has been inaugurated to spread the message to the general public as, sadly, even the imposition of an Order cannot be a guarantee against illegal quarrying of pavement. A survey carried out in 1991 identified 47 pavements in the National Park that were worthy of protection. So far less than half have been saved.

They simply must be protected as an integral part of a special landscape. Aside from this aesthetic reasoning, the botanical diversity of ungrazed pavements is stunning. The grykes are miniature gardens in themselves and can provide a secure habitat for a wide array of ferns and flowering plants, some of which are exceedingly rare, and many of which are more reminiscent of woodland flora.

Life in the Iron Age and Romano-British Period

By 700 BC the period known in everyday prehistory as the Bronze Age was coming to an end after maybe 1000 years of technological and social stagnation. There was no sudden change to the Iron Age at this time. Rather it was a slow and halting process by which new ideas filtered north to the Dales. Bronze still continued in use for another two centuries, and flint tools had not yet been abandoned, but iron was coming into greater usage. It was more easily worked, more durable and more effective than bronze.

By the start of the Iron Age the climate had deteriorated to become cooler and damper than previously and the Dales then, as now, were very much a marginal area in terms of settlement and agriculture. In some areas the Iron Age folk still practised transhumance, a pastoral system involving seasonal movement of people and stock. In the summers stock were moved to the upland pastures from permanent settlements in the lowlands of north Lancashire and the Vale of York. It is difficult to imagine how people and cattle could have survived a harsh winter in some of the remote, upland farmsteads within the Dales.

The dominant form of settlement in this period was the isolated farmstead or cluster of small huts. Villages as such were comparatively rare in the Dales. The one above Grassington is one of the larger, having an enclosed village area less than one hectare alongside 32 hectares of field enclosures. (One hectare is roughly the size of a football pitch.) Raistrick, the pioneer archaeologist in the Dales, has identified almost 250 Iron Age sites in the southern Dales, mostly small. To get an idea of what their huts were like, bring to mind the stereotypical image of an African hut today: round, three to five metres across, with a conical roof of thatch. In our case the wall footings were made of roughly placed stone blocks. They had living huts, storage huts and huts for animals. The enclosures also had stone footings with some kind of paling on top to keep in domestic stock and keep out predators.

Life was hard and no doubt desperately poor for the majority. Certainly none of the material riches associated with Iron Age sites in southern Britain are in evidence here. The British North-South divide is perhaps older than sociologists think.

They led a mainly subsistence existence though there are signs of trade. Cattle and sheep were kept, along with goats and pigs, and they were cultivators, who knows how successfully? A range of crops were planted: hardy cereals (emmer, spelt, oats and barley), vetch crops and legumes. One hectare of such could have supported two or three families.

As regards the appearance of the people themselves, archaeology as yet can give us no clue. It is known from Roman writings that the Silures, in Gwent, were short and dark, and that some of the tribes in Scotland were tall and reddish, but what were our folk like?

The Iron Age peoples of the Dales were the Brigantes. There is some controversy as to their origin. Some prehistorians say they were a mixture of native Bronze Age folk and the descendants of Celts, immigrants from the continent. Others totally reject this hypothesis, believing that the last pre-historic migration occurred in the early Neolithic, and that the Celtic language and culture developed from that. The Brigantes were not one tribe or one people: they were a loose and often disorganised and schismatic confederation of tribes. They seemed to lack any sort of cohesion, whether political or social, and certainly lacked vision. They were, though, the largest tribal grouping in pre-Roman Britain, occupying a territory that the geographer Ptolemy later described as stretching "from sea to sea".

To Roman commentators, prior to the invasion, they were the Britons, brithon, meaning painted men. According to another geographer, Strabo, they were "madly fond of war" but not evil. To themselves they were simply Cymru, the countrymen and, of course, this word is still in use today as the Welsh name for Wales and as the name of England's most mountainous county, Cumbria.

By 100 BC another wave of ideas had reached the Dales from the south, and Celtic society took on a more organised complexion. A distinct ruling class developed, possibly centred on Almondbury near Huddersfield. The population was growing more rapidly and, as prime areas of land disappeared under cultivation and settlements, conflicts ensued. There is nothing like land hunger to turn friend into foe.

And then in AD 43 the Roman invasion of Britain began, and rapidly moved north to subdue tribe after tribe. However for the continuation of this story you will have to read "The Northern Dales". Suffice it to say here that our country entered what is known as the Romano-British period, really the bridge between prehistory and written, recorded history in these parts.

Traditional life for the mass continued as before. Those who had some status and wealth prior to the invasion either welcomed the Romans and thus prospered, or resisted and lost all. The rest, the majority, continued to eke out a meagre existence from the soil. Perhaps the most pronounced visible change in the archaeological record was the transformation from round huts to rectangular structures, as at Lea Green. Without doubt this came about owing to Roman influence.

In many respects, though, life remained unchanged from 1000 BC to 1000 AD.

On from Lea Green

After the sycamore in the pavement the path continues as a green track, crossing a lead vein with early workings. Further on there is a line of shallow, rectangular lead workings, called coffin workings for obvious reasons. These date back to the fifteenth century, or possibly even earlier. The records of Fountains Abbey, for example, relate how the monks purchased lead from one Adam Cokeson in 1484. He is thought to have lived in a house, whose lower wall courses survive, in the dry valley called Kimpergill to the east of the long wall parallel to your route. Pottery was found at the site dating from the monastic period through to the seventeenth century.

The remains of Kimpergill House

As your track starts to descend slightly you come to a fork. The left track heads uphill again. You take the right track downslope, to another track junction. At this point walk straight across to the wall, at the south end of Lea Green. Go through the stone stile in the first wall and the squeeze stile in the second. You are now in late medieval Grassington.

A Lost Village

Old Grassington was situated in this and adjacent fields, the walls of which post-date the settlement. Excavations have turned up little other than large quantities of medieval pottery, but then why should there be anything more exciting? The last people to live up here probably re-located downhill as early-modern Grassington was beginning to grow, and they would have taken their few possessions with them.

Set against the north wall of this field, to the left (east) of the path, are the foundations of three houses, the furthest of which has a small croft attached. The wall bases are very sturdy and one of the houses has a floor paved with slabs of limestone. In front of them was a midden (rubbish dump). In it were found some metal objects and a profusion of pottery, dated to the fourteenth century and later.

What of daily life in the Middle Ages? In many respects it had changed very little since the Iron Age. Language and culture had completely changed with the various influxes of immigrants in the Dark Ages, but much of the drudgery remained. The people still occupied simple huts, little changed in over 1000 years. They still scraped an existence from the land, keeping cattle, sheep and pigs and growing a range of crops the Iron Age folk would have recognised. In addition the noble cabbage had come to the fore and beans were an important staple. The phrase "down to my last bean" originally reflected a lack of food in the larder rather than money. Leeks, onions and garlic also appeared on the menu, home-grown, and played a major role in ameliorating the distaste of less than fresh meat, the stench of the midden and animal dung and the not so wholesome smells of the house. Let us be careful, though, not to judge and condemn the ways of the past. We have no more right to pass critical comment from our own twentieth century perspective on the past, than future generations have on us.

As you cross the village look carefully as the whole of its eastern half has lumps and bumps indicating houses, stores and enclosures. Think of the people who lived here: of the Westcott family and of Elizabeth Newton who were among the last inhabitants of old Grassington.

Back to the Start

Head on through the lost village to another squeeze stile at the south end, at the top of the rise. (I think this was designed by somebody on the tall and thin side!)

Look back here, for a last look at the old village and the two houses down below, with their small house sites (tofts) within their garden enclosures (crofts). South-west of the village site is a limestone scar, simply called The Cove, and beyond that the mass of Grass and Bastow Woods, coppiced in earlier days to provide timber and chopwood for the lead mines of Grassington Moor (see Walk 8).

Two more small fields lie ahead and then the outskirts of present-day Grassington. Pick your way through the cow yard, round to the left of the main buildings, and out onto Chapel Street by the farmhouse. Before you return to the Town Hall, the frontage of sixteenth century Town Head farm deserves more than a glance for its fine decorative plasterwork.

Place-name meanings

Bare House	ON	the house on a hill
Botton House	ON	the house in the (valley?) bottom
The Cove	ON	the recess
Grassington	OE	the grazing farmstead
Grass Wood	OE	the wood with grass for deer grazing
High Close	OE	the high enclosure
Lea Green	OE	the green forest clearing
Sweet Side	OE	the sweet (i.e. not acidic) hillside

Discovery Walk 7

A Ramble through Langstrothdale Chase

Start and Finish: By the beckside upstream of Yockenthwaite, 3km along the by-road from Buckden to Hawes (Grid reference SD902 792).

Parking: There is ample roadside parking all along this stretch of road, beyond Yockenthwaite. Those wishing to split the walk into two loops could park on the roadside near Hubberholme.

Public transport: A bus service from Skipton and Grassington operates as far updale as Buckden. Check with Pride of the Dales (01756 753123) or Keighley and District (01535 603284). Keighley's Dalesbus service, run in conjunction with Harrogate and District (tel. 01423 566061) passes through Buckden en route from Harrogate, Leeds and Bradford to Hawes or Leyburn (summer only). A park-and-ride scheme operates frequent buses from Grassington to Buckden in July and August. Contact any tourist information centre.

Facilities: The White Lion at Cray and the George Inn at Hubberholme offer the usual services. There is a National Park Information Point and a new National Trust centre in Buckden.

Outline of the walk: Yockenthwaite – Scar House – Cray – Hubberholme – Dalesway to Yockenthwaite.

Length: 8.5km (5.3 miles) for the full route. It could be divided into two loops of around 5km (about 3 miles) each, starting at Hubberholme. To include the Deepdale circuit add another 2.5km.

Ordnance Survey Map: Outdoor Leisure 30. Landranger 98.

Introduction

Langstrothdale forms the uppermost part of Wharfedale. The Wharfe itself begins its long journey, to join the Ouse south of York, at Beckermonds. Here Green Field Beck converges with the infant Wharfe (called Oughtershaw Beck further up the dale).

Much of the dale (2400 hectares) is owned by the National Trust, thanks to a magnificent bequest in 1989, and extensive purchases of land in 1994 utilising funds from the Yorkshire Moors and Dales Appeal and another major legacy. The Trust has set itself the task of conserving the herb-rich hay meadows and the woodland tracts that distinguish Langstrothdale from much of the National Park. It has also embarked on an ambitious programme of restoring dry stone walls and traditional stone barns. With 160 hectares of woodland, eight SSSIs and one hundred barns to oversee, the task is somewhat daunting.

This walk has much to offer the discerning walker, wildlife aside. As you trace the route in these pages a story will unfold of a great medieval hunting chase, of lost roads, of a Quaker hideaway, and of subterranean passages to daunt all but the most determined cavers.

If you intend to split the walk into two loops, use Hubberholme as your base. For the western loop first read the section "The Last Lap" and then "Yockenthwaite" and "Langstrothdale Chase".

For the eastern loop start with "Hubberholme", then read "From Scar House to Cray" and the ensuing section.

Up Dale and Down

From wherever you have parked, or been dropped off, there is a stretch of riverside to ease you into the walk. You may choose to head downstream directly to Yockenthwaite, but I hope you will find the diversion to Deepdale worthwhile, so follow the road upstream. This is one of those stretches of river that can either be peacefully idyllic or reverberating to the sounds of Sunday picnickers and paddlers. The stream itself – the infant Wharfe – varies from a collection of quiet pools linked by gentle trickles, to a tremendous force of frothing water, depending on the weather.

It is also a stretch of water where you can see dippers all year round, and pied and grey wagtails through the summer.

As you begin to approach Deepdale, particularly during May and June, you might look out for two special flowers. Opposite and beyond Cow Garth Barn the south bank of the road is steeper, more rocky and distinctly wetter than elsewhere. The flowers in question are found in close association as they favour similar conditions. One is the delicate pink bird's-eye primrose *(Primula farinosa)* and the other is butterwort *(Pinguicula vulgaris)*. This has very distinctive pale yellow-green leaves, low to the ground, and it resembles a starfish in shape. It derives its sustenance in a fascinating way. Its leaves are covered in sticky hairs which trap any unsuspecting insects. The captive is then digested by the plant which thereby gains the nutrients it cannot obtain from the acidic soil. Its flower is purple: there is only one flower per plant.

Two pieces of folk lore are associated with butterwort. A baby fed on milk from a cow that has eaten the flower is sure to grow strong while the leaves, if added to milk, will stop it separating. So why was it not called milkwort

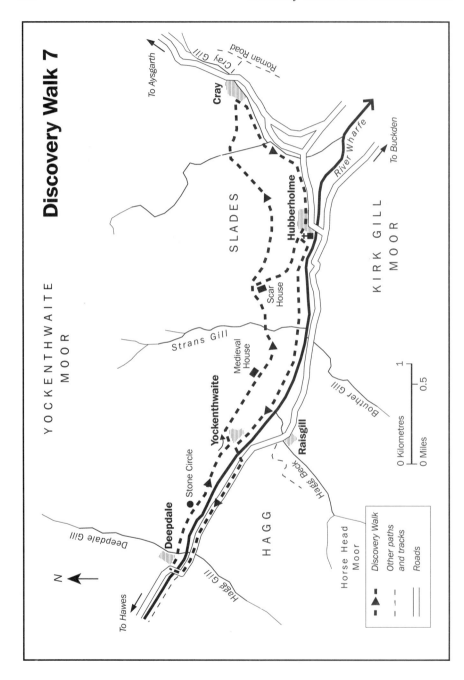

instead of the little blue-pink-white flowers that have laid claim to that name? Part of the dale around Deepdale forms the Deepdale Meadows Site of Special Scientific Interest (SSSI), one of several in Langstrothdale, thus recognising the local botanical diversity.

There are almost fifty caves and pot-holes in the dale, a few of which I intend to point out to you. Personally I find caving an enjoyable and stimulating pastime but I do find some of the caves not quite to my liking. In fact I would not even descend them to escape Armageddon. The first such is here, between road and beck, opposite the junction of Deepdale Beck. It is called Deepdale Rising, is only 35 metres long and little more than 10 metres deep, and is a Grade I cave (i.e. easy) but it is a horrible tight, wet and rough crawl. There is another one opposite the barn but this is Grade III, so forget it.

Cross the river by the recently renovated Deepdale Bridge and turn up the access road to the hamlet. On the first bend a gate marks the start of the riverside path, another section of the Dales Way.

There is not much left of Deepdale now but in its heyday there were thirteen households and two inns. This was in the days when Langstrothdale carried the main coach road from Lancaster to Newcastle-upon-Tyne. It came over the top from Ribblesdale, down Green Field to Beckermonds and then followed the Wharfe to Hubberbolme before turning north to Wensley-dale and beyond. Deepdale was an important staging post on this route, the first one to the east of High Birkwith in Ribblesdale.

Deepdale also lay on a monastic route, one of the many Monk's roads in the Dales. Green Field, further up dale, was a grange of Fountains Abbey but the road also served estates belonging to Jervaulx Abbey.

It must have been quite an adventure, in an unheated coach, with no springs, and a road that would have varied from a rutted quagmire to boneshaking rocks and stones.

A map of 1770 shows a third road, almost certainly a packhorse route, climbing up Deepdale Gill over the moors to Raydale and Semer Water. Absolutely no trace of this road has survived.

Drop down the paddock, noting the ancient and gnarled elm pollard. You do not see many pollarded trees in the Dales: in fact you see few trees, full stop! Timber was harvested from a pollard every few years and, by cutting the wood above head height, the new shoots were sure to grow, safe from cattle and deer.

Pass over Deepdale Beck by the footbridge, climb up the bank and follow the edge of this meadow to the ladder stile at the other end. You now enter the National Trust's huge Upper Wharfedale Estate. **The path lies ahead and becomes an easy stroll on the river's flood plain, all the way to Yock-enthwaite.**

There is another cave coming up now in Great Pasture: look for a stream, just left of the path, which emerges from a slit between beds of limestone, only to disappear after a couple of metres. This slit is the entrance to Yockenthwaite Cave. The caving handbook recommends avoiding it except in drought! It can be followed, believe it or not, for 150 metres much of which is a flat-out wriggle. I went in once, for maybe three metres – and promptly reverse wriggled out. There is an even more bizarre cave further on today.

Between the cave and the gate ahead lies Yockenthwaite stone circle, which has been dated by excavation to the Middle Bronze Age. It has been mentioned in print on several occasions as a stone circle for ritualistic use, but a more plausible theory is that it was a burial site. Elsewhere in the Dales features of a similar size and shape occur, though with the stones buried in a circular earth bank. The burial would have been placed within the ring. If indeed it is from the Middle Bronze Age, the tomb should only have contained ashes as cremation was then the preferred method of burial. The big, unanswered question is where did these people live?

The path continues through the beckside pastures, past a field kiln, and into Yockenthwaite.

Yockenthwaite stone circle

Yockenthwaite

This, too, is a mere shadow of its former self. Like Deepdale it lay on the coach road but Yockenthwaite lay near a more important road junction. The fell on the south side of the valley is called Horse Head Moor (the haunt of golden plover and dunlin, by the way) and Horsehead Pass was a major packhorse road for centuries, linking Ribblesdale, Malham and the south, via Halton Gill, with Wensleydale and the north. The old road is now a bridleway. The village started to decline in the early nineteenth century, as the old roads were superseded, a decline accelerated by the advent of turnpikes (see "The Northern Dales") and the railways. By the 1851 census it had shrunk from having sixteen households, an inn and a school, to only four households.

The big house (Yockenthwaite Hall) was rebuilt before 1769 by the Tennant family in a somewhat grandiose Georgian mode. It has been quoted as a "good" example of this architectural style, indicating entry into the ranks of the gentry by this yeoman family. Behind it is a house dated 1681 and immediately east of that was another, now a barn. Behind the main house, also, is the rubble of another seventeenth century house: Top Farm lies at the north end of the village and, nearest the river, is Yockenthwaite Cottage, once the main farmhouse. Rescue excavations were carried out in 1992 where the new barn now stands, and medieval remains were unearthed, but nothing spectacular, as well as Neolithic and Early Bronze Age flint tools.

The bridge was built – or rebuilt to replace an earlier one – in the early eighteenth century.

Yockenthwaite bridge

Langstrothdale Chase

You should leave Yockenthwaite on the track that swings between the main house and the isolated barn, left of the track. It is hard to imagine now that this was a three-bay seventeenth century cottage, used as the village school two centuries later. As the farm track climbs away from the village look for the large copper vessel, now filled with rubble, set into the bed of a small stream. This is a posser, or set-pot, formerly used for doing the laundry! **When you reach the first trees go through the handgate onto the gravelled path that contours along the bottom of the wood.** Look across the valley and you can see the old Horsehead road zigzagging up the fellside by Hagg Beck, above Raisgill farm. This place name indicates some kind of burial cairn and at the lower end of one of the fields running down to the Wharfe there is a massive mound topped with stones.

Very shortly the path strikes uphill, in a mini-scramble onto a higher ledge, a higher bedding plane. For nearly five kilometres now the path follows one bedding plane or another and makes easy and delightful walking 100 metres or so above the valley floor. The rocks here are some of the most northerly exposures of Great Scar Limestone. The rising ground to the north also contains bands of limestone, but of the younger Wensleydale Group, interspersed with beds of sandstone.

Bear right at the top of the climb and immediately you find yourself in a medieval landscape. For almost a kilometre the path cuts through a series of small enclosures, all bounded by very crudely built walls. In places boulders balance precariously on boulders, in others the edges of low scars have been utilised to give extra height to the wall.

Approximately 300 metres from the top of the climb there is a ruin left of and above the path. It is quite distinct from the barns dotted around. They are made of sandstone: this one is limestone. Have a close look at it. The style and the size, and the lack of properly-framed windows, are sure signs of an early date. The steep pitch of the surviving gable was designed to take thatch, probably heather. Here stand the remains of an early house. In nearby fields are the remains of three more with small and equally old walled enclosures.

After the Norman Conquest vast areas of land were granted to noble families to add to their new found status and wealth in vanquished England. Much of these lands was very thinly peopled and the new, absentee lords set aside tracts of country as hunting grounds called Chases. Within the Dales as a whole there were ten Chases and Forests, the difference being that a forest was in royal as opposed to baronial ownership. At the maximum it has been estimated that one-third of England was set aside as hunting grounds of one sort or another. Langstrothdale was the playing fields and meat larder of the Percy family, from the Conquest one of the most powerful families in England and Earls of Northumberland from 1377. All forest and manorial rights in the dale were held by the family until 1534.

Hunting chases were organised in a uniform way, each applying the same set of laws and having a similar body of officers. The laws were not just designed to uphold the owner's rights: there was an ulterior motive. Fines imposed on miscreants were an important source of income for our noble lord, the more the better for him.

There were so many rules and regulations, in fact, that it was hard for the peasantry not to infringe them in their daily struggle for survival. Perhaps that was the general idea!

The Laws

There were three classes of offence: against the person; against vert which included trespass on the chase or enclosing part of it for cultivation as well as causing any damage to trees or unlawfully taking brashings; and against venison, which included poaching by any method of "the four beasts of the chase" or Campestris, These beasts, protected from the peasantry and reserved for the lords, were roe deer, fallow deer, fox and marten.

Cases were heard in the first instance in the local Woodmote court. This met every forty days and passed cases on to the higher Swainmote court. The courts had a jury made up of twelve sweins (freemen), and forest verderers (officials) presided over court proceedings. Any serious cases were referred to the highest court, the Justices of Eyre, which worked on a slow rotating circuit around the whole of the north of England.

Officials

The lord's agent was the Keeper. It was he who ran the Chase and acted as the final arbiter, except when the lord was in residence on a hunting spree. Beneath him were lesser officials. The agister was the medieval equivalent of the rent collector. He collected rent from the peasants for pannage and supervised grazing within the Chase. The woodward (hence the origin of the surname) was the warden responsible for the timber stock in the wooded sections of the Chase. The verderers had charge over vert and venison.

Organisation

Although the laws of the Chase were many and far-reaching, local villagers and existing farmers did maintain certain rights. With permission they could collect firewood (the right of firebote) and honey, they could turn their pigs loose to forage in wooded parts of the Chase (the right of pannage), and they had the right to cut peat on the moor tops (the right of turbary).

The village of Buckden was established in the twelfth century by the Percys, as the centre of Langstrothdale Chase. The forest keepers were based here and their role soon became an institutionalised and hereditary position in the family of the de Knolls.

To ensure sound organisation and secure control, the Chase was partitioned into divisions, each centred around a lodge (the equivalent of a vaccary in a royal forest). Langstrothdale had seven lodges in addition to Buckden itself: Yockenthwaite, Cray, Hubberholme, Raisgill, Deepdale,

Medieval forester's house

Beckermonds and Oughtershaw. Each of these still exists, either as a village or a collection of farms.

In addition there were a number of isolated homesteads dotted about, especially on south-facing slopes. I believe these were originally Norse farmsteads which were incorporated into the overall organisation of the Chase. I am quite sure that the ruins you see here, as they stand, are medieval rebuildings of Norse farmhouses. I am also quite sure the Chase keeper came to a mutual understanding with existing settlers: live and let live, within reason.

The End

The terminal decline of the feudal system in the late fifteenth century made Forests and Chases untenable in the English social scene, and they in turn began to lose their identity although they lingered on in parts of the country far beyond then. Charles I resurrected the full idea and extent of the medieval Chases and Forests, in his desperate attempts to wring yet more money from his subjects. An Act of 1641, however, reversed this. The hunting grounds did not finally meet a legislative end until the mid-eighteenth century.

Strans Gill and Scar House

Carry on from the ruined house through the old enclosures and eventually

through a later Enclosure wall where there is a gap stile. At this point the path turns uphill parallel to the wood, to a footbridge.

On the same level as the bridge, and about fifty metres west of it, there is a small stone circular feature. I have no idea of its date or purpose! On the rise to the north of this is a large depression, marked by a few saplings and a ruinous wall. This is Strans Gill Old Pot. It is only about 14 metres deep but is dangerous.

In quite a different league is Strans Gill Pot next to the stream, above the bridge. You cannot miss it if you have a mind to find it. On the surface it is a very narrow slit but in a series of vertical pitches the cave drops over 100 metres and has a total length of 500 metres. Apparently, hidden in its innermost recesses are some of the most beautiful stalactite formations in England. I, for one, have no desire to test the validity of this claim: it is classified as Grade V, the most difficult of all, with a hideous entry pitch.

Like the infant Wharfe, Strans Gill is a stream of many moods. Most of the time the water flows underground but, when the pots and rifts can take no more, the flow cascades down the gill in a spectacular fashion.

Before you leave the bridge peer over the side: it is considerably older than its top side might indicate.

The path cuts through the top part of Rais Wood and then follows a limestone ledge along the top edge of the wood, a section of path that will surely delay the botanist in spring and early summer with its broad array of flowering species. **The wood comes to an end and the path cuts across a small section of pavement to a gap stile by the gate. Climb through this and you are at Scar House.**

If you are walking the Hubberholme to Yockenthwaite loop, rather than the full route, take the farm track downhill to the church.

I may be sentimental but I hate to see fine old houses standing empty and forlorn, but I suppose reality prevails. The house belongs to the National Trust and has been a problem for them. What can they do with it? It is remote and at the top of a long, hard climb, and needs a great deal of attention internally to make it habitable again. However, their intention is to renovate it as a holiday cottage, and by the time you read this, work should have been completed.

It may have had an uncertain few years but it can look back over a long and illustrious past. It sports two date-stones: the latter (1876) bears the initials of the owner at the time it was substantially rebuilt, remodelled and enlarged, Sir John W. Ramsden, who sold it just three years later. The older datestone bears the initials of the Tennants who lived here for generations but even this date of 1698 is not the beginning of the story. That, too, represented perhaps a rebuilding or modification. Scar House goes back way beyond 1698. An extant will of Christopher Tennant, dated 1570, suggests a long lineage. An inventory also exists for 1719 when the house contained, amongst other items, five beds and 24 chairs.

The rear of the house suggests an early seventeenth century style with its small mullioned windows, and the old roof line can be traced on the east gable. I suspect that the back door, facing west, with its plain stone lintel, was moved from the front of the house in one of the re-building phases.

The Tennants were devout Quakers in the times when break-away sects were suppressed and their adherents persecuted. In the seventeenth century – and probably later – the Tennants held illicit meetings here. George Fox, the founder of the movement, is known to have been here in 1657, and in 1677 when by contemporary accounts he preached to a large gathering. One Tennant – James – died for his faith in York jail. The family lived here until 1740.

Nearby, in a small rectangular enclosure, is the old Quaker burial ground. A plaque on the wall gives the date of 1650, but it was in use into the nineteenth century.

Also nearby are the remnants of a hollin, a holly wood. Hollins were prized possessions in the early modern period as a source of winter fodder for cattle.

From Scar House to Cray

If your intention is to complete the full route clamber up behind Scar House to regain the path on a slightly higher limestone ledge. The walking is easy all the way to Cray. Initially the path contours along the top edge of Black Wood which has recently been completely stock-proofed with wire netting. The idea is to keep out sheep and rabbits though I suppose some rabbits found themselves fenced in.

The woodland on this side of the valley is continuous from Scar House to Crook Gill, but has different names: Black Wood gives way to Hubberholme Wood which, in turn, merges into Todd's Wood. This extensive wooded tract is one of the best examples of a broad-leaved, semi-natural wood in the dales. The dominant tree species are ash, wych elm, hazel and holly, with rowan, bird cherry and the invasive sycamore here and there.

The area had been suffering from over-grazing, hence the Woodland Guardianship scheme entered into by the owners of Black Wood in 1993. The hope is that the ground flora will re-establish itself while the existing and newly planted trees will be left in peace to regenerate. Even in the depth of winter the success so far is evident to the casual eye.

The National Park has an excellent woodland advice and grant scheme so hopefully more woods within the Dales will receive similar remedial treatment.

These woods are a haven for a variety of birds. A slow walk along the edge of the woods, binoculars poised and ears pricked, is a rewarding experience especially before the trees come into full leaf. Flycatchers, treecreepers and pipits are common enough in addition to the normal range of resident

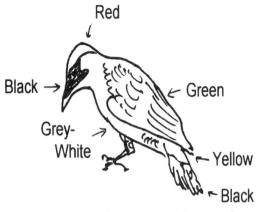

Red

Black →

Grey-

White

← Green

← Yellow

← Black

Green woodpecker (average size: 30cm)

species. If you happen to hear a very loud and raucous kind of laugh, long drawn out, it will be a green woodpecker flitting from tree to tree.

As you proceed a spectacular view opens up on your right. You can see right down Upper Wharfedale from Buckden below, past Starbotton in the middle distance, to Kettlewell where there is a noticeable constriction in the valley. This is a textbook example of a glacial trough, gouged out by successive glaciers: steep-sided and broadly U-shaped, the gentler pre-glacial valley sides visible higher up on each side, and flat-bottomed, indicating infill with sediments from the fells.

Straight ahead, across the tributary valley of Cray Gill, lies the massive bulk of Buckden Pike (702 metres high) falling away southwards to Starbotton Fell. The successive bands of limestones and sandstones stand out clearly on the flanks of the Pike.

This delightful stretch of strolling – and it is ideal strolling terrain – comes to an end at Crook Gill which is crossed by a footbridge. The path swings right now, past a barn (and television booster), through three meadows to the hamlet of Cray. If you intend to take advantage of the White Lion's facilities, go through the farmyard on the topmost track and return to this point later.

If you are continuing on, turn sharp right and down by the entrance to the first farmhouse. A narrow path, signposted, leads between walls to a handgate and open pasture.

Cray to Hubberholme

From the gate the path continues along the slope for a few metres before dropping diagonally towards the valley bottom. There is a post part way down to mark the way. Beyond this the track is clear and you can tell it has been engineered, not recently either. This is part of yet another ancient packhorse route from Wensleydale to Wharfedale and Ribblesdale.

At the foot of the slope, hidden in the thicket, the track crosses Crook Gill. Spend a moment here and scramble down to the streamside to examine the bridge. Many of the so-called packhorse bridges are nothing of the sort: they are rebuilt versions of older structures. Here, though, we have the genuine article, an unaltered and traditionally constructed bridge. The whole structure is held in place by the central V-shaped key stones. Knock them out and it will collapse. In the building process, incidentally, an arched wooden framework would have been erected to keep the stones in place.

The path hugs Cray Gill now and every bit of the way is to be savoured for the falls and quieter pools, the wayside flowers and the birdlife. The occurrence of limestone grassland, semi-natural woodland and water in such close proximity have guaranteed biological diversity par excellence.

The path ends at Stubbing Bridge and you should turn right along Stubbing Lane into Hubberholme. Throughout mid and late summer the verges of this lane form a flower bed of giant bell-flower *(Campanula latifolia)*. Growing up to a metre in height, with striking pale blue, pinkish or white flowers, you might not expect it to be a close relation of the comparatively tiny blue harebell *(Campanula rotundifolia)* you will already have seen today.

Hubberholme

Hubberholme (or "Ubberam") may originally have been a Norse settlement, though the place-name suggests an Anglian foundation. Its existence as a permanent recorded settlement begins in the thirteenth century: Hubberholme was one of the lodges of the Chase. The church then was only a forest chapel, and not a parish church as now. It began life dedicated to St Oswald, changed its name two centuries later and, later again, to its present title.

An excellent guide is available in the church, which is a must, so I need say no more here. The George Inn across the river used to belong to the church and, in January, there is a gathering of church and farm community for the long-established land-letting ceremony. A nearby field is let to the highest bidder, a local farmer invariably, and the rent traditionally goes to the old of the parish.

The bridge has had a chequered history. Lying on the old Lancaster to Newcastle coach road it obviously formed a vital link, the river here being too deep and steep-sided to ford. The records relate how it had to be extensively repaired, three times in the seventeenth century alone. The inn, too, was indispensable as a stopping point on that long and arduous journey.

The route recommences through the large gate next to the churchyard, along the gravelled track round and alongside the north of the church.

If you are only walking the eastern loop, from here to Cray and back, stay on the track uphill to Scar House and join the full route there. If you are following the western loop, to Yockenthwaite and back or on the full route, then read on here.

The Last Lap

Behind the church a small path branches off Scar House access track and stays close to the river most of the way. The route finding could not be

easier: the path is clear and, in places, has been recently improved and waymarked by the National Trust to keep you to a specific line. Please stick to this through the meadows. To farmers, hard-pressed enough these days, grass is not just grass. It is vital to see their stock through the long winters. Of the riverside meadows between the two settlements, no less than six contain the name *Holm*, a word of Norse origin, meaning water meadow.

Black

White

Pied wagtail (average size: 18cm)

Once again this is a stretch, only two kilometres or so, that should not be rushed. The river itself has its picturesque reaches, there will be dippers to look out for as well as grey and pied wagtails, and the botany is sublime.

The valley here is in the care of the National Trust but the tenant farmer has day to day responsibility for managing and conserving the two Sites of Special Scientific Interest. One is Strans Gill, which you cross by a footbridge, and west of the bridge is Yockenthwaite Meadows SSSI. In the flush of summer no one need ask why this SSSI was designated, nor why it must be conserved sympathetically. Recently the farmer stockproofed Strans Wood, west of the gill, so that the ancient woodland of native ash and hawthorn can again regenerate, under English Nature's Wildlife Enhancement Scheme.

I once counted the number of flowering species in one square metre by the path side in one of these meadows. This was my count, in no particular order:

knapweed	*Centaurea nigra*
ox-eye daisy	*Chrysanthemum leucanthemum*
hawkweed	*Hieracium sp.*
devilsbit scabious	*Succisa pratensis*
lady's bedstraw	*Galium verum*
betony	*Betonica officinalis*
pignut	*Conopodium majus*
dropwort	*Filipendula vulgaris* (not common at all, in fact)
tormentil	*Potentilla erecta*
yellow vetchling	*Lathyrus pratensis*
lesser stitchwort	*Stellaria graminea*

– eleven colourful flowers.

Do you like conundrums? Why did the devil bite the scabious? Because he was so jealous of its numerous medicinal properties, so the folk tale would have us believe.

On the approach to Yockenthwaite, leave the riverside and look for a stone stile and the way into the hamlet. Either return to your starting point over the bridge, or turn right up the track if you are following the western loop. Pick up the route description earlier in this chapter.

Place-name meanings

Beckermonds	ON	the meeting of streams
Black Wood	OE	the dark wood
Buckden	OE	the valley where there are deer
Cow Garth	ON	the enclosure for cows
Cray	Brit	fresh waters
Crook Gill	ON	the winding stream
Deepdale	OE/ON	the deep valley
Dubb's Lane	OE	the lane by the pool
Green Field	OE/ON	the green open area
Hagg	ON	the place where trees were felled
Haw Ings	OE/ON	the enclosed meadows
Hubberholme	OE	*Hunberga's* (fem.pers. name) homestead
Langstrothdale	ON	the long,marshy valley with underbush
Oughtershaw	OE	*Uhtred's* (pers. name) copse
Rais Wood	ON	the wood near the ravine with a cairn
Slades	OE	the low,flat valley
Strans Gill	ON	the ravine near the shore (ie of the Wharfe)
Stubbing	OE	a clearing in the forest
Todd's Wood	-	from a local family name
Wharfe	Brit	the winding river
Yockenthwaite	OIN	*Eogan's* (pers. name) clearing

Discovery Walk 8

Yarnbury and Hebden Gill

Start and Finish: Yarnbury (Grid reference SE015 658) at the top of Moor Lane, 2km from Grassington Town Hall.

Parking: there is ample space to park at the road-head at Yarnbury, either before or just beyond the end of the tarred road. Do not drive over the cattle grid into the mine area.

Public transport: none beyond Grassington. For bus services to the village, see Walk 6.

Facilities: Grassington has a wide range but there are none on the walk.

Outline of the Walk: Yarnbury – Mire Ridge – Hole Bottom – Hebden Gill – Bolton Gill – Coalgrove Beck – Yarnbury.

Length: 5.5km (less than 3½ miles) for the full circuit, with an extra 3km (less than 2 miles) or so for a tour of the main mining remains at Grassington Out Moor.

Ordnance Survey Map: Outdoor Leisure 10. Landranger 98.

Introduction

Almost without exception so far, the walks described in this collection have concentrated on areas dominated by limestone. This walk happens to completely avoid it by sticking to Millstone Grit from start to finish. The greys and whites of limestone are here replaced by browns, weathered to a very dark shade on the outer surfaces. The soft, bright green turf of the limestone gives way to longer, yellower and more tussocky grassland, except where the hand of mankind has altered the natural scheme of things. Gritstone landscapes could not be more different from those developed on limestone.

This walk introduces yet more aspects of the Dales, so far mentioned only in passing. Grassington Moor and Hebden Gill bear the scars of a major mining venture as lead ore was won here over a period of almost three hundred years on a very large scale indeed. In the previous walks the only signs of mining have been small and isolated. Up here, from 1603, mining was big business involving large-scale investment in technology and

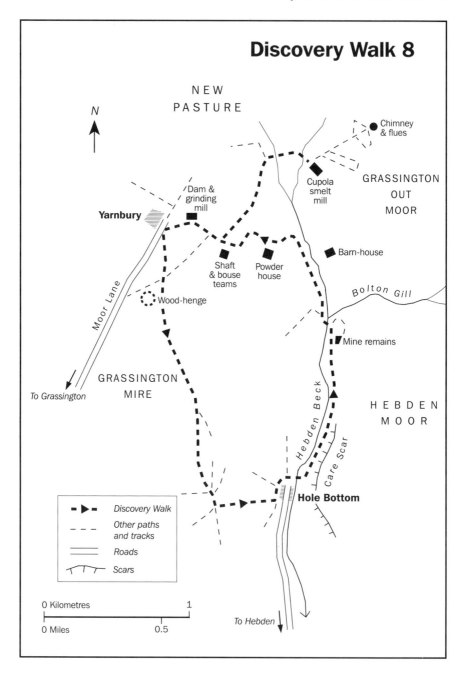

Discovery Walk 8

methodology. The mining has long since gone but the signs are there above and below the ground.

You will come upon a henge monument, dating from three or four millennia in the past. You may come upon one of our shyer birds, the ring ouzel, in the recesses of Hebden Gill; and you will learn how the gritstones were laid down as sands in a vast delta.

As the route is less than six kilometres in total, no "short-cuts" are provided, but you have the option of extending the walk to explore the mine areas. Please do not be tempted to venture into any of the mine entrances: they can be unstable and full of dangers for the inexperienced.

Yarnbury

The impressive nature of the buildings at Yarnbury is indicative of former importance for this isolated settlement. The buildings date from 1826 and formed the core of a major lead mining enterprise on Grassington Old Moor, the area between Yarnbury itself and Blea Beck. From the late eighteenth century the mines were owned by the Dukes of Devonshire.

The most impressive building, Yarnbury House, was the mine office and the residence of the Duke's mine Agent, who effectively superintended operations on a day to day basis. Behind this is Yarnbury Lodge. Here were two cottages for lesser agents, a carpenter's shop, timber yard and stores. The single-storey building, now converted to a residence, was the smithy. There are also two very small structures. The one set well back from the road, and having a stone sphere on the roof apex was the powder store. The other, on the road side, was the weighing house. Before any lead ingots could be despatched from the mine area, they had to be weighed and recorded.

We shall be exploring the area east of the road later on during this walk but you may wish to have a brief look around the vicinity of Yarnbury. Moor Lane continues northwards as an unmade track, Old Moor Lane, which served the mining areas of Grassington Moor until the commissioning of the Duke's New Road, to the east. Branching off Old Moor Lane just beyond Yarnbury is another lane, Lime Kiln Lane. This connected the scattered settlements of Grassington New Pasture, and joined up with the major route from Conistone via Sandy Gate to Upper Nidderdale.

Where Lime Kiln Lane dog legs below New Pasture Edge an apparition appeared on the horizon a few years ago. A mature, yet near dead, tree spouted overnight from nothing, a mansion was newly built in a matter of days, though it seemed weather worn and in need of urgent maintenance. Wrought-iron gates spanned the lane ... but it was all an illusion. From the rear, scaffolding poles gave the game away. House, walls, gates and all manner of objects were made of plywood and papier mache; the "tree" was bolted together. Within weeks it was all reduced to a pile of waste. In its short life it had served as the set for the filming of "Wuthering Heights", which you may have seen at the cinema.

The area south of this lane has been heavily worked for lead over the centuries, and there is place-name evidence of very early mining in an elongated field south-west of Yarnbury, a field full of mining remains. This was the New Rake mine, and nearby is Bayle Hill, neither of which are named on the 1:25,000 map. A "bale" or "bayle" was a simple form of smelter, in use elsewhere in Europe from Bronze Age times and probably in use in the Dales from the Iron Age. They continued in use until the advent of better technology in the sixteenth century. It is likely that this particular bayle dates from the medieval period though, without firm evidence, this cannot be taken as hard fact.

Yarnbury Henge

It is time to leave Yarnbury now. Opposite the entrance to Yarnbury Lodge there is a stone squeeze stile in the wall. From this an undefined footpath heads south past some bell pits (see later) to the corner of a wall where there is another, gated, squeeze stile. I would recommend a very short diversion now, so turn right and cross the adjacent field to a second gated stile.

On the other side of the wall lies a large circular banked feature, more than 25 metres in diameter. This is Wood Henge, our answer to Wiltshire's Stonehenge. The henge is marked on the Ordnance Survey map. What can one say about such monuments?

The term "henge" refers to the earth bank and ditch, rather than to any standing stones a henge may have contained. This one may have had a wooden structure within the henge. The very earliest henges are situated in Orkney, dated to about 5,000 years ago in the Neolithic period. Yarnbury Henge may either be similarly Neolithic, though not as old, or it may date from the Early Bronze Age. Does it really matter, though, bearing in mind that some prehistorians now reject the arbitrary divisions and labels we have fixed onto the past, because cultural changes occur gradually and in an evolutionary manner, rather than suddenly?

There is healthy argument concerning the role henges played in contemporary society. It is generally agreed that they were the ceremonial focus of settlement in the surrounding area, but for how far? Were they constructed by settled farmers who found they had spare time on their hands to undertake communal projects? Or were they erected by semi nomadic peoples who slowly began to settle down, the monument acting as a catalyst for permanent settlements? Questions, questions ... and a dearth of answers.

Along Mire Ridge

When you have finished pondering the imponderable go back through the stile and turn sharp right to follow the long boundary wall. The Ordnance

Survey map would seemingly have you practice tight-rope walking along the wall-top. **In fact you should have the wall on your right.** The wall follows Mire Ridge though it hardly fits my understanding of a ridge. The mire is genuine enough though, south of the ridge.

Part way along, the line of the path negotiates old quarries, presumably used as a source of walling stone. You then come to a gated stile by the four-way wall junction and continue to follow the wall to a second wall junction and a gated stile. Across the fields to your left is the very isolated New House farm, at the end of a long and circuitous route from Grassington.

Two narrow fields follow. You cross them both diagonally, in each case exiting by a ladder stile. The third field is broader and you need to make for its south-east corner where another gated stile lies adjacent to a field gate. At this point no less than six footpaths converge from almost every point on the compass.

A few metres beyond the last stile is the north-south track called Tinkers' Lane. In the Good Old Days the itinerant tinker (the mender and vendor of pots and pans) and the chapman (a pedlar: know anyone with that surname?), spent their time on a circuit of outlying farms and hamlets with a pack pony or two. The panniers would be laden with spices, trinkets, wares and frills, hopefully to tempt the wife into parting with a little of her hard won money. The tinker's or chapman's arrival was something to look forward to, not just for the "window shopping" but also because he was the deliverer of news and a fount of knowledge and gossip from near and far.

A Tropical Interlude

Turn south (right) down the lane but only for 50 metres or so, to the first wall corner on the left of the track. At this point you can see the village of Hebden down below, to the south-east, and in the distance the bulky mass of Barden Fell and Simon's Seat.

Turn off the lane at this wall corner and drop straight downslope towards the inevitable gated stile in the bottom (east) wall. Pause awhile at this point and look to the south, across the Wharfe valley. Nestling below the brooding mass of Burnsall and Thorpe Fell is a line of conical and bright green hillocks. There are thirteen of them in all, Elbolton being by far the biggest, and individually they make up the Cracoe Reef Knolls SSSI. So what is a reef knoll, and why are they here?

During the early Carboniferous period (around 360 to 350 million years ago) the higher ground to the north was land, part of the Askrigg Block. This was bounded on its southern edge by the North and Middle Craven Faults which run roughly west-north-west to east-south-east in what is now this part of Wharfedale. To the south of the faults was an ocean whose continental shelf sloped gently away from the coastline. At this time "Britain" lay on or near the equator so the ocean waters were warm, and also clear – in fact the stereotypical image of a tropical sea today.

Along the coastline, in a belt at least 20 kilometres long, a continuous coral reef built up with isolated conical reef knolls in particular places, as here and at Malham and Attermire near Settle. Faulting during the Carboniferous broke up the reef belt but the knolls continued to grow on the shallowest parts of the shelf. They did not consist of coral, as we understand that term. They were not like the present Great Barrier Reef off Queensland or the reefs off the East African coast. Rather the Cracoe reef knolls were more akin to the reefs found today in the Bahamas where marine conditions were more analogous. The predominant constituent of our reef knolls is a gelatinous algal mud: in other words limestones containing a high proportion of mud and gooey algae.

As the Carboniferous period progressed, conditions changed. The clear ocean gave way to a muddy sea and the reefs were gradually buried – and thus preserved – beneath a thick layer of mudstones, what we know as Bowland Shales. Later still the muddy and ever shallower sea became a huge delta (see later in this chapter), so the shales in turn were buried by the Millstone Grit.

As you stand and look at the reef knolls now, it is as if someone has been gently scraping away the later layers to expose the knoll. Indeed this is what is happening except that the "someone" is the erosive forces of Nature. What you see now is almost certainly the original shape of the knolls as they were when active in the Carboniferous. They are now being exhumed like a precious archaeological find. They are special, hence their being granted SSSI status.

Hole Bottom and Care Scar

It is time to move on now so leave the gated stile in the field below Tinkers' Lane and cross the next two fields, crossing a step-over stile in the fence and then a stone stile in the wall left of the field gate. Continue downslope, sticking close to the north wall alongside the small covered reservoir, and down to the bottom corner of this field. While you were coming downhill I am sure your eyes were drawn to the massive gritstone scars and screes across the valley, and to the farm houses that seem to be perched precariously on the scar top.

At the bottom corner of this field, turn right to follow the fence for a short distance to a step-over stile. Beyond this you should head left again to the barn at the bottom: here another step-over stile and a small gate allow access to a narrow and deeply etched path left of the barn: you rarely see paths like this in the Dales, sandwiched between a wall and a ha-ha. At the far end another small gate delivers you to the road at Hole Bottom, a former lead mining community.

Turn left past the cottages and through the gate marked "bridleway", then over two foot bridges and across Hebden Beck, to enter the depths of Hebden Gill. You now have over one kilometre of easy walking alongside the beck, with plenty of distractions, so do not hurry.

Between the two footbridges, down below the track, are the foundations of three rectangular buildings. Across the main beck are the scant remains of further buildings and a flue making up what was Hebden Gill smelt mill, which processed lead ore from mines further up the gill from 1858 to the 1870s. The three rectangular buildings are thought to have been used for storing lead ingots while waiting for despatch to the markets.

Hebden Moor ends in precipitous crags on its western edge where glacial meltwaters have carved the gill now occupied by Hebden Beck. Care Scar is one of the most dramatic gritstone crags in the southern Dales. The massive fallen boulders, and the carved rock faces bear witness to the erosive forces constantly wearing away the earth's surface.

Millstone Grit

Millstone Grit is a rock more typically associated with the Pennines of West Yorkshire and the Dark Peak. There are few areas in the Southern Dales where it is the dominant surface rock. Hebden Moor, however, is almost the southern extremity of an extensive belt running up the eastern boundary of the Park from Bolton Abbey as far north as Wensleydale.

Millstone Grit is a coarse sandstone. Hold a piece to examine it closely and you will see it is made up of large grains of hardened sand with crystals of white quartz liberally interspersed. If you find a freshly shattered piece, the friability and coarseness will be apparent. Coarse sandstones are referred to as gritstones in geology and the "millstone" epithet is derived from the rock's suitability as a stone for grinding corn.

Grits are the product of river deposition in a delta. It requires a good deal of faith to accept that a single delta once extended across much of the Dales. Picture the size of present day deltas, however, and it is a more believable hypothesis. The Nile delta, for example, extends for more than 200 kilometres along its east-west axis, and most of Holland is the drained and reclaimed delta of the Rhine. Our delta, associated with a totally different late Carboniferous geography, has long since lost its deltaic appearance: it is the nature of the rock itself, and the ripples and current marks that the knowing eye can detect on its vertical faces, that give the game away.

The thickness of the deltaic sands in Care Scar is immense and, for me, these crags are second only to Brimham Rocks beyond Nidderdale.

Part of Hebden Moor is called Backstone Edge and this is connected to the main road by a lane of the same name. Some gritstones were found to be especially suitable for baking, in that they could withstand the intense heat from the fire, and also for lining chimneys. Such flagstone (a type of thin gritstone) only occurred in certain locations which often bear the name Backstone or Baxton.

Bolton Gill Mines

The track follows the east bank of Hebden Beck, through a succession of gates, and the scattered remains of past industrial endeavour, to eventually enter an area of substantial remains shortly before the confluence with Bolton Gill. The track was cut in the late 1850s to improve access from Hebden to the mines. Before this the only routeway climbed steeply from Hole Bottom to the Mere and Tinkers' Lane, a roundabout and difficult route.

You may feel this site warrants closer inspection. In the vicinity there are three easily accessible adits – horizontal mine tunnels – which have been gated to keep out over eager but probably ill-prepared explorers. There are the remains of a dam which stored water for the washing floors and stone crusher. The pit that held the water wheel is clearly recognisable as such. On both sides of the valley are old mine shafts. A short way up the eastern slope, above the dam, are the stubby remains of stone pillars. It is impossible to fathom what purpose they may have served, just by looking at them. Reconstruct them in your mind's eye: build them up higher and extend the line of pillars down the valley. Attach a 600 metre cable system to the pillars and imagine tubs of lead ore trundling along the wire to the smelter. Advanced technology for those days, but unfortunately it was never really successful.

The most impressive mine remains here lie high up in Bolton Gill. The building you can see is the restored engine house above the main mine shaft into Bolton Gill mine, a major operation until a changing economic climate forced its closure in 1873.

Just beyond Bolton Gill you will ford Hebden Beck near the point where Tinkers' Lane joins the valley track, and then pass through the gate to the left of the main beck. Carry on along the track, up and through an extensive area of mine spoil. Keep an ear and an eye primed for two local but not common birds. You may disturb a flight of red grouse or see them flying low, noisily complaining at being interrupted in their daily routine. The other is more likely to be heard than seen. He (or she, as they are very similar) is the size of a small blackbird and could at first glance be mistaken for a cock blackbird. There is one crucial and distinguishing difference: the ring ouzel has a white throat line, more particularly the male. They are very shy and will go into hiding if they perceive any threat but their voice is distinctive, and in a way quite eerie, being loud and scolding. Sadly, ring ouzels are by no means secure these days.

On the other side of the valley, just above the beck, is another adit, this one ungated. It is wet and potentially dangerous, and you must not think

Black-Brown
Yellow
White

Ring ouzel (average size: 24cm)

Barn house and adit at Cockbur Mine

of entering it. Tunnels like this can end up as spider's web for the unwary though I find it unbearably difficult to resist a good hole – properly equipped, of course! This particular one is quite short: it was cut as a trial dig towards the end of Cockbur Mine's life.

Above the adit stands a tall building which was somebody's home at one time (though in the filming of "Wuthering Heights" it was dressed up as a very convincing chapel). This particular barn house is rather unusual in its design, and it is exceptionally well-preserved, down to the interior details like the stone sink and fireplace, and the lath and plaster ceiling. At the front – the end you can see – the building has three storeys. The upper two housed the domestic quarters with a "living" area below a sleeping area reached by a ladder. The ground floor of the entire building housed cattle, and the boskins are still intact complete with some tying posts and rings. The bulk of the building above the byre was a hay loft. At the rear is the access for forking the hay in and in the floor was a hatch to allow access from the byre by ladder. The size of the loft is immense. How they ever managed to fill it is beyond me, and how the floor managed to support the weight of hay is equally difficult to comprehend.

Grassington Mines

The track from the beck side passes through a gateway in a crumbling wall and past a crumbling lime kiln, before zigzagging uphill out of the valley.

Barn-house at Cockbur Mine

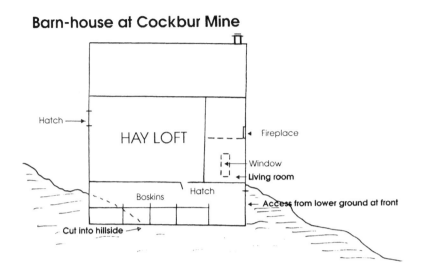

When you are near the top look away to your right, east of north, where a tall chimney dominates that particular tract of moor. To the left of that you may be able to pick out an ugly concrete structure. This is the relic of a post-World War Two operation to re-work the spoil heaps. Later on it served as a location for one scene in a James Bond film: I think it was "From Russia with Love".

The track soon forks and you should turn right through the gate. Away to your left, near the wall, is a small building that was the powder house for Cockbur Mine. Gunpowder was, understandably, kept in secure conditions and handed out to miners as and when needed. Like many of the mining remains in the area, this was restored by a dedicated band of enthusiasts from what is now the Northern Mine Research Society.

You then come upon an area of bell pits (though properly the term bell pit is reserved for coal mining). In the seventeenth century lead ore was won from bell pits. A shaft was sunk to a depth of no more than ten metres, and tunnels were cut along the line of the vein to extract the ore. However I have discussed lead mining in more detail in "The Northern Dales" as Swaledale in particular has a far greater wealth of mining archaeology.

From this point onwards I am leaving you to your own devices. You can return to the start by following the main track you are now on, if time and weather are against you today. Alternatively you may wish to explore the general area between here and Yarnbury. Dotted around the Beever Mine area are a number of small, numbered display boards, giving brief details of what is to be seen at each locality. Do not waste time hunting for numbers 1 and 2: they disappeared! Numbers 3 to 10 are, at the time of writing, intact though.

Bell pit

A third alternative, for the energetic or the enthusiast, is to turn right beyond the top gate on the main track onto another wide track. This is the Duke's New Road, ordered by the 6th Duke of Devonshire in 1826. It runs for nearly a kilometre to the remains of a huge cupola smelt mill (where there is a large display board). **Beyond that you could follow the long flue to the chimney.** And while you are up there ... the world is your oyster.

Place-name meanings

Blea Beck	ON	the dark stream
Bolton Gill	OE/ON	the ravine near the dwelling house
Bolton Haw	OE/ON	the hill near the dwelling house
Care Scar	OE/ON	the rocky cliff
Cockbur	OE	the hillock
Grassington	OE	the grazing farmstead
Hebden	OE	the valley where brambles (or rose hips) grow
High Garnshaw	ON/ME	the demon's wood
Hole Bottom	OE/ON	the hollow bottom
Loss Gill	OE/ODan/ON	the spring at the pigsty in the ravine
New Rake	OE	the new, rough road or path
Yarnbury	OE	the ancient earthwork

Discovery Walk 9

In Sight of Simon's Seat: a walk in the Appletreewick area

Start and Finish: Appletreewick village on the east bank of the Wharfe between Burnsall and Barden Tower (Grid reference SE 05 60).

Parking: There is ample parking down by the river, accessed by a track opposite the New Inn. A reasonable charge is levied: the honesty box is at the entry gate.

Public transport: Appletreewick lies on the route from Skipton via Bolton Abbey to Grassington operated by Keighley and District (tel. 01535 603284).

Facilities: The Craven Arms and New Inn in Appletreewick offer the usual facilities to visitors. Teas are available in season at the weekend at Andra's Farm at the upper end of the village and at the cottage at the entrance to Parcevall Hall Gardens . There is a shop and cafe at Howgill Lodge caravan and camping site. There are public telephones at Appletreewick and Middle Skyreholme.

Outline of the Walk: Appletreewick – Howgill – Middle Skyreholme – Trollers Gill – Appletreewick Pasture – Kail Hill – Appletreewick.

Length: 8.5km (5.3 miles) for the main route, with an optional extension to 10.5km (6.6 miles). The shorter route is 8km (5 miles).

Ordnance Survey Map: Outdoor Leisure 10. Landranger 98.

Introduction

This walk takes you almost to the eastern edge of the National Park, and towards the lower reaches of Upper Wharfedale. The area to be traversed today lies between two honeypot sites: the village of Burnsall to the north-west and Strid Woods between Barden Tower and Bolton Priory. On a busy weekend these are perhaps best left to the less adventurous day-trippers. Appletreewick itself can be busy, particularly alongside the Wharfe, but you can soon escape the throng.

I could not describe the Wharfe, where it passes by the village, as an attractive stretch of water, but it does have much to commend it both to the north and south, at the beginning and end of today's walk. On the other hand no one could dispute the beauty of the wider valley here, and of the tributary valleys around Skyreholme. Limestone abuts against millstone grit; the crags of Barden Moor provide a fitting backdrop to the detail of the valley with its patchwork of irregularly arranged fields and extensive tracts of woodland. And, surely, Trollers Gill must be one of the highlights of this walk.

Inevitably the past makes its presence felt, and I shall touch on a late medieval feud between two land-owning families, a local lad made good, and a glimpse of industrial enterprises that might seem out of place in such a peaceful area.

Today's route is by no means long. The full route is 8.5km but it can be slightly shortened early on or lengthened by 2km towards the end. I have made clear in the text where the decisions are to be made.

For motorists with a limited amount of time, the walk could readily be divided up into loops. You could park in Appletreewick and follow the route from there to Howgill or Skyreholme, returning by road from either. Alternatively, if you park up on New Road you could modify my route by using the path down from road to river near Parcevall Hall. Then again you could make a loop out of Howgill, Eastwood Head and the Skyreholmes.

Appletreewick: an amble through the village

Apart from some mid-twentieth century housing tucked away to the north of the village, Appletreewick is basically one long street. In plan – and this is seen best on a much more detailed map than the 1:25,000 – it is very simple and retains its medieval form. Cottages and farm houses faced each other across the street, each sitting on its own plot, or toft, with a narrow croft running away from the toft at right-angles to the road. It is quite remarkable that there has been so little development to upset the symmetry of the village.

It is also remarkable, for such a small village, in having two substantial halls: Low Hall at the western foot of the street, and High Hall at the eastern, top end. Each is a fine example of its architectural style. To some High Hall is too much on the grand side; to others Low Hall is stern and plain. To me they are both fine buildings. High Hall, as you view it now, is largely the result of an early seventeenth century restoration. Low Hall has known construction dates of 1597 and 1658 though, like High Hall, it most probably goes way back before then. Low Hall was also restored in 1868.

Appletreewick has yet another hall, downhill slightly from High Hall, with a most distinctive architectural style. Mock Beggar Hall stands on the site of a monastic grange. It was rebuilt in 1697 but could well have monastic stonework in its courses. The external stone stairway to the upper door, the ornate lintel designs and the pigeon holes, all help to put this building in a class of its own.

On an altogether different scale is the old Prospect Farm house diagonally opposite and uphill from this hall. With a datestone of 1688 and a functional

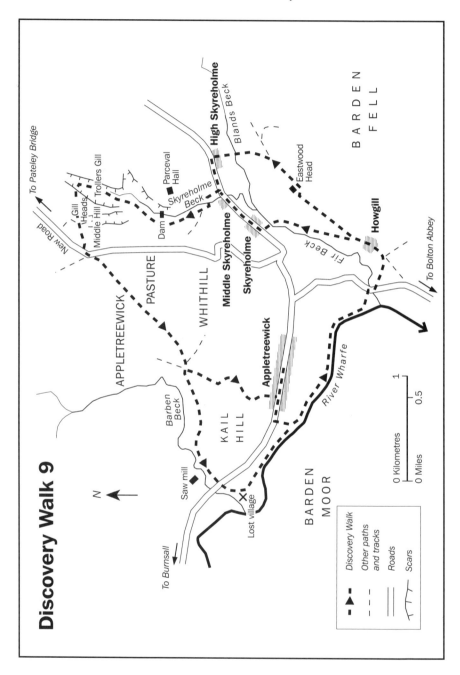

Discovery Walk 9

and unfussy architectural style, it proclaims itself for what it was: a substantial and prosperous farm. The string course above the windows is particularly fine and typical of later seventeenth century farm houses. The letters T.N. on the datestone are the initials of one Thomas Nussey.

String course

String course

Is it any wonder that the village was awarded Conservation Area status?

The parish church, dating from 1897, opposite High Hall, and subsidiary to Burnsall, is quite unprepossessing – and all the better for that, some would suggest. I dare say many others would find greatest succour from two of Appletreewick's other buildings, both at the bottom of the hill. I refer, of course, to the Craven Arms and the New Inn! The Craven Arms is obviously the older of the two inns and, like many remote inns, had another function. The Court Leet met here till as recently as 1926, hearing and adjudicating on petty offences. It is perhaps fitting that the village stocks stand outside the inn! By the New Inn was the village pinfold.

Other points of interest in the village include the Pounder Stone outside the old smithy (just below Andra's Farm). When metal rings were being fitted to wooden cart-wheels they were placed on this stone red hot and pounded with a hammer. The parallel grooves represent rims of different sizes.

Opposite Mock Beggar Hall, through the white gates, is the former Cork Street (leading nowhere now) which had stone troughs for stock to quench their thirst. Another old and formerly very important road heads north from the village, opposite High Hall. This, called Sandygate, connected Appletreewick with Nidderdale.

A Potted History

In 1300 the manor of Appletreewick passed into the tutelage of Bolton Priory, and prospered almost immediately. Ten years later it was granted licence to hold a two-day October fair which survived into the middle of the nineteenth century. It was considered to be one of the more important fairs in Wharfedale, being particularly noted for its sales of ponies as well as cattle and sheep. Interestingly it was also famed for onions!

The village lay near an important junction of drove roads. One ran alongside the Wharfe from Bolton Priory to Kettlewell and beyond, a second branched off over Skyreholme Bank to Pateley Bridge and the east, while

Sandygate was the third. Apart from stock and general merchandise that was carried away in packhorse trains, quantities of lead were also despatched southwards from the Priory's mines in the parish.

When Bolton Priory was dissolved, along with all other religious foundations, the manor was sold off and within the space of ten years had passed through three different owners until the Yorke family purchased it in 1549 and gave it stability. There were two other major land owning families in Wharfedale, the Nortons and the Cliffords, Earls of Cumberland. The former owned Rylstone Hall and Norton Tower, now a scant ruin above Rylstone, while the latter owned Barden Tower, Skipton Castle and a good deal more.

The Nortons and the Cliffords were notorious rivals and came to blows on more than one occasion, the cause being a hunting dispute. The Nortons backed the wrong side in the Pilgrimage of Grace in 1536, a northern rebellion against Henry VIII. The Cliffords had the last laugh on this occasion. Henry was vicious in his response to the rebellion, having ordered:

"such dreadful execution to be done upon a good number of the inhabitants of every town and village that hath offended ... as well as by the hanging of them upon trees as by the quartering of them and the setting up of their heads and quarters ... without pity or respect."

The orders were dutifully carried out, and Appletreewick suffered alongside many other parishes in the dale.

The Nortons, I fear, were rather slow to take a hint because they were also involved in the Rising of the North in 1569, again against the Crown. This, too, failed and was suppressed even more viciously than thirty years previously. This time the Nortons were well and truly consigned to history.

To return to feuding and brinkmanship, the Cliffords had a number of disputes with the Yorkes, also over respective rights to hunt deer. The date 1621 stands out in the records when open fighting between the two rival camps broke out at the Fair. Shades of the Wild West!

On to Howgill

It is time to make a move now, before the day's best is over. You must first go down to the riverside, either by using the right of way at the camp site at Ainhams House beyond Low Hall, or by paying the token fee to use the private track opposite the New Inn. The gently sloping fields that lead down to the river below Fold Bottom are where stock were fattened up and "re-conditioned" before the Fair. It is still called Sheep Fair Hill.

The walk alongside the river can vary from restful on a quiet day to quite traumatic on a hot summer's day when the day-trippers descend complete with footballs, cricket bats and all manner of adjuncts they seem unable to leave at home. **You will soon leave all this behind, though, once you cross Foul Sike and enter the wooded slopes of Haugh.** This stretch of path is delightful and, unlike the Strid downstream, it is free for you to enjoy. It is only a few hundred metres from one end to another but it is worth lingering over. Bluebells and dog's mercury (the one with the green flowers) are locally in utter profusion within, and beyond the edges of, the wood. The main attraction must be the river itself, especially when in spate, as the torrent foams and thrashes its way around and over the massive rock barricades. The river here has cut a deep but narrow channel through resistant rock bands, just as at the Strid, changing its mood from placid to tormented and back to placid. At times of low water you really do see just how narrow the main channel is here, and you can surmise how deep it must be to cope with the volume of water passing through. Do not be tempted onto the rocks mid-stream.

The Wharfe above Howgill

At the far end of the wood the path swings away from the river, passes through a corner of the wood and joins the tarred lane below the old Howgill chapel. Cross Fir Beck, where a water-powered corn mill once stood until destroyed by flood. Immediately turn left up the stony lane and follow it to the cross-roads by How Beck.

Straight on is a permissive path onto Barden Fell, a very popular and badly eroding route onto the Access Land that stretches away over the fell top and beyond. Your route lies to the left. Follow Howgill Lane uphill past the almost suburban camping site at Howgill Lodge. Just past the Howgill Lodge Barn conversion, you have a decision to make, as the route forks.

The Skyreholmes

If you want the slightly shorter – and downhill – route, turn left through the first gate. If you want the longer – and gently uphill route – stay on Howgill Lane.

The Shorter Alternative

At first the path follows an old green track between wall and bluebell-covered bank, then passes through a gate and alongside the other side of the wall, beginning to lose height gradually. Beyond the next gateway your line of march is straight ahead making for a ladder stile in the wall, and then diagonally downslope to a footbridge over the sike and a stile by the wall. Stay parallel to Fir Beck now through the riverside meadows until you reach a footbridge across the beck. On the opposite side are the remains of a paper mill. The new housing development lies on the site of the mill.

When you reach the road in Skyreholme turn right, past the row of former mill cottages. It takes a moment or two to work out why the row is so massively broad in the gable, until you realise they were built as a row of back-to-back cottages. Yet again we have an example of an aspect of urban industrial development in a remote upland dale. This very remoteness is what helped to kill off the mill: it could not survive in the way that Langcliffe's paper mill has. The roads are too circuitous and narrow, the water supply too unreliable, for any hope of success nowadays. There was another factor, of which more later.

Carry on along the road until you reach Middle Skyreholme, cross over the bridge and look for the footpath sign a few metres up on the left. You rejoin the longer route here.

The Longer Alternative

Stay on Howgill Lane and, as you pass the first gate in the side wall, notice the old guidepost built into the wall, indicating an old road to Pateley Bridge. I would guess it to be no later than eighteenth century. The inscription is fading as weathering takes its toll, but it reads "To Patley Bridge m. 6". There is also a rather crude hand with a pointing finger. After a few hundred metres you will see a ruined barn at the bottom of the field below the lane: a careful look, even from this distance, indicates that it had a cruck frame and was originally thatched. A roof pitch as steep as that could not have supported stone.

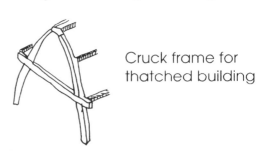

Cruck frame for thatched building

As you follow the lane to Eastwood Head farm you have a clear view across the valley to Whithill beyond Skyreholme with views up Wharfedale to the west, and to Black Hill in the east. Directly to the north you can probably make out Parcevall Hall set amongst woods.

Parcevall Hall

Carry on through the farm yard and then look for the second gate in the left-hand wall of the lane. The path downslope is waymarked through three fields: by the gable end of a lost building and over two stiles. There is a footbridge over Blands Beck at the bottom. Have a look back at this point as you can see right up to the top of Barden Fell with its gritstone outcrops of Simon's Seat and Hen Stones. These are massive chunks of rock that have, so far, resisted erosion except on their fluted and wind-carved faces. Simon's Seat is one of those airy places of pilgrimage, a goal that has to be grasped, perhaps because its very form proclaims it to be something worthy of grasping. Not today, though.

Anyway hop over the bridge and clamber up to the houses at High Skyreholme. Mind your head if the washing is hanging out, as the path leads between the two houses onto the road. **Turn left and walk downhill to the footpath just before the bridge at the road junction, to rejoin the shorter alternative.**

Skyreholme Beck

From the road the next section of path is very short. **Head up the bank into the next field and continue ahead parallel to the wall to your left, and next to the wall in the third field.** Notice the recesses in this wall. The only explanation I can think of – and I may be wrong – is that they were bee-boles for keeping bee-skeps in. These were like miniature beehives, made of straw.

Climb over the stone stile onto the tarred lane at Ridge End. In the season teas and light refreshments can be obtained at the cottage. If you have sufficient time I would recommend a diversion to the grounds of Parcevall Hall. The hall itself is not open to the public as it is a retreat and conference centre for Bradford Diocese, but the gardens are. These are the responsibility of the Walsingham Trust which requests payment towards the upkeep. The Trust offers a programme of holiday breaks for those of a contemplative mien (tel. 01756 720311).

The hall started life as a yeoman's farmhouse built, or rebuilt, in stone in 1653 though the manor was held by the powerful Yorke family from 1549. The house was substantially altered during a restoration in 1928.

When you are ready, **cross the bridge by the cottage and go through the gate immediately on the right, to follow alongside Skyreholme Beck. (If you took the option of parking up on New Road, you will join us now in the second field.)** The flowers are delightful along the valley, especially in early summer, and particularly on the opposite bank. Ramsons or wild garlic *(Allium ursinum)* with its white flowers and pungent aroma, bluebells *(Hyacinthoides non-scripta)* and dog's mercury *(Mercurialis perennis)* are all ancient woodland indicators. There are also two yellow flowers common in the valley. Lesser celandine *(Ranunculus ficaria)* is small and low to the ground with distinctive glossy heart-shaped leaves. It grows everywhere and, while it is a tiresome weed to some, it is one of the earliest harbingers of spring and better days to come. On a sunny day celandine forms a bright yellow carpet: in dull conditions they close up: by June they have withered and gone.

The other yellow beauty, also one of the buttercup family, is down by the stream, the marsh-marigold or kingcup *(Caltha palustris)*. This glorious plant is at its best in May though it has a much longer flowering season than its cousin the celandine.

Listen out, and watch out too, for great spotted woodpeckers along the wooded stretch of stream. Their short, sharp sound is unmistakable.

Very shortly there is a ladder stile just before a breached earth-filled dam. This was built to impound water for the paper mill down at Skyreholme. In times of low flow the water was released down the beck to a leat just south of Ridge End which diverted the water to power the mill's water wheel. I have a theory that the dam was designed and sited on a Friday afternoon, probably pay day: how could anyone build a dam on highly permeable limestone and expect it to hold water? On one day in 1899 the dam burst ... and that was the end of that.

Across the beck, level with the dam, is a cave entrance and mine working. This is Trollers Gill Cave and, though only 60 metres long, is classified as (medium) Grade II. Two lead mining levels intersect the cave but neither was very productive. They could be very old workings, however, as mining was certainly underway and important in the general area in the seventeenth century. There is also a record of an early mining death, in the 1260s, when a local man called William was killed after falling into a mine shaft somewhere on Appletreewick Moor in the reign of Edward I.

Carry on upstream to where the paths fork, just past a wall. It is time for another geology lesson now.

The Skyreholme Anticline

I have discussed in other walks in the book how important earth movements, or tectonic forces, have been in shaping the relief of the Dales. I have discussed the North Craven Fault (Walk 3) and folding processes (Walk 2) and their influence on the present landscape and scenery. Those forces and the features resulting from them are apparent here also.

For much of this walk Barden Fell and Simon's Seat have dominated the view to the south, yet that upstanding mass of Millstone Grit is actually the lower part, the core, of a syncline (a downfold) while the lower limestone hereabouts is the remnants of the anticline (the upfold). The gritstone has resisted erosion more so than the limestone and intervening Bowland Shales and thus stands proud today. Another factor has played a part here, too. The anticline, by being over-stretched, sheared and fractured along a number of near parallel faults. These are lines of weakness and therefore more prone to attack by past and current erosional processes. If you study the simple geology map and section, it should be easier for you to appreciate the lie of the rocks. It is, of course, this faulting that was responsible for the mineralisation that gave rise to lead mining.

A Geological section between Bolton Abbey and the North Craven Fault

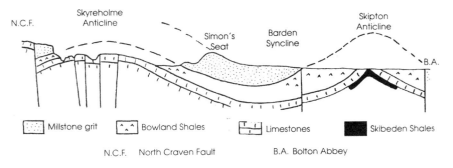

Redrawn from "Yorkshire Rocks and Landscape" with the permission of the Yorks. Geol.Soc. and Ellenbank Press of Maryport.

Geological map of the area between Bolton Abbey and the North Craven Fault

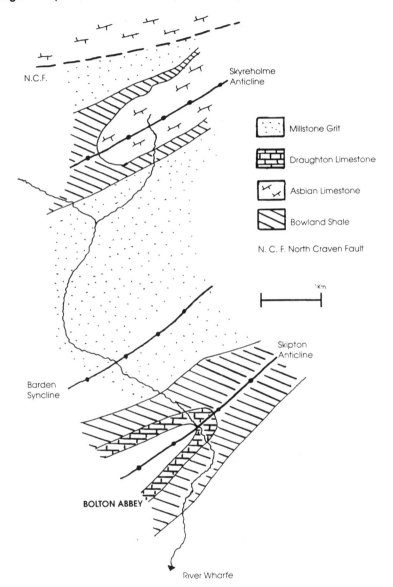

Redrawn from "Yorkshire Rocks and Landscape" with the permission of the Yorks. Geol.Soc. and Ellenbank Press of Maryport.

Beyond the present horizon, to the north, there is more gritstone and the North Craven Fault ... but more on that later. One final point before you move on. If you focus on the east side of the valley in particular, at Nape Scar to the right and Old Man's Scar to the left, look carefully at the bedding of the limestone. Apart from being a massive thickness, indicating a very long, calm period of uninterrupted deposition, the beds are gently dipping downwards. This is the lower part of the anticline.

Incidentally, miners in latter centuries always referred to older workings they encountered as evidence of the Old Man. The scar here perpetuates that.

Trollers Gill and Gill Heads

From the path junction you can go one of two ways up diverging valleys. I would recommend you take the right fork which initially follows the beck, though much of the valley beyond is dry in all but the wettest weather. There is no right of way through the gorge, called Trollers Gill, but an agreement was made in 1992 to provide a permissive path from here to Black Hill Road on the moor top.

Trollers Gill is a less dramatic, but still impressive, example of the type of gorge carved by glacial meltwater that can be see at Conistone Dib and Gordale Scar. It is thought that the upper part of the gorge may well be a collapsed cavern. In fact, in the time of Edward II in the fourteenth century, Trollers Gill is referred to in a document as "Gordale in Appletreewick".

Trollers Gill

As you approach the cross wall with a ladder stile, look upslope on the right where two veins of lead were followed in eighteenth century workings, leaving clear gashes in the landscape. **At this point you could scramble up the faint path on the left side of the valley, over the flanks of Middle Hill, to a step-over stile in the fence above. Alternatively you could retrace your steps through the gorge to the original junction and then double back up the other dry gill, interesting in its own right, and round the west side of Middle Hill.**

In either case you will come to Gill Heads and another old mining area. This was originally focussed on mining lead (until 1884) but there was intermittent working for fluorite or flourspar until as recently as 1981. You can see the actual workings at the foot of the dry valley below very steep and disturbed ground. An incline carried the rock from the valley to the ore dressing floors on the tops and a tramway ran from there to New Road in a direct line.

Head away from the dry valleys on the broad track but only to the point where it swings sharply to the right. Look for a small path cutting off to the left, to the west. You may notice a shallow ditch just to the left of path and track. This was a leat that collected water from the moors and carried it to more mine workings around Whithill to the south-west.

Very shortly the path passes by a fenced-off swallow hole. This is Hell Hole, both in name and by nature. It is one of a series of pot-holes where water from the impermeable Bowland Shales above sinks into the limestone below. For the budding geologist it is of interest because a feature called the Girvanella band can be detected in rock surfaces at the entrance. This consists of nodules of algae, about 1cm in size, forming a distinct band between two divisions of the Great Scar Limestone. As for the hole itself and its hellish reputation? It is "only" five metres deep and runs for just over 200 metres in length but, after an easy walk in, it soon deteriorates to a series of vertical pitches, crawls and occasional larger spaces. It is classified as Grade III, in other words beyond me thank you.

Beyond the pot-hole the path soon brings you, via a bell pit and the leat again, to New Road at a ladder stile. To the north are some prominent gritstone crags, Fancarl Crag. I mentioned earlier that Skyreholme is a planed off anticline and that Simon's Seat is the south end of the upfold. Fancarl Crag is the north end so this will give you an idea of the magnitude of the folding: nearly four kilometres from end to end. Just beyond the crag, and more or less following the Hebden to Stump Cross road, is the line of the North Craven Fault.

Turn left at the stile and follow New Road southwards to where there are gates on both sides of the road, where the old mine tramway used to cross. Turn through the gate on the right. You will notice the Ordnance Survey map shows the path slightly to the north of the gate. This is an anomaly the National Park is aware of.

Appletreewick Pasture

It is unfortunate sign of the times, I suppose, that the National Park has to erect signs like this one forbidding vehicular access. Some four-wheeled drive owners seem to think they can go off-road at will, and it is an escalating problem in the Dales as in other Parks.

Once through the gate you have over one kilometre of easy and more or less level walking on the broad track. This was the bed of a mineral railway built to carry ore from the mines of Appletreewick Pasture to the dressing floors above Gill Heads. About 200 metres from the first gate across the track you may see a trace of another leat crossing from north to south, to feed a small mill dam. At this point a new vista opens up, affording a look around the mass of Langerton Hill up the Wharfe to Burnsall and beyond. Clearly visible are the rounded reef knolls between Burnsall and Thorpe. The nearest one to you is Kail Hill.

Eventually you come to a track junction at which point you should bear right, on the Hartlington path. Pass through the gate ahead into the narrow, walled lane, noting once again the dominance of limestone in the landscape.

It is choice time again now.

Shorter Option

In little more than 100 metres down the lane there is a cross-roads where you turn left, on the path signposted to Appletreewick. Follow the clear track along the wall-side, past Turbot Gate Lathe barn to a gate in a new length of wall. There are more signs here of lead workings which are peppered across the whole area, as well as a number of former railway tracks.

Appletreewick Mine is documented from 1709. There were shafts and levels as well as two dressing floors, one having been supplied with water by the leat you crossed earlier. As with so many lead mines falling prices, increased production costs and cheap imports (it sounds like coal in our own time!) led to the closing of the mine in 1884. As with Gill Heads there was further sporadic fluorite activity this century, including the cutting of a new level on the hillside in the wooded Reynard Gill behind the New Inn. There was no smelt mill for lead in Appletreewick: the dressed ore was sent by horse and cart to Greenhow and Nidderdale to be smelted, though some went the other way to Grassington Moor smelter.

Carry on down the track past a second barn beyond which there is a steep and rather stony descent down the Rakes to meet the road at the Craven Arms inn ... and back whence you came.

Longer Option

Continue down the walled track, ignoring the cross-roads 100 metres along, and drop gently down to the barn called Kail Gate Lathe. The track

now transforms itself into a real green lane as it curves round Kail Hill (or Hartlington Kail). This is the south-eastern extremity of the reef knolls that can all be so clearly seen from above Grassington (see Walk 8).

When you get to the small roofless building, look up the valley where terraces on the hillside indicate more mine workings and an incline down to an ore dressing floor. If you look down the lane, across the Wharfe, you will see, as a blot on the landscape, the limestone quarry at Skirethorns, recently granted an extension to the year 2020. Further down Kail Lane, across the gill, is Hartlington Hall, the building you see dating from 1894 but being a successor to a medieval manor house.

Just before the track begins its final descent you pass by an old dew pond which no longer holds water, and see the roof of a building down on the road to the right of your vista. This is Spout Yat (= gate). It used to be an inn and derived its name from the water spout which fed water from a spring to stone troughs for passing drove cattle. In the mid-eighteenth century it was occupied by the Bland family, but the building you see dates from 1882. Opposite, just upstream from Hartlington Bridge, stands a large building with water wheel attached. The wheel powered what was a saw mill and provided electricity for the Hall.

Eventually Kail Lane meets the road. Cross straight over down Woodhouse Lane opposite to Woodhouse farm. Turn left here and follow the path over two stiles to the free-standing barn. This is Water's Laithe and it is more than just a barn. The first clue is the fine chimney stack on the gable end. Look over the wooden gate (do not enter) at the front of the stone barn and you see the unaltered frontage of an early seventeenth century farm house. The datestone, which you cannot see, reads "JW 1635". The house was reputedly given to the Water family by the Cliffords for rescuing one of the latter's daughters from a gang of rogues.

The laithe, the farmhouse and High Woodhouse on the roadside are all that remain of the manor and village of Woodhouse.

Very shortly the path brings you to the riverside and a short stretch of woodland walking. The flora in spring and summer are sublime. The following is a far from comprehensive list of the more common flowers here:

white pignut	*Conopodium majus*
yellow Welsh poppy	*Meconopsis cambrica*
pink red campion	*Silene dioica*
white cow parsley	*Anthriscus sylvestris*
green dog's mercury	*Mercurialis perennis*
yellow cowslip	*Primula veris*
purple-blue bugle	*Ajuga reptans*
blue forget-me-not	*Myosotis sp*
blue germander speedwell	*Veronica chamaedrys*
white greater stitchwort	*Stellaria holostea*

Beyond the wood is a delightful stroll down the riverside. The Ordnance Survey map marks Mill Island: this is the only reminder of Appletreewick's corn soke mill, washed away in a flood in 1673. Before that, below Fold Bottom, is Sheep Fair Hill, site of the annual stock fairs held at the end of October at the Feast of St. Simon. **To return to the village, either take the private track up to New Inn** (and pay at the gate) **or take the right of way by the first camp site.** I think this is Onion Lane, whose walls were festooned with bundles of onions during the Fair. Quite why onions were so important is beyond me.

Postscript

I must not end without mentioning Appletreewick's own Dick Whittington. William Craven was born in 1548 of a not-so-humble family opposite High Hall. His parents had ambitions for him and sent him off to London to learn a trade and make a living. (I do not know if William had a cat.) He prospered in merchant tailoring and entered civic life, becoming Alderman and later Lord Mayor of London in 1610. Prior to this, in 1603, he had been elevated to a knighthood. He did not forsake his roots, though, but in 1601 moved across the road from home to live at High Hall which he restored. He was a great local benefactor, particularly in Burnsall where he restored the church, repaired the bridge and built and endowed the then grammar school. He died, a multi-millionaire by today's standards, in 1618. Two of his sons were created Baron Craven in their own right: one of them was later elevated to a viscountcy and to an earldom, being the 1st Earl of Craven (the 9th Earl is alive today).

Not quite rags to riches ... more of a local lad making good!

Place-name meanings

Appletreewick	OE	the dairy farm with apple trees
Barden	OE	the bare valley or the valley where barley grows
Blands Beck	–	named after a local family
Burnsall	OE	Bryni's (pers. name) piece of land
Dibb	OE	the deep pool
Fancarl Crag	–	originally Fan Cairn Crag
Foul Sike	OE	the dirty or muddy stream
Hartlington	OE	Heortla's (pers. name) farmstead
Haugh	OE	enclosure
Howgill	OE/ON	the hollow ravine
Kail Hill	OE/ON	the hill with cabbages growing
Langerton Hill	OE	the long hill near the farmstead (?)
Parcevall Hall	–	named after the local Percival family

Skyreholme	ON	the bright water meadow
Trollers Gill	ON/OE	troll (a goblin) and ... ears ... so it may mean the rounded hill like ears or buttocks. It has been translated as ... ahem ... "the goblin's arse"!
Wharfe	Brit	winding river
Whithill	OE	the white hill

Discovery Walk 10

On the Packhorse Trail – Ribblehead

Start and Finish: Gearstones less than 2km east of the road junction at Ribblehead (Grid reference SD778 799).

Parking: There is roadside parking just west of Gearstones.

Public transport: Bus services connect Ribblehead with Hawes and Swaledale on summer Sundays; and with Settle and Ingleton more regularly, all operated by Ingfield – Northern Rose (tel. 01729 822568). Trains stop at Ribblehead station on the Settle – Carlisle line.

Facilities: None except for an ice cream/teas van at Ribblehead junction in the season.

Outline of the Walk: Gearstones – Thorns Gill – Nether Lodge – Birkwith – Ling Gill – Cam End – Gearstones.

Length: The full route is 10km (about 6 miles), while the short route is just over 8km (over 5 miles).

Ordnance Survey Map: Outdoor Leisure 2. Landranger 98.

Introduction

The Dales National Park possesses a number of honeypot areas, sacrificial lambs to the popularity of walking. The majority are focussed on specific attractions, such as Malham Cove, Grassington or the Ingleton waterfalls. There is also a linear honeypot that stretches for around 40 kilometres. I am, of course, referring to the Three Peaks Challenge route, taking in the summit of the mountains that flank upper Ribblesdale. Tens of thousands set off with determination, and often trepidation, to attempt the circuit. Rather fewer manage to complete the round. You can well imagine the impact of so many feet on one narrow route, and the headache the Park staff have in trying to keep on top of maintenance.

On this walk you will have the noble peaks in view much of the day, and you will be following the challenge route for one stretch, but you will have most of the rest of it to yourselves, particularly on weekdays.

Every metre of this walk follows ancient roads, some still in use as roads,

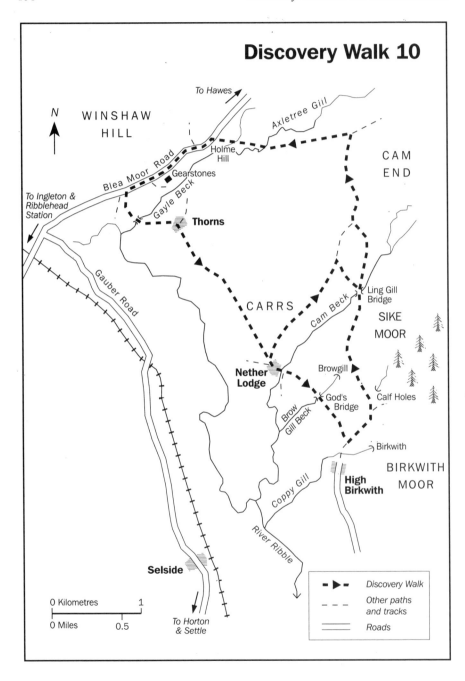

Discovery Walk 10

N

WINSHAW
HILL

To Hawes

Axletree Gill

CAM
END

Holme
Hill

Blea Moor Road

Gearstones

Gayle Beck

To Ingleton &
Ribblehead
Station

Thorns

Gauber Road

CARRS

Cam Beck

Ling Gill
Bridge

SIKE
MOOR

**Nether
Lodge**

Browgill

God's
Bridge

Calf Holes

*Brow
Gill Beck*

Birkwith

BIRKWITH
MOOR

**High
Birkwith**

Coppy Gill

River Ribble

Selside

0 Kilometres   1

0 Miles   0.5

To Horton
& Settle

Discovery Walk

Other paths
and tracks

Roads

some recognisable for what they were, others lost and reclaimed by years of disuse. You will touch packhorse routes, coach roads and turnpike roads; there are two former inns of renown and an abandoned hamlet. You will see the massive viaduct carrying the Settle-Carlisle railway across the moss, and pass alongside a very important National Nature Reserve, and a collection of drumlins telling a distant glacial story.

And ... there are spectacular views.

The walk can be completed in full, to make a good day's outing, or it can be shortened by omitting the southern portion. If you intend to follow the short route, that could be fitted into a half day, omit "The Long Route to Birkwith", "Birkwith" and "Calf Holes".

If you intend to have a look into either Birkwith Cave or Browgill Cave, on the long route, ask permission from High Birkwith farm. If you want to enter Ling Gill National Nature Reserve, on both routes, telephone the site manager on 015242 42021.

Limbering Up

If you are setting off from the railway station, walk east along the B6255 road for one and a half kilometres. If you are starting at Gearstones, walk west along the road for about 300 metres. In either case you leave the road at Ribble Head House. Do not look for a house because there is none there – just a small farm building and sheep pens. **Two paths start here: yours is the eastern one, starting at a gate where a signpost directs you to Nether Lodge.**

Nether Lodge and Whernside

Drop down through the pens, through a field gate and downhill by the wall-side. The view is quite something from here. Whernside (736 metres), the highest but perhaps least imposing of the Three Peaks, dominates the skyline beyond the railway viaduct. Across the valley of Chapel-le-Dale stands Ingleborough (723 metres) showing you its precipitous northern profile, the cliffs and screes of The Arks, with the rounded contours of its offshoots Park Fell and Simon Fell between the mountain and the railway. If you look south down Ribblesdale, you will see the knobbly lumps that are Warrendale Knotts above Settle, and the long whaleback of Penyghent (694 metres) and Plover Hill (680 metres) beyond the thickly forested northern slopes of the ridge called Cosh.

Viking Settlement

A study of the Ordnance Survey Map in the Ribblehead area emphasises the high proportion of place-names with a Norse (Viking) origin: the farms of Winterscales, Gunnerfleet, Ivescar, Bruntscar and Scales are just a few such names. All these have survived as farmsteads for a thousand years or more. On the other side of the valley, near the quarry, is the site of a settlement that did not survive, maybe because it is north-facing or because water is scarce nearby.

The earliest Viking raids along the east coast occurred in 789 and continued sporadically for the next seventy-five years, until some Vikings crossed the seas not as marauders and pillagers but as settlers bent on permanent conquest. At this time the population of our islands was no more than one million and life was a perpetual battle against the elements and the seasons. Hygiene and nutrition were at appalling levels, every third child died before the age of six, and life expectancy was a mere 21 years. The appearance of foreign raiders must have been the final straw for many peasant folk.

In 954 the Viking settlers were expelled but less than thirty years later they were back in force, Danes, Swedes and Norwegians together. Soon after, the humiliation of Danegeld was introduced, tribute or protection money paid to the Vikings to stay away, but by 1016 the English and Danish crowns had been united.

For the populace as a whole, once the initial trauma of the raids was past, life changed little. Only the landlords were different ... and they were always a different breed anyway to the oppressed. As the number of Scandinavians settling in what had been the Anglian kingdom of Northumbria grew, pressure on land brought about a movement up the rivers into the Dales.

The greatest Viking push into our area came not from the east, though, but from the west, from Ireland via the Isle of Man, Cumbria and Morecambe Bay. Indeed the Vikings and their offspring were expelled from Ireland in 902 and came to England. It may have been this push of people that added so many Norse words to our local dictionary and landscape. No less than 200 -*by* place-names have been identified in Yorkshire, as well as 155 -*thorpe* elements. (The word *by* meaning homestead or village has been preserved to the present day in the term by-law, that is the law of the village.) Almost half of all place-names in Yorkshire have Norse origins. But let us be prudent here. A Norse name need not necessarily imply Norse settlement or presence. Just think of the influence in the twentieth century of Americanisms in our everyday language, personal names and habits. It far outweighs the number of Americans living here. By parallel logic this may have been the case in the tenth century. Yet another imponderable.

The site at Ribblehead is not an imponderable, however. It was a farmstead consisting of a long-house and two out-buildings, with fields enclosing nearly two hectares. The people were self-sufficient, as they would have to be, living up here. They farmed a range of food crops: wheat for flour, barley for beer, oats for gruel and rye for winter feed for their stock. They hunted and trapped fox and hare and birds, all for food. There is evidence elsewhere of Norse eating curlew, woodcock, golden plover and black grouse, all of which occur in these fells even today. They made their own tools, clothes and basketware.

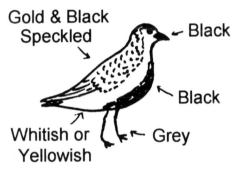

Gold & Black Speckled

Black

Black

Whitish or Yellowish

Grey

Golden plover (average size : 27-30cm)

They were also, perhaps, fortunate. In the Bronze Age, in the late Iron Age and in the Middle Ages, our climate took major turns for the worse, causing famine and population crashes. In the ninth and tenth centuries the opposite happened. Summers were longer and warmer than today, and winters correspondingly milder. Great tracts of the Dales were settled and brought into cultivation in this period. The "English" population probably doubled by the time of the Domesday Book in 1086.

Another historical cameo slots into place.

A Note for Railway Buffs ... and Others

It is a strange world we live in. People these days mount campaigns to preserve "monuments" like the railway viaduct: calling them "part of our heritage, a reminder of past endeavour and achievement, a vital addition to the landscape" and other such cliches. I wonder how the world would react if a company were to seek planning permission to build such an obtrusive feature today?

The story of the construction of the Settle-Carlisle railway, and particularly of the viaduct and Blea Moor tunnel, is a fascinating one. It happened because of the stubbornness of the Midland Railway company which wanted its own line to Scotland: the east and west coast routes had already been grabbed so Midland was left with Hobson's Choice, to build up the middle or nowhere. So up the middle it went. The surveyors came to Ribblehead in 1869 but it was not until 1875 that the first train ran. Blea Moor tunnel alone took five years to build, and for those years there was almost a town at Ribblehead. Some sources say two thousand people lived here in a series of camps that surely resembled the Klondike in the gold rush. There were navvies, engineers, brick makers, lime burners, surveyors, shebeen keepers, ladies of loose disposition ... and a whole host of hangers-on. There was a hospital, a school, a library, a post office, a policeman no doubt vainly trying to keep the peace, and a Methodist Mission no doubt equally vainly trying to maintain minimum standards of morality.

There were five shanty towns at Ribblehead itself, and numerous others elsewhere; their names invoke something of the conditions therein and of the fortitude, fatalism and humour of the inhabitants: Sebastapol, Inkerman, Battlebarrow Bank, Garlic Huts. Higher up, away from the squalor and the mire, was Belgravia, the camp for the site managers and other "higher" mortals ... literally looking down on the plebeians!

The correct name for the viaduct is Batty Moss, not Ribblehead, Viaduct. There are Batty Green and Batty Wife Hole nearby, the former having been one of the biggest shanties. Why Batty, you might think? Now this is a true story!

Mrs Batty ran a popular shebeen and, by all accounts, was a very forceful and domineering lady. As might be expected Mr Batty was mild, inoffensive ... and henpecked. In the end he conceived a dastardly plan! He persuaded the wife to tie him up and push him into a deep pool. She obliged with the first part but was thwarted on the second. In the nick of time he jumped aside and his dearly beloved fell headlong into the pool and drowned. Could there be a moral here?

Originally the station here was to be called Batty Wife station ... but perhaps Ribblehead sounds better.

To bring the story up to date, the National Park announced, in 1995, the commissioning of an archaeological survey of the remains of the railway camps and shanties at Ribblehead, such is their importance in railway and industrial archaeology.

Thorns

Continue down the wall from the sheep pens and through the bottom gate just before the beck. Cross by the footbridge and stop awhile. This stream is Gayle Beck, the main head-water of the Ribble which rises as Jam Sike high up on Grove Head at Gavel Gap. The bridge is one of the most aesthetically pleasing and beautiful packhorse bridges in the Dales. It is very simple and crude of construction but so perfectly in tune with its surroundings. The full autumn flush of rowan berries in the gill provides an almost magical setting, especially if the beck is in full spate.

The gill – the gorge, that is – displays the results of typical limestone processes. The acid waters of the beck are steadily dissolving away the rock along natural joints: in dry weather the waters actually flow underground here. The bed of the gill is also pock-marked with pot-holes, carved out by rocks and stones in the swirling waters of Gayle Beck in flood.

Once over the bridge, swing uphill to the left past a huge limestone erratic and around the contours of High Flat Hill. It passes by a number of shake holes (see Walk 5), ruined walls and the remains of a small field kiln to enter an old walled lane into a deserted hamlet. This was Thorns. Apart from the big barn, it is now mainly a collection of lumps, bumps and ruins, everywhere festooned in nettles in summer. Thorns began as a monastic grange and lay on a packhorse route that ran north-south, climbing out of Dentdale by the Craven Way, north of Whernside, to Little Dale, across the bridge at Thorns Gill, and south through Thorns and Nether Lodge to Birkwith where it joined up with other medieval and early modern routes. You will be following its course all the way to Birkwith, if you adopt the full route today.

In days when superstition reigned, and when strange happenings were given mystical significance, the humble thorn – the hawthorn – was held in great symbolic esteem. The thorn was venerated in the pre-Christian era and Christ's crown is said to have been hawthorn. There was a widespread belief, even into my lifetime, that bad luck came to those who harmed the hawthorn. Because of the awe attached to the tree, many villages were named after the thorn: Thorns is but one of several in the Dales.

Just before the remains of the farmhouse, turn right through a small gate, again signposted to Nether Lodge, and then over the ladder stile at the other side of the paddock. Attached to the signpost is a wooden plaque with a carved symbol that many find difficult to decipher. It is actually RW, the logo of the 115km long Ribble Way that loosely follows the river from source to mouth.

Plod uphill beyond the stile staying close by the wall on the east side of this field, then downhill through the next field once you have passed the rounded crest of Back Hools Hill. Stop at the isolated barn.

Whoever built it wanted more than just a functional barn and took pains in its construction. The coping stones and corner quoins, and the door lintels, all cut from sandstone, could not have come cheap, nor can the water trough and boskins made from Helwith Bridge flagstones. The present state of the roof is not so impressive, however!

A Basket of Eggs

Over the years people have ascribed to the Dales a number of adages like "the best of this" or "the most of that". The uppermost section of Ribblesdale, between Ribblehead and Horton, is said to possess the best collection of glacial drumlins in the country. I can remember from distant school-days being dragged up here to look at these very special drumlins. However, with the wisdom of years, I have come to realise there are thousands of them all the way from east of Windermere in a massive swathe south to Lancaster

Drumlin Fields of Ribblesdale

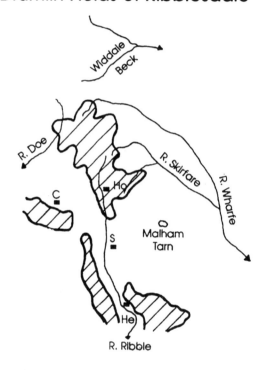

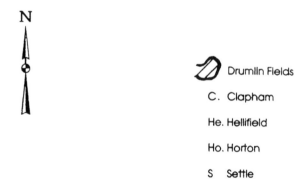

and then east to Settle, Hellifield and Skipton. Altogether a vast area of drumlins of which Ribblehead is a mere fraction of the whole.

One of the pioneer geologists and physical geographers, one Arthur Holmes, coined a phrase that has passed into the annals of geographical analogies. He decided these drumlin swarms are reminiscent of a basket of eggs. He must have been thinking of dinosaur eggs.

So what is a drumlin? I hear you gasp. It is a small hill, of the general shape you can see here, and with the variation in size you can observe around you. They are made up of unsorted glacial deposits (till) and were laid down under an ice sheet or glacier. Why are they all this general shape and why are there so many here? Why do they vary so much in size but not in shape? I possess a massive and recent tome on geomorphology whose author admits these questions cannot be answered satisfactorily, so I would not dare to suggest any solutions. Sorry.

Carrs and Nether Lodge

Pass around the bottom side of the barn and over the wall stile onto Thorns Moss and follow the faint path, above another defunct lime kiln to a ladder stile in the wall corner ahead. Beyond the stile the line of the path is again not well-marked on the ground but, if you look ahead to the crest of the far drumlin, you will see a fence with a stile. Make your way across the marshy dip where the twin arms of Crutchin Gill twist.

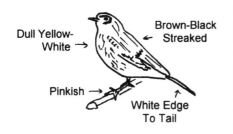

Dull Yellow-White →

Brown-Black ← Streaked

Pinkish →

White Edge To Tail

Meadow pipit (average size: 15cm)

In spring and summer the air here is full of bird song: the haunting, plaintive cry of the curlew; the harsh, nasal sounds of the lapwing dive-bombing you to distract you from its nesting site; the sweet warbling of the skylark soaring high in the sky, its song abruptly curtailed as it plummets earthwards; and the rather thin whistling and trilling of the meadow pipit as it flits about, always in a hurry.

Climb over the somewhat elaborate stile in the fence, with its click counter (your presence has been recorded) **and carry on straight towards Nether Lodge farm. Drop down from Low Rigg,** one of many riggs hereabouts, **cross the stream and stay close to the foot of Swinesett Hill.** As the path approaches the farm there are signs of a sunken track, part of the old packhorse track.

When you reach the farm, there is a four-way path junction. It is here that the short and full routes diverge.

Much of the land around Ribblehead was granted to Furness Abbey near present day Barrow. Nether Lodge was one of the farms or granges which became the centre for monastic farm activities. When one compares the high quality of land given to other Cistercian abbeys, like Fountains or Sawley, to the barren and windswept lands here, one wonders whether the donor had a grudge against Furness. It was by no means a poor foundation, though, and has been ranked as the second most wealthy Cistercian house in England.

The Short Route

Turn left back on yourself at the signpost and climb up the steep banking on the track signposted to Cam End. Follow the wall, keeping it on your right, over the east side of Swinesett, down the dip, up the next slope and over the step-over stile. Stay with the wall until it becomes a fence, climb over the stile here and follow the fence without losing any height until a third step-over stile is reached.

The path now contours on a ledge between Scald Bank and the enclosed meadows of Gill Rigg as far as a ladder stile by New House Barn. Turn right here and follow the wall beyond the barn to join the main track and the full route at Ling Gill Bridge.

The Long Route to Birkwith

Enter the farmyard of Nether Lodge: there is a ladder stile next to the gate. Tread speedily and considerately through here as the occupants must be heartily sick of walkers at times. The famous, or perhaps it should be infamous, Three Peaks Challenge is routed through here then down the main track to Lodge Hall. I am surprised they have never requested a footpath diversion around the farm ... or maybe they have in the past. I do not know.

The right of way passes between the present house and its crumbling seventeenth century predecessor, over the footbridge and left across the field to a ladder stile. Turn right here along the stony track which soon reduces to a grassed surface. After 500 or so metres you are ushered by enclosing walls to another stile by a gate. Look up Brow Gill Beck towards the barn high up. Between the barn and you is one of the more popular caves in the Dales, one that is used by caving instructors and novice groups – but more of this later.

You are at present at God's Bridge, a natural "bridge" as some would say. To be more exact the beck just disappears below ground for eighteen metres along an easy cave passage, before emerging again.

Carry on along the track but stay close to the wall. Ignore the track when it swings away from the wall uphill ... unless you happen to be hitching a ride on a passing tractor. This track later rejoins the wall. Stay on the track now all the way to the junction above High Birkwith farm.

Birkwith

Birkwith lies at an important junction as five rights of way converge here. All of them were important roads from monastic times to the coming of the turnpike roads in the eighteenth century. There was the packhorse road you have been following which continues south to Settle as a tarred road; there was the packhorse and later Lancaster to Newcastle coach road which came from Clapham via Selside and on over Birkwith to Green Field and Langstrothdale; and the packhorse and coach road that ran northwards to Hawes.

Birkwith enters the written record as a monastic grange and its focal position undoubtedly led to its providing shelter and vittels for travellers. In the centuries following the dissolution its occupants combined farming with innkeeping. Whether travellers and wayfarers had approached from north, east or west, they surely must have been heartily glad to see Birkwith. The nearest inn in each of those directions was a very long and bumpy day's ride away. Three cheers for trains and tarmac!

There is no need for you to drop down to Birkwith. **Turn left at the junction above the farm and climb uphill. Another track soon branches off to the right.** Here you can wave goodbye to any Ribble Way devotees you may have encountered; you can also put out of your mind the Three Peakers as you will see no more of them. If you have time you may care to take a short detour here. At the head of the wood just along that track is the entrance to Birkwith Cave. This is the main resurgence for a complex system of caves in this general area. It is a magnificent system, though definitely not for the uninitiated: the guidebook warns of the danger of being literally flushed out in wet weather. Being a major resurgence it does flood easily and quickly. Permission is required to enter the wood.

As with so much of the Dales this area has been designated a Site of Special Scientific Interest, for its caves and moorland scenery.

Carry on up the main track from Birkwith, past the entrance to Old Ing Farm (though Old Ing is actually hiding behind "new Ing"), **and through the gate ahead.** Coaches and packhorse trains for Newcastle turn right, those for Hawes turn left. You will not see any of those, except perhaps their ghosts, but you may just happen upon a hardy and determined soul, laden down with mighty rucksacks treading the Pennine Way. It is a long way from Edale to Kirk Yetholm.

Turn left here and follow the Pennine Way.

Calf Holes

At the first gate across the lane a stream plunges underground into Calf Holes cave. There is a stone stile so you can peer into the chasm if you so wish as long as you promise not to emulate the luckless calf that fell in. Various passages, suitably embellished with crawls, squeezes and other interesting bits connect this sink with Browgill Cave, mentioned earlier, to make a trip not far short of a kilometre. It is very popular with novice groups under instruction as it is safe and offers a variety of troglodytic experiences. I have seen disabled youngsters being lowered down, apprehensive but thankful for the experience.

Like so many cave systems, Calf Holes can flood very rapidly. There has been so much artificial draining of the moors that storms or heavy showers higher up soon find their way here. An experience more than ten years ago comes to mind. Two of us were lowering a group of teenagers down, having carefully checked the weather situation previously. When we had half the group at the bottom the stream began to rise so we took the decision to bring them back up again thus aborting the venture. All safely and easily reached the surface with a combination of climbing and being pulled up ... except for the last one. He got half way up and froze. He could go no further. As fate would have it, he just happened to be a prince of (foreign) royal blood. Eventually we managed to physically haul him out, cold and wet but otherwise fine. My colleague and I expected to be banished or sent to the gallows but father decided it had been an excellent character building experience for his heir! The experience haunts me still and I have never been down there since. I learned a great deal that day.

A short distance beyond the gate there is a ladder stile in the left-hand wall. That permits access to Browgill Cave, though there is no right of access. Permission should be sought from High Birkwith farm.

Carry on past Dry Lathe barn, hopefully enjoying clear visibility as Whernside, the viaduct, Simon Fell and Cam Fell come into view. **The track adopts an easy line through the drumlins and then comes alongside a gorge.** This is Ling Gill.

Ribbledale from above Ling Gill

Ling Gill

Ling Gill has been a National Nature Reserve since 1958, its creation due to the survival of the limestone gorge woodland, or "Pennine Gorge Woodland" as it is now called, woodland that would have covered much of the limestone dales before the advent of humans with their sheep until around 6,000 years ago. The gill is very deep and obviously steep-sided and, because of its sheltered nature, is almost always slippery even if the beck is not flowing. You should not enter the Reserve but, if you do have a particular botanical interest, you could telephone the Site manager for permission.

The gill has wide species diversity in terms of trees, understorey and grasses. The details of slope angle, soil depth, drainage and sunshine incidence result in a localised ecological patchwork quilt. Ash and wych elm dominate the more sheltered spots while rowan, bird cherry, birch and aspen have found their niche on the more open sections. Hawthorn and hazel also grow throughout the gorge. There are far too many flowers to list, not to mention ferns, mosses and lichens ... and let me not forget the crayfish. Holes again – there are seventeen little caves in the gill.

At the head of the gill the beck, called Cam Beck except in the gorge, is crossed by Ling Gill bridge.

It is here that the long and short routes combine again.

Ling Gill Bridge

The track that you have been following from Old Ing, and are to follow to Cam End, is the old Hawes to Settle road. It was both a packhorse and a coach road. The bridge was built in stone in the sixteenth century and it is not known whether a wooden bridge existed earlier or whether the beck was forded.

The wily and astute Henry VIII, never one to waste an opportunity, passed a long lasting law to the effect that any damaged bridge in his realm was to be put right at local cost rather than with funds from the Exchequer. This explains the reasoning behind the message inscribed on the plaque. The weather is taking its toll on the sandstone, but the inscription can be deciphered:

> *"Anno 1765*
> *This bridge*
> *was repair*
> *ed at the*
> *charge of*
> *the whole W*
> *est Riding"*

It was also repaired, at the charge of Settle Rural District Council, in 1932! Just upstream of the bridge there used to be two cottages but you will be hard pressed to find any signs of their existence.

The road was still in use in the nineteenth century. At the end of the first decade it was apparently still on the main route from London to Askrigg via Halifax, Skipton, Settle and Hawes. By 1864 an author and keen rambler, William Dobson, wrote that it had become more or less disused and "seldom traversed" except by shepherds and their flocks, a new road having been built on the western side of the Ribble, the present tarred road.

As you walk along the rutted and stony surface, spare a thought for those who had to travel this way, especially perhaps those gentle folk who travelled in unheated, unsprung coaches. **The road heads northwards across windswept and desolate moors, finishing with a long drag to the junction on Cam End. Leave the Pennine Way now and join the Dales Way, as you tramp downhill.**

Cam High Road

You are now on Cam High Road (or Cambesgate as it used to be) and it, too, has a long pedigree. It was a Roman road, connecting the Roman camps on the River Lune with Bainbridge (more on the Romans in "The Northern Dales"), later on the main road from Hawes to Ingleton and, from 1751, part of the Turnpike Road from Lancaster to Richmond, one of the earliest such roads in the Dales. It was superseded, however, in 1795 by being re-routed via Widdale and Newby Head along the line of the current tarred road. Lancaster and Richmond have been connected by road since the medieval period because, surprisingly, Lancaster was part of the Archdeaconry based on Richmond. So much for counties and the Wars of the Roses. The consistory court met in Richmond to hear all cases involving breaches of ecclesiastical law within the Archdeaconry, even from the Lancastrian fringes.

The track is in a variable state of repair now and Axletree Gill is doing its best to destroy one section. It is Gayle Beck that presents the greatest problem, though you will use the footbridge. The beck is fickle and not content to leave the crossing point alone. At least the latest efforts of the National Park team seem to be working – so far.

From the bridge cross the flood-plain to the ladder stile and head up to the road. A few tens of metres downstream, below the small crag, is the entrance to Holme Hill Cave, one of thirty-seven caves and pot-holes in the Ribblehead area. This used to be a show cave years ago, though a wet one. The total length is just short of 400 metres of which the first quarter of the passage is an easy walk through.

Turn left along the road for almost one kilometre back to where you parked at Gearstones – or on to the railway station.

Gearstones and the Drove Trade

Gearstones has almost followed Thorns into oblivion, as a place that was. I suppose only the tarred road saved it from total decay. From monastic times it fulfilled a role at the junction of several packhorse routes and much later sat astride coach and turnpike roads. It was the only civilisation for many a medieval mile. An important market was staged here, though our traveller noted in 1864 that it was by then merely a "ghost of a fair". Nevertheless it struggled on almost to the end of that century. Corn and oatmeal from Wensleydale were traded here to merchants from the west and south, and to passing cattle drovers.

There was a school serving the sizeable community here and at Thorns, and an inn. This mainly saw to the needs of the drove and packhorse teams but won the jackpot with the coming of the railway navvies, to such an extent that it was rebuilt in 1880. The actual inn, which lost its licence in 1911, stood on the opposite side of the road to Gearstones Lodge (a former shooting lodge) but it has been demolished.

The inn had rather an unsavoury reputation, in some quarters at least. One aristocratic traveller, John Byng, 5th Viscount Torrington, came down off Cam in 1792 to what he described as a "seat of misery" in an area of scenic "horror". He was appalled by the coarseness of the Scottish drovers and the English whatever, by the degree of drunkenness and fighting. He mentions seeing huge numbers of Scottish cattle being driven southwards. He also talks of grouse shooting in the area, and disdainfully dismisses the inn as a "hovel".

Further up the valley, at the crest of the way over to Widdale and Hawes, stands a farm called Newby Head. This too was an inn, said to have been

England's second highest, and again of significance to cattle drovers and packhorse teams alike and, from 1795, to travellers on the new turnpike. It is perhaps a pity Torrington had not waited three years more to make his journey because his road would have taken him there first rather than to Gearstones. In the following century Newby Head was praised for being "clean" and "respectably" run.

The cattle droving trade really needs a book to itself, but I have discussed it at some length in "The Northern Dales".

Place-name meanings

Axletree Gill	ON/ME	the ravine with an axle-tree (= an axle rod!)
Birkwith	ON	the birch wood
Blea Moor	OE/ON	the blue moor
Broad Ray	OE	the wide sheep walk
Bruntscar	OE/ON	the burnt,rocky hillside
Cam End	OE/ON	the end of the ridge
Carrs	ON	a marsh
Gayle Beck	OWS	the stream in the ravine
Gearstones	OE	the triangular piece of land or the land alongside the stream or the piece of land with marker posts (for the old Roman road perhaps?)
Green Slack Hill	OE/OWSc	the hill with the green hollow
Gunnerfleet	ON	*Gunnar's* (pers. name) stream
Holme Hill	ON	the hill by the water meadow
Ingleborough	OE	the fort on the hill
Ivescar	OE/ON	the cliff where ivy grows
Ling Gill	ON	the heather-covered ravine
Nether Lodge	-	the lodge below (Lodge Hall)
Old Ing	ON	the old meadow
Penyghent	OWelsh	the hill (in open country or near the border?)
Swinesett Hill	ON	the hill shieling where pigs are kept
Thorns	OE/ON	the place with thorn trees (hawthorns)
Whernside	OE	the hill where grinding stones were won
Winterscales	OE/ON	the winter shieling

Discovery Walk 11

From Conistone Dib to Conistone Pie

Start and Finish: West of Conistone Bridge, on the road connecting Conistone with Kilnsey (Grid reference SD978 675).

Parking: There is room to park on the roadside.

Public transport: Buses stop at Kilnsey on the Skipton-Grassington-Buckden route. Contact Keighley and District (tel. 01535 603284) or Pride of the Dales (tel. 01756 753123). There is also a frequent Park and Ride scheme up the dale from Grassington on Sundays in July and August; and the Dalesbus stops in Kilnsey (see Walk 6).

Facilities: Kilnsey Park has extensive facilities for the visitor, including meals and a tourist information point. The Tennant Arms provides meals and morning coffee. There is a telephone in Conistone.

Outline of the Walk: Conistone Bridge – Cool Scar – Kilnsey – Conistone – Conistone Dib – Capplestone Gate – Highgate Leys – Conistone Pie – Wassa Hill – Conistone Bridge.

Length: 11km (under 7 miles) for the main route, with almost an extra 3km (under 2 miles) if the Kilnsey loop is included. The short version is around 7km (over 4 miles).

Ordnance Survey Map: Outdoor Leisure 10. Landranger 98.

Introduction

This is a walk of contrasts. West of the River Wharfe lies the hamlet of Kilnsey, its park and trout farm, its pub and quarry all bringing an air of endeavour and bustle to this side of the valley. Conistone, set at a junction on the minor road east of the river, is a relative backwater, unspoilt and unhurried.

The flatness and dampness of the broad valley floor contrast with the precipitous nature of Kilnsey Crag and the stepped rising ground to the east. The gentle contours of the lower slopes are offset by the ruggedness of the many limestone scars and by the chasm of Conistone Dib. The greenness

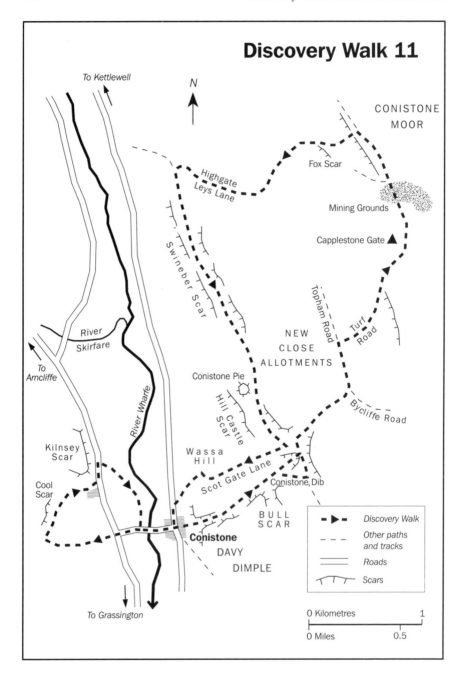

Discovery Walk 11

To Kettlewell

N

CONISTONE
MOOR

Fox Scar

Highgate
Leys Lane

Mining Grounds

Capplestone Gate ▲

Swineber Scar

Topham Road

Turf Road

NEW
CLOSE
ALLOTMENTS

River
Skirfare

To
Arncliffe

Conistone Pie

Bycliffe Road

River Wharfe

Hill Castle Scar

Kilnsey
Scar

Wassa
Hill

Scot Gate Lane

Conistone Dib

Cool
Scar

Conistone

BULL
SCAR

DAVY
DIMPLE

To Grassington

- ▶ - *Discovery Walk*
- - - *Other paths
and tracks*
——— *Roads*
⌃⌃⌃ *Scars*

0 Kilometres   1

0 Miles   0.5

and gentleness of the limestone in much of the area also provides a marked contrast to the barren moorlands on the gritstone slopes of Conistone Moor.

As with all the walks in this book, the parish of Conistone with Kilnsey is steeped in history. Here the most visible story is the medieval one. The eastern slopes of the Wharfe valley possess some of the best-preserved early medieval fields in the North, while Kilnsey itself enjoyed a high status in the monastic period.

There are various options open to you. You could follow the entire route in one go, taking a full day over it. You could perhaps walk the Kilnsey loop in the morning, combining it with a visit to Kilnsey Park, and leave the main section of the walk for the afternoon. If so, read "Kilnsey".

A third option would be to split the whole walk into two loops of more or less equal length though, of course, there will be overlap to climb out of the valley. If this is your choice, follow "Kilnsey", "Conistone and Conistone Dib" and "Scot Gate" for the western, lower loop. For the eastern route, start with "Conistone and Conistone Dib" and follow the text through all the ensuing sections to finish with "Scot Gate".

Kilnsey

From Conistone Bridge make for the junction with the Kettlewell to Grassington road and turn left. If you are starting at the bus stop in Kilnsey, simply walk south along the main road past Kilnsey Park and the junction.

Approximately 100 metres south of the road junction a track turns west next to a bungalow. Follow this track up Howgill Beck beyond the farm units, crossing from one side of the stream to the other. On the approach to a collapsed barn the track forks. Take the right fork, over the single slab footbridge and straight up the field for a short distance. There is a field gate above but ignore that. Half way up the wall you meet a clear, and partly sunken track coming down the field. Follow this to the left as it contours up to a stile and small gate in the wall. This short stretch of track is the line of the original Mastiles Lane. It continued in the same direction, across the head of Sikes Beck into Kilnsey but is no longer a public path.

When through the gate you are on the modern Mastiles Lane. Turn right down the quarry road into the village. The first building on the left is Kilnsey Hall or Old Hall. What a magnificent building it is.

Old Hall

It is more than thirty years since the Old Hall was last used in a substantive way, other than as an agricultural store, though general planning applications have been lodged over the years for residential renovation. As I write the latest attempt has just been passed by the planners. If it is a sympathetic plan I hope it manages to restore the hall to its former glories.

The present set of buildings reflect architectural styles of various periods.

Kilnsey Old Hall

The barn, the small building just above the hall, has tentatively been described as the chapel that served the monastic community here until Dissolution in 1539, though this has to be conjecture. However, it was clearly more than just a barn in its prime: the doors, with their chamfers and spandrels in the doorheads are far too grand for a utilitarian building. I am no expert but I am tempted to ascribe this building some function in the post-monastic period.

There has been a hall on the Old Hall site since the twelfth century but it was only built in stone sometime in the fourteenth or fifteenth century. The evidence for this is the surviving portion of the gate-house which dates from then, and thus has monastic origins as the entry to the monastic grange. The masonry suggests there may have been an arch, and the door on the inner side of the building was probably the gatekeeper's door. The chamfers and spandrels above this are similar in a way to those on the "chapel" ... so are they in fact contemporary after all, or have old stones been re-used in the barn?

The medieval hall was completely rebuilt in 1648 using stone from its demolished predecessor. The new hall was a three-storey structure and the original mullioned windows survive on all except the rear wall. Later, nineteenth century alterations – or desecrations to the purist – added the large, arched barn doors and totally changed the detail of the north elevation of the hall.

Hood Moulding

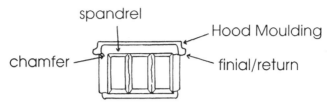

spandrel

Hood Moulding

chamfer

finial/return

When Fountains Abbey, owners of the site, was dissolved in 1539 the lands at Kilnsey were sold by the Crown to the Gresham family, rich and powerful merchants from London. They soon re-sold (at a profit) much of the estate to the tenants, and Kilnsey itself was sold to the Yorke family, one of the "big" names of the North. They have lived, in an unbroken line, on the fringes of the Dales since the fifteenth century, having once owned much of Nidderdale, large areas west and south of Settle and along the Wharfe.

Within a hundred years ownership of the estate had passed to the Wades and it was Christopher who built the hall in 1648 but his son, Cuthbert, developed the estate into a major and profitable operation. He must have been quite a man, having had three wives who between them bore him a baker's dozen children. His son, another Cuthbert, was less fortunate and did not long survive his father. Cuthbert's widow re-married, took her son, yet another Cuthbert, and did the unforgivable by moving to live in Lancashire! When he died in 1745, the last of his line, the estate was sold off: blossomed, flourished and gone in less than a century. By 1800 the hall was being used as a barn ... and so it has largely remained.

Monastic Kilnsey

I have mentioned the grange at Kilnsey several times already in other walks and hinted at its importance. For a long period of time Fountains Abbey, a Cistercian foundation west of Ripon, owned one million acres (this sounds more impressive than 4,000 square kilometres) in the Dales, and Kilnsey was their centre of operations, their corporate headquarters. All life and work centred around the grange. Kilnsey then consisted of the monastic hall, seven other large houses, a court house, a chapel and all manner of stores, barns and hovels, all originally of timber and wattle until the more important ones were rebuilt in stone.

The estates in the Dales had been granted to the abbey from 1156 by Alice de Romille of Skipton Castle, and the monks soon took advantage of these enormous bequests by developing a wool industry second to none in medieval England.

In addition to the buildings at Kilnsey, the monks had two mills, one for corn and one for fulling, at Mill Scar Lash on the Wharfe south of Kilnsey, and they had a series of fish ponds where Kilnsey Park now is. Conistone Bridge was built to a standard that could take loaded wagons, in monastic times. Fields and woods were enclosed by stone walls, some of which still stand today, and a huge stock enclosure, bounded by ditch and bank, was constructed a short distance along Mastiles Lane. It is marked on the Ordnance Survey map as Cool, and in part can still be traced on the ground.

Kilnsey Crag

From Kilnsey Hall take the left fork to come out at the main valley road next to the Tennant Arms. Turn left for two hundred or so metres of road walking alongside White Beck. Towering above the beck is Kilnsey Crag, a limestone cliff forty metres high with a massive overhang. You often see climbers pinned to the crag like flies, usually with onlookers on the road either stationary – or mobile, with eyes anywhere but on the road. I once saw one car load of southbound gapers cross the road, plough through the wall and end up in the beck. The yellow lines have not made one jot of difference. Coming back to the climbers, though, I have yet to see any trying to negotiate the overhang. Personally I have never been one for hanging about. Life is all too short.

Just before the crag proper there is a barn, called Scar Lathe. Leave the road here by climbing over the step-over stile into the field. The path on the ground is unclear but head south-eastwards to clip the two wall corners, then follow the wall south to Conistone Bridge. Climb onto the road and turn left over the Wharfe. From early March these riverside meadows team with lapwings and curlews. Stray too near a nest and you will invoke the wrath of the former, while the latter wheel and display noisily above. On the river banks, just above and below the bridge, there are holes in the sand "cliffs". These are home to nesting sand martins that arrive as summer visitors, though there seem to have been fewer of them in recent years.

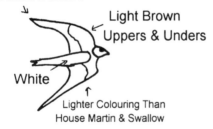

Tail Less Forked Than
House Martin & Swallow

Light Brown
Uppers & Unders

White

Lighter Colouring Than
House Martin & Swallow

Sand martin (average size: 12cm)

The river is fast-flowing here at the best of times but, in flood, it can be a sight to behold, a raging foaming torrent. In the serious floods in early 1995 the whole valley floor was awash and two long lengths of roadside wall were demolished by the torrent, the stone being splayed far across the field. On the road the water was over half a metre deep.

Follow the road into Conistone village. I suppose you could pick up a sturdy steed at the trekking centre if you are tired of walking. Perhaps not.

Conistone and Conistone Dib

Pass to the left of the village maypole (no elongated barber's pole here, thank you) **towards the village green.** I would recommend a visit to the church, on the northern edge of Conistone. It is simplicity itself but no less interesting for that. It is an ancient foundation and some Saxon stonework survives.

In the churchyard there is a monument to one of caving's worst ever tragedies. In the summer of 1967, six young but experienced cavers were trapped by rising waters in the recesses of one of the passages of Mossdale Caverns, high up on Conistone Moor, and drowned. The passage became their communal tomb and was sealed off when the rescue attempts had clearly failed. This incident sent shock waves through the caving community that reverberated for years.

When you are ready to leave the village walk east through the village green towards the rising limestone slopes. At the far end, by the old school house, there is a field gate and a path leading past an old railway carriage into a narrowing gorge below the unusually named Davy Dimple.

It is a very easy scramble up through the gorge, locally known as Gurling Trough. The water-smoothed rocks and water-worn grooves and the potholes tell of the times when the glaciers were receding and enormous quantities of meltwater were rushing into the valley below. You will not find water flowing through here but that is perhaps just as well.

The gorge soon opens out into a wider but still deep and steep-sided valley, carved out between Wassa Hill on one side and Conistone Old Pasture on the south side. **The walking is easy and gentle as you pass beneath the limestone crags of Bull Scar,** capped with a small Iron Age site, into the enclosed, elongated bowl that is Conistone Dib. **There are two ladder stiles now, one ahead of you and one to the right. You need to decide which one to use, depending on your spirit of adventure or agility.**

The way ahead is shorter but involves a mild scramble out of the gorge onto the broad track carrying the Dales Way. The alternative is to climb to the right through the gentler valley to the south to also meet the Dales Way. In either case turn left and through the gate at the track cross-roads, where the ancient north-south road crosses the east-west road, again one of great age.

If you are following the shorter, western loop you need to turn left here and pick up the route description under "Scot Gate". Otherwise turn right up Bycliffe Road.

New Close Allotments

The road leads upwards, flanked by limestone pavement to left and right, through the nick and across an open pasture. The track is soon enclosed by walls as the gradient steepens to a cross-roads. This is Cappleside Gate. Bycliffe Road turns sharply right here.

Bycliffe Road was an important packhorse route in the Middle Ages, connecting Conistone and Mastiles Lane to the west with Middlesmoor in Upper Nidderdale over the top of Mossdale and Friar Hood where the road is called Sandy Gate. In later times Bycliffe Road provided access to Conistone township's stone quarries on the moor top, and to the small lead mines of Silver Rake and Mossdale.

The track that runs straight ahead from Cappleside Gate simply leads to the fields above. **Your route is through the gate on the left.** This is Conistone Turf Road though it does not look much of a road nowadays. You will be walking the Turf Road up onto the gritstone moorland way beyond the present horizon. In the days before coal, villagers had the right to cut peat for fuel up on the township (or parish) moors. There are many such turf, or turbary, roads in the Dales and Pennine fringes.

Follow the road up the field, parallel to the wall on your right, to the corner just before the plantation. The road divides again here. Straight on, west of the plantation, Topham Road links the various fields that make up New Close Allotments. There is, however, nothing new about New Close: the area was enclosed as early as 1587, significantly earlier than the main Enclosure period. They were only "new" in comparison to the existing fields nearer Wharfedale.

The Turf Road turns between the plantation and the wall, over a stile. You can see its course higher up, edging below the long, low limestone scar. Pause to admire the panorama below. Rylstone Fell and the tops near Skipton give way to the less aesthetically pleasing quarry at Skirethorns. Mastiles Lane climbs steeply up Kilnsey Moor almost due west from where you are standing while, north again, lies Old Cote Moor, between Littondale and Kettlewell, with Starbotton Moor completing the view in the north.

The track crosses a wall by the scar and heads over the rise. Note the marked changes in vegetation now. The limestone here has a blanket of glacial drift, giving rise to more acidic soils and a different plant community. Further on, **on the final climb to the skyline,** limestone gives way to Millstone Grit and a total vegetation change. The hill top with the triangulation pillar has no name other than that more properly attached to the wall crossing, Capplestone Gate.

Conistone Moor

Look west from the wall and most of what you see is limestone: look east and the scene is very different. This is real gritstone moorland, complete with windswept peat haggs and groughs. You are in grouse territory now, a land as harsh and forbidding as the limestone pastures are soft and welcoming. **Press on, with stout heart and firm tread, to follow the track diagonally away from the ladder stile, meandering between soggy patches.** You could stick to the wall but that is not the path.

Looming ahead of you – as often as not half hidden in the clag – is the brooding mass of Great Whernside, great not in height (704 metres) but in bulk, and also in relation to its near neighbour Little Whernside (604 metres). **After five minutes or so the path leads into the middle of an area that has been extensively worked for lead in the past centuries.**

There were two mining fields on Conistone Moor, in addition to Mossdale: a kilometre to the east of you are the Out Moor mines around Silver Rake and Swarth Gill; while here are the remains of the Moorhead lead mines. They were only small-scale operations, largely developed and worked by local freeholders. Shallow bell pits were sunk, at least from 1686, with deeper shafts seeking more profitable veins in the nineteenth century. Eight veins were worked up here but profits were never large, and production was finally abandoned in 1870.

A footpath, once a miners' track, heads in a bee-line from the mine to Kettlewell where most of the lead was smelted. Smaller amounts were sent for smelting at Yarnbury, but this proved to be a long and somewhat tortuous journey.

In the midst of the mine stands a three-way fingerpost. You could follow the old miners' track (signposted to Kettlewell) over the stile and diagonally downhill to a second stile, but I would urge you to stay high and take the more northerly path along the moor edge for several hundred metres.

This path crosses a small stream and then boundary stones on the border between Conistone and Kettlewell townships. **Very shortly beyond this is a ladder stile by a gate. Climb over this and literally plunge downhill on the zigzag track,** back onto limestone. **At the bottom of the field go through the collapsing wall and turn slightly north to pass above Fox Scar.**

The way then meanders the length of the next long field, passing a small expanse of limestone pavement and a line of old lead workings. The path swings from one side of the field to the other, and back again, to end up at a gate in the bottom, north-west, corner. Once again you are presented with a wonderful view from Buckden Pike in the north to Amerdale Dub and Kilnsey Crag in the south.

Beyond the gate the track, here called Highgate Leys Lane, is very clear, and so are the old sunken holloways, **as it drops down to a major track appearing from within the wood. You are now once again on the Dales Way.**

Within the woods, a little to the north, is Scargill House, complete with a fine chapel built in 1960. This is a holiday and conference centre run by a Christian community offering facilities for quiet relaxation, worship and fellowship, as well as a programme of holidays and breaks year round (tel. 01756 760234).

Scars and Screes

You now have 2.5km of immensely pleasurable and easy walking, contouring along limestone bedding planes between scars and screes. You cannot fully appreciate the fact, unless you see it from below, that there is quite a drop on your right, especially along Swineber Scar and Hill Castles Scar further south. Facing south-west these limestone bands had been heavily shattered by frost action in the post-glacial and inter-glacial periods. Water settled in cracks and joints in the rock, expanded in times of frost, contracted in the thaws, and thus exerted pressure on the rock, shattering and splintering it into ever smaller pieces that make up the scree below the scars.

At the first ladder stile there is a view across the valley to Amerdale Dub, the confluence of Wharfe and Skirfare. Above that is the gently sloping High Wind Bank, or Dead Man Rigg to give it an earlier, gruesome name. At some time in the past, so it is said, a highwayman was strung up on a gibbet here. Served him right!

Between this stile and the third you will cross a number of "lost" walls, remains of an earlier farming landscape. You will also notice a number of engineered tracks up through the screes on your left: they led up to the enclosures of New Close. A particularly clear track heads upslope just before the third stile, to be truncated by the later walls. This one is marked on the 1:25,000 map passing through an Iron Age field system and settlement further south, and then cutting across Bycliffe Road to Conistone Old Pasture. If you look downslope between the third and fourth stiles you can pick out a medieval field pattern of irregular shapes and sizes.

Conistone Pie looms ahead now, a freak of nature, protected by a particularly resistant cap of limestone. I guess it is obvious how it earned its name.

Anywhere along this stretch of path, as indeed in any similar landscape, you may well spy a busy little bird, the size of a robin. He and his wife can be seen hopping along the coping stones of the walls, or flitting from boulder

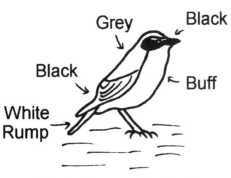

Grey **Black**

Black

Buff

White Rump

Wheatear (average size: 15cm)

to boulder, keeping an eye on you while keeping just ahead of you, too. This is the wheatear, a summer visitor from Africa. The male has the more distinctive markings: a grey back with buff-coloured unders with a white belly. When he takes to the air he displays white prominently on his rump. Now, he has no ears and eats insects not grain, so why is he called wheatear? Is this a linguistic corruption of white rear, I wonder?

Beyond Conistone Pie you climb another ladder stile and almost immediately are in the middle of a lost settlement with enclosures stretching all the way to Bycliffe Road. There is Iron Age material on the next level above but this lot may be later.

Below you is Hill Castles Scar and High Hill Castles and there was a monastic sheep-house, with grazing for four to five hundred sheep, like the one on Malham Lings (see Walk 3), near Conistone Pie and between the two scars. Fountains Abbey owned no lands around here, but leased grazing rights. So, once again, we have field evidence of multi-period, but not necessarily continuous, occupancy on the limestone uplands.

Scot Gate

Just beyond Hill Castles Scar the Dales Way meets Bycliffe Road. Turn right here. If you are walking the western loop only, you should slot back into the narrative here.

Below this point Bycliffe Road is called Scot Gate Lane and it is an easy descent over the flanks of Wassa Hill, through a major and very important set of early fields which you may not be aware of until you reach the bottom of the lane and look back up.

Some of these fields take the form of long, narrow terraces, parallel to the valley side. These are lynchets (from an Old English word for ridge) and they could first date from an expansion of population and settlement in the Anglian period, in the eighth century, though there is every reason to accept their intermittent usage throughout the medieval period.

Lynchets near Amerdale Dub

Lynchets were not deliberately cut as terraces: they evolved that way. The plough of the day could only turn the soil one way so, at the end of each furrow, the oxen were walked back to start again. The effect of this would be to turn the soil only one way, and downslope had to be easier than turning it against gravity. In addition, the peasants removed any large stones, again downslope to the edge of their strips ... and thus the terraces came to be.

Ideally a lynchet is a furlong in length – a furrow long, that is how far an ox could pull the plough without rest. In width they are a perch (or rod or pole: do you remember these old measures? I do not!). Multiply a furlong by a perch and you have a quarter acre. Magic.

Towards the bottom of the lane there is a stretch of newly rebuilt wall, built by a craftsman in my humble opinion. Let's hope he is given plenty of work around here as there are almost endless lengths of wall in need of such restoration.

When you reach the tarred road – possibly a Roman road and definitely part of the London to Richmond coach road – **turn left back into Conistone and ... home?** Note the finger post at the junction: eleven miles to Middlesmoor. Now in those days that was truly a long, hard day's trek for pony or foot traveller, especially over terrain such as Conistone Moor. They were tough in those days.

Place-name meanings

Bull Scar	-	as it sounds
Bycliffe	OE	near the cliff
Cappleside	OE/ON	the hillside with horses (nags)
Capplestone	OE/ON	the stones where horses graze
Conistone	OE	the king's farmstead (it was held by the king's thanes)
Cool	ON	the stock enclosure / hill with cows
Davy Dimple	OE	*Davy's* (pers.name) deep pool in a pit
Dib	OE	pool
Friar Hood	OE/OFr	the hill like a monk's cowl
Gurling Trough	ME	the rumbling valley
Highgate Leys	OE	the high road near a clearing in the wood
Hill Castles	OE/ME	as it sounds
Kettlewell	OE	the bubbling spring
Kilnsey	OE	the lime kiln near the marsh
Skirethorns	ON	the bright thorn trees
Skirfare	ON	the bright or sparkling river
Swarth Gill	OE/ON	the dark or black ravine
Swineber Scar	OE/ON	the cliff on the hill where pigs graze
Topham Road	-	named after a local family
Wharfe	Brit	the winding river
Whernside	OE	the hillside where grinding stones are won

Discovery Walk 12

Beyond the National Park – a walk in Nidderdale

Start and Finish: In Pateley Bridge at the foot of the main street near the car park entrance.

Parking: Pay and display car park by the riverside.

Public transport: Buses run from Harrogate on a regular basis, operated by Harrogate and District (01423 566061). The Nidderdale Rambler connects with Grassington in the summer only, also operated by Harrogate and District. The Rambler also runs through Wath once a day. A "shared hire car" service also runs through Wath at set times and must be pre-booked (01423 711312).

Facilities: Pateley Bridge has all the services you would expect of a small town. The Sportsman's Arms in Wath offers bar meals and there is a public telephone in the village.

Outline of the Walk: Pateley Bridge – Ladies Riggs – Brandstone Dub – Providence Mine – Heathfield – Wath – Pateley Bridge.

Length: 11km (less than 7 miles) for the main route with extensions of 4km to Merryfield and 1.5km for Gouthwaite Reservoir.

Ordnance Survey Map: Pathfinder (1:25,000) no. 652. Landranger 99.

Introduction

This final walk in the Southern Dales takes us beyond the bounds of the National Park into upper Nidderdale. I cannot understand the reasoning behind the decision to exclude the dale when the Park was created as, structurally, it is part of the larger whole and is affected by the eastern extremity of the North Craven Fault. Scenically, also, it was surely worthy of inclusion. Perhaps the large-scale water abstraction scheme in the upper-most dale was the deciding factor against inclusion? For those who campaigned for its inclusion, justice of sorts has now been done: recently the whole valley, stretching from the Park boundary almost to Ripon and Harrogate, was gazetted as an Area of Outstanding Natural Beauty.

Nidderdale has been influenced, shaped and styled by similar processes as throughout the Dales. The geology is basically the same with limestone

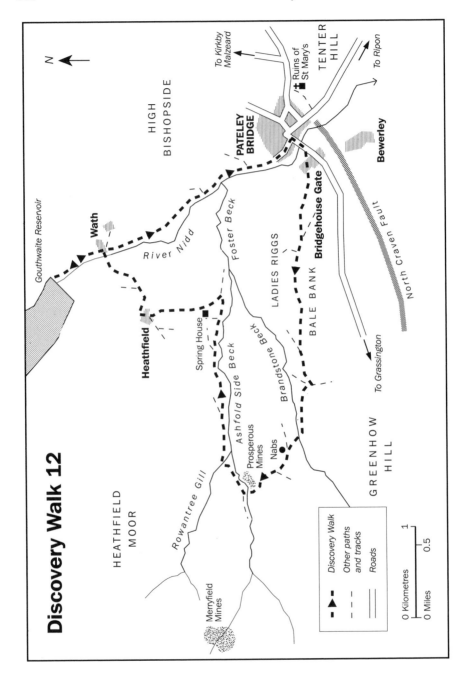

Discovery Walk 12

and deltaic gritstones being paramount; glaciers have left their mark on the landscape; lead has been extensively worked west of the Nidd; and industries have come and gone. There are, I suppose, two main differences between this dale and the others we have journeyed through. Farming here is on an altogether larger scale between Wath and Pateley Bridge, though it is still pastoral in essence. Secondly, whereas most of the Dales concentrated on woollen and cotton textiles, here in Nidderdale, linen held sway.

This walk allows you the option of extending or truncating it according to your needs and interests. I have indicated in the text where options present themselves. In all, the route divides itself into three diverse parts: the upland section as far as Providence in the west, the rich farming country around Heathfield and Wath, and the riverside south of Wath.

Motorists with limited time, or young families, could adapt any of these sections for a shorter circular walk, using Pateley Bridge, Wath or the Watermill Inn at Foster Beck as the focus of the walk.

Whatever you opt for, do have a look round Pateley Bridge at some point. I can fully recommend the museum below St Cuthbert's church at the upper end of town, as well as a circuit to the ruined medieval church abandoned in 1827, high above the town on Tenter Hill.

Pateley Bridge

A number of villages in Nidderdale, as far north as Pateley Bridge, have the element ley in the place-name. This denotes a clearing made in the forest, suggesting the dale was well-wooded in Anglian times when the settlers pushed north in search of new lands. Pateley owed its early survival, if not success, to its site at the junction of three early tracks: one from the Ripon area, one from Kirkby Malzeard over Pateley Moor, and the other from over Greenhow Hill. These routes are actually documented from the twelfth century though the bridge does not appear in the records until 1320.

Throughout the Norman period upper Nidderdale lay waste, devastated by the brutal suppression of the North ordered by the new king. Great swathes of the dale were alienated as hunting grounds with the royal Forest of Knaresborough in the south and Nidderdale Chase to the north. (See Walk 7 for a discussion of hunting forests.)

The growth of Pateley Bridge as a settlement worthy of note dates from 1320 when the lord of the manor, so to speak, the Archbishop of York, was granted a market charter.

The township remained small – just a huddle of houses – until the development of industry and trade, more of which later. It was the establishment of the turnpike roads and later on the coming of the railway that gave the town the impetus to shed its rural slumber in favour of the ups and downs of manufacturing and mining. Downs there certainly were and the size of the workhouse, enormous in relation to the size of the town, testifies to times of hardship. All was obviously not well in the running of the workhouse and, within one five year period in the middle of the nineteenth century, no less than three wardens were shown the door. The first was dismissed for inebriety, the second for incompetence, and the third for pilfering. The present building, now housing the museum and offices, dates from after this episode. As you will see later on today, its severe bulk dominates the town seen from afar.

From Bridgehouse to Brandstone

When you are ready to set forth, turn your back on the town and the parish of Bishopside and cross the Nidd into the twin settlement of Bridgehouse Gate and Bewerley parish. On the left, just beyond the bridge (still made of wood in Tudor times at least) lies Bewerley Park. There stood here one of the ancestral seats of the Yorke family, one of the most prominent families in the dale until they sold up in 1924 and moved elsewhere in the Dales. The great house was demolished not long after they left.

Ignore the first turning on the right but turn along the side road by the post box. Look out for the old brewery part way along. Pateley Bridge also had a brewery, and a substantial one at that, another sign of an industrial past. I digress once again ... I had a rather militant grandfather who maintained that the ruling and managerial classes took great pains to ensure a ready supply of beer for the working classes to keep them content and compliant. H'mm!

More or less opposite the brewery, bear to the left up a track between the houses. This soon turns into a grassy track leading to a gate to the left of a field barn. Note the left-hand gatepost with three squarish notches carved into it. This is a relic of the days before hinged gates. It would have had a matching gatepost and poles would have been inserted through the holes of the other into these cuts to form a stock barrier. **Carry on up the field, keeping to the left-hand edge** by the rather grand display of mature trees: sycamore, holly, rowan, hawthorn, hornbeam and a particularly majestic oak. **At the top, pass through the kissing gate into the next field and continue on the same course.**

If you halt awhile now and look over to starboard, there is a panoramic view of the town. St Cuthbert's stands out clearly but is almost dwarfed by the former workhouse.

Shortly ahead you pass alongside the grounds of Eagle Hall on the edge of a field that radiates with the yellow and white in early summer of meadow buttercup *(Ranunculus acris)* and pignut *(Conopodium majus)* a tiny Umbellifer. Both are common natives in the Dales and both had their uses. The latter had a definite use: an alternative name for pignut is earthnut. Taste one of the radish-like tubers and you will understand why. The use of the buttercup, however, is speculative. I am sure as a child you held one under your friend's chin to see if (s)he liked butter or not (unless you grew up in a concrete jungle) but have you ever felt moved to rub it on a cow's udder? It is said that this improves milk yield. I asked a farmer friend to verify this but he looked at me askance!

Have another look back somewhere in this field, as the view of the town opens up more to the south. There is a rather prominent cemetery and just behind it a church tower. This is the ruined church I mentioned earlier.

The ruined church of St Mary

At the top corner of the field find the stone step stile into the beech wood and onto the tarred lane. It is best to amble up the lane, I feel, because the wayside flowers are colourful and diverse to say the least. There is that very common Umbellifer, the tall and stringy cow parsley *(Anthriscus sylvestris)*, ladies mantle *(Alchemilla sp.)* with its almost apologetic yellow flowers, the superficially similar yellow-petalled crosswort *(Galium cruciata)*, forget-me-nots *(Myosotis sp.)*, the white greater stitchwort *(Stellaria holostea)* and the deep blue of the common milkwort *(Polygala vulgaris)* ... and others I cannot recall just now.

Further on you pass Riggs House where the closely farmed land to the north contrasts vividly with the open, bleak aspect of the moors rising away to the south. Rudyard Kipling's Learoyd, one of the Soldiers Three, has something to say about these moors in the short story "On Greenhow Hill". Reminiscing of home, in a remote posting in northern India, Learoyd talked of:

"moors an' moors an' moors, wi' never a tree for shelter, an' grey houses wi' flagstone rooves ... And cold! A wind that cuts you like a knife ... Miners mostly, burrowin' for lead i' th' hillsides ... It was the roughest minin' I ever seen."

Obviously, Kipling knew these parts well.

Down in the valley beyond the crest of Ladies Rigg is Bale Bank Farm, the name suggesting early lead smelting. To the north-west, across that valley, stands Throstle Nest farm below a series of medieval banked fields. Now, I thought a throstle is another name for a song thrush but the origin of the place-name suggests the raven. I cannot fathom this out.

The track begins to drop more steeply and brings you to a four-way junction of paths and tracks. Stay on the lane down to the bridge, leave the tar here and swing round right on the stony lane past Hillend. This lane leads you to Brandstone Dub Bridge.

Providence Mine

The track swings round and uphill becoming sunken between banks covered in bilberry, ling and birch seedlings (downy birch, I think). In among the bilberry (*Vaccinium myrtilis*, otherwise known as whortleberry or blaeberry depending on where you live. The leaves make passable tea, by the way) in early summer, is a white flower with clover-like leaves. There is no plant actually called shamrock but this wood-sorrel *(Oxalis acetosella)* must be it. If you want a salad to go with your bilberry tea, try the leaves of the wood-sorrel. It cannot be worse-tasting than cress!

Very soon the track forks and a prominent mound looms in front of you, partly covered in loose stone. It is worth clambering up, noting on the way two small white flowers that grow on the mound in profusion, right through from April – May to August. Both are national rarities and appear in the 1994 edition of "Scarce Plants in Britain" (published by the Joint Nature Conservancy Council). However, both can be locally very common on old lead workings. The minute one with four petals is alpine penny-cress *(Thlaspi caerulescens)* a pioneer colonist of lead spoil: the slightly larger one, distinctly star-shaped with five petals and narrow leaves, is spring sandwort *(Minuartia verna)* or leadwort. This latter grows neither in sand nor only in spring, so why ...

At the top of the mound – an old spoil heap – is Sir Thomas Shaft, sunk in 1843 in a desperate attempt to return this mining field to a profitable state. Its success was limited. The shaft is fenced off but do be careful as it is very deep.

At this junction stay on the main track, the Nidderdale Way, ignoring the next fork to the left but passing through a gateway ahead, noting the benchmark (a known level for early map surveying) carved into the rock to the right of the gate. **You are now in the thick of the mining area associated**

with Providence and Prosperous Mine. It was actually well-named as it proved to be among the most productive mines in the southern Dales. That was true until cheap foreign imports brought about a serious slump in the 1830s, after which the venture could no longer claim to be prosperous. It all came to a sad end in 1889, the end of an exceptionally long mining story, which is recorded as early as the thirteenth century in the records of Byland Abbey, Ashfold having been a grange for the abbey's estates west of the Nidd.

Ashfold Side gill lies on an extension of the Bycliffe Fault, which extends here from Grassington and Conistone Moors. To its south is the eastern extremity of the North Craven Fault: between the two is a fractured and fragmented shatter belt of cross-faults (see Walk 1). The mineralisation is rich and extensive because of the scale of the faulting.

The size and spatial extent of the spoil heaps give a clear indication of the amount of rock brought from underground. Across the beck is one of the levels or adits driven along the lead veins to extract the ore or to drain the mine, but the most impressive remains are those on the south bank. This heap was Prosperous Smelt Mill built in 1785. The sketch might help you to make some sense of the remains. The filled in shaft with the upstanding ironmongery was Smelt Mill Shaft which held three water wheels at different levels to bring out water from the mine. The uppermost wheel powered the ore dressing plant and bellows between buildings and beck. The mill closed down in 1872.

Prosperous Smelt Mill

Prosperous smelt mill

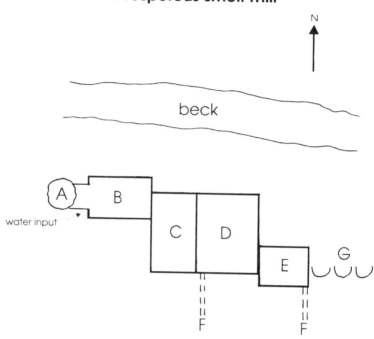

A - engine shaft
B - wheel house
C - bellows room
D - smelter
E - roasting hearth
F - flues to condenser
G - bouse teams or bingsteads

When you have had your fill of Prosperous, cross the beck and clamber up to the main track parallel to the beck. If you wish to extend the walk now, or if you have a particular interest in mining history, turn left and follow the main track upstream to the extensive remains of **Merryfield Mines** including the partially restored boiler house, reminiscent perhaps of Cornish tin mines, and a well-preserved circular stone buddle (which follows a similar principal to modern sewage settling tanks).

Otherwise turn right and head off downstream.

The track parallels the beck, apart from diverting "inland" to negotiate **Rowantree Gill,** where rowans still maintain a sturdy presence. **Pass through the gate** and look down into the valley bottom where there are further mine remains and the low, dark slit indicating the entrance to an adit.

Eventually the former mine track is tarred as you continue through the never-ending caravan sites, past Low Wood and its hive of activity, to the entrance to Spring House. A Nidderdale Way sign directs you to the tarred access to the farm.

Heathfield

If you are pressed for time, head on down the road, past the caravan park office buildings (a restored smelt mill rebuilt in 1855 to treat lead from these parts and from Appletreewick) to the main road at Foster Beck. At the junction a path leaves the road, passes by Brigg House, near the site of a lost bridge, and follows the Nidd back into town.

For the full route, head up to where the drive enters the farm complex, turn right and pass around the complex (keeping all buildings on your left) into an open, gravelled yard. The Ordnance Survey map is confusing here so be careful. Another path does come up through the complex from below, but this is best left alone. At the top end of the open yard, behind the buildings, a field gate allows access onto a clear bridleway that heads gently uphill, alongside the wall. Go past the field barn, straight across the

Foster Beck linen mill and water wheel

middle of the next field, and out of the last field to join the access track
from Highfield. Carry on in the same direction as the track drops down
through Heaton Wood (or bluebell wood in spring) to the hamlet of
Heathfield.

One of the cottages gives an indication of an earlier Heathfield: Grange
Cottage perpetuates the village's rebirth as a grange of Byland Abbey. I
discussed at some length the grange at Kilnsey (see Walk 11) which belonged
to Fountains Abbey. Both these Cistercian foundations played a major part
in the development of the Dales and of the medieval wool trade to the
continent.

There were close links between Nidderdale and Kilnsey. Fountains owned
the manor and the lands of Bewerley, their main grange in the dale. Every
May the sheep that had over-wintered in Nidderdale were driven to the
summer pastures around Darnbrook, Malham Moor and Bordley.

Back to Heathfield ... a grange was a centre for the abbey's estates and the
base for farming operations in a particular area. There may have been a few
monks in residence, but more likely just lay brothers (members of the
monastic community and subject to its rules but exempted from monks'
choir duties) who ran the place, and oblates, those lesser monastic mortals
who did more of the donkey work than the brain work. Like all great religious
houses, Byland had to raise the money to construct its magnificent buildings:
one of the lucrative sources of revenue was wool.

A fulling mill, scouring and beating the wool, utilising a type of clay called
fuller's-earth, is recorded in Heathfield in the sixteenth century and could
well have existed in monastic days.

The only overt sign of recent religious activity in the village is a tiny tin
chapel, opened in 1890 and closed in 1976.

**From the village, turn right past the old chapel along Grange Lane but
only as far as the first house. Turn left here on the drive to Spring Hill, pass
round to the right of the buildings, following the waymarks into and
through a paddock in front of the house to a step-over stile. Two paths
diverge: your's heads steeply downhill past a spreading oak to a second,
similar stile. Drop diagonally down the next field to a third stile at the
bottom next to a gate. The way continues through three small fields to meet
the main valley road at Wath Bridge.**

Wath

The bridge here was originally called New Bridge when first erected in the
sixteenth century to replace the ford that had been there since at least the
early Middle Ages. **A short diversion may appeal to you here, barely one
kilometre in total return length.**

**To make the diversion, turn left immediately over the bridge and follow
the riverside to Gouthwaite Reservoir,** built in 1901 as part of a massive

scheme to harness the Nidd to supply Bradford through an aqueduct 51km long. The whole construction scheme lasted from 1893 to 1936 when Scar House reservoir updale was completed. The purpose of Gouthwaite is to release water into the Nidd when large quantities are extracted from the upper reservoirs. In other words it is there to compensate in times of low flow. Gouthwaite is now a Site of Special Scientific Interest (SSSI), rich in wildfowl and waders especially in winter months. A path runs alongside the east side of the lake though the best bird watching is to be had on the mudflats at the northern end. Leave that for another day, perhaps.

From Wath Bridge it is a mere hundred metres or so to the start of the village which is split into two halves. The first house you come to, on the right, was a station on the railway from Pateley Bridge to the upper dale. You can see the now grassed track clearly. It was built and operated by Bradford Corporation for transferring materials to the dam construction site. but it also ran passenger services up to 1929. When the construction was complete, the line closed.

Next to the Sportsman's Arms is a large building with an inscription telling you it was rebuilt in 1880. It was a textile mill.

The Linen Industry

Wath mill was a flax spinning mill, operated by water power, and successor to a medieval corn mill.

Nidderdale concentrated on woollens until the seventeenth century when linen became more dominant. The linen trade goes way back into the monastic period but on a domestic basis for local consumption until machines were patented to spin flax and hemp, in the 1780s. The industry became prominent in Pateley Bridge and downstream partly because the soft waters of the Nidd, having an origin in sandstone, were especially suitable for soaking the fibres. By 1835 there were 60 mills in the dale, of which Wath was but a minor example. Pateley Bridge alone had nine such mills.

The industry began to contract around 150 years ago in the face of competition from the more accessible and favoured coalfields, and the mills either closed shop or were turned to other uses. In Pateley Bridge, for example, rope making took over.

The Stone Industry

Return to Wath Bridge and follow the Nidderdale Way downstream, across a series of meadows and pastures. For much of the way you will be walking on or next to the old railway. At Low Green House you pass by ornamental ponds where coot are normally in residence, and **south of here the path closely follows the riverbank for the final kilometre into Pateley Bridge.**

As you begin to approach the town, look high up on the valley side to the east. You will see, beyond a wood, a very disturbed area of ground, and the line of an inclined plane rising from the edge of the town. This was connected with Scot Gate Ash stone quarries.

Stone working has been recorded in Fountains Abbey records as early as the thirteenth century and it became one of the three main exports of the dale (alongside lead and cloth) by the late seventeenth century. Its importance is attested by plans, drawn up in 1818-19 by none other than Thomas Telford to link Pateley Bridge by rail to a canal at Knaresborough for despatching stone. This did not materialise, however, until 1862. At one time there were three dozen quarries in the Pateley Bridge area, but Scot Gate Ash was probably the most industrialised and productive. Its sandstone, in quarryman's terms "Delphstone", was used in the construction of such nationally important buildings as London's National Gallery, the Albert Memorial and the museums in South Kensington.

All good things come to an end and the quarry was killed off at the start of the First World War ... by concrete and brick.

As you enter "suburbia" alongside the old mill you leave behind the river and rural solitude for the relative bustle of Pateley Bridge. Mill Lane brings you back to the centre of town and the end of the walk.

Place-name meanings

Ashfold	OE	the enclosure with ash trees
Bale Bank	OE	bales were an early kind of lead smelter
Bewerley	OE	the forest glade with beavers
Bishopside	-	the hill in the fee of the Archbishop of York (as part of his manor of Ripon)
Brandstone Dub	OE	the pool on the steeply flowing stream
Gouthwaite	ON	the clearing with cuckoos
Greenhow	OE/ON	the green hill
Heathfield	OE	the open place with magpies
Nabs	ON	a hillock
Nidd	Brit	the bright river
Pateley Bridge	OE	the bridge near the path junction in the forest clearing
Tenter Hill	ME	the hill where frames were laid out for stretching cloth
Throstle Nest	OE	the small house with ravens
Wath	ON	the ford (originally *Àki's* ford: an OD pers. name)

Glossary of terms used in the text

acid soil	having a low pH owing to high water content within the soil
agister	a forest official responsible for monitoring cattle grazing
algae	primitive organisms akin to simple plants
Angles	One of the Germanic peoples who, with the Saxons and Jutes, migrated to Britain after 400 AD and dominated the country till the Norman Conquest in 1066. The word England derives from Angles
anticline	an upfold of beds of rock
A.O.N.B	Area of Outstanding Natural Beauty: extensive areas of outstanding scenic and ecological value, protected but not promoted as fully as national parks. Introduced first in 1956
bale/bayle	an early, simple form of lead smelter
bed .	a layer or thickness of rock, representing an unbroken period of deposition
bedding plane'	the break or divide between any two beds
bee-bole	a recess in a wall to hold a bee-skep
bee-skep	a small beehive made of straw
bell pit	a shallow mining shaft, the spoil from which makes the rim
boulder clay	a mixture of stones, boulders and clay laid down by glaciers
Campestris	the four animals of the hunting forest reserved for the lord
carbonation	the process by which dissolution occurs in limestone
carbonic acid	a natural constituent of rain, formed by the reaction of water (H_2O) with carbon dioxide (CO_2) to give H_2CO_3
cave-earth	deposits that build up in caves from natural infill and from human waste
chamfer	the bevelled edge of a lintel, mullion or transom added as extra decoration
chapman	an itinerant trader or pedlar
chase	a hunting forest owned by a lord rather than the king
clint	the blocks within a limestone pavement
coffin working	shallow, rectangular lead workings from an early date
conglomerate	a mixture of rock fragments, naturally cemented together
cool	an early stock enclosure, bounded by ditch, bank or stone wall
coping stones	a row of cut stones edging a roof at the gable ends
croft	the garden plot attached to a house or toft
Danegeld	tribute exacted by Danish invaders from the English to leave them in peace
dew pond	an artificial, lined stone depression for holding water for stock
dilation	see pressure release
Direct-Entry plan	a house with no entrance hall : entry is directly into a room
dissolution	the process by which rock reacts with rain water to chemically decompose

Dissolution	the act of closing down all monasteries, between 1536 and 1539
drift	fine material laid down by water from melting glaciers
drove road	a road developed for driving cattle long distances to market
drumlin	an oval hillock of glacial boulder clay
Enclosure Movement	the period, mainly from 1780 to 1820, when great tracts of open land were enclosed and divided up by Act of Parliament
erratic	an isolated boulder brought and deposited directly by ice
Environmentally Sensitive Area	an area whose environment is special enough to warrant extra protection, and in which farmers can claim grants to manage the land in sympathy with nature. Introduced in 1987
fault block	an area of high land, uplifted between faults
fault-line scarp	an escarpment marking the line to which a fault scarp has been eroded back
fault scarp	an escarpment actually along the line of a fault, along which movement may occur
feudalism	a medieval system in which the peasantry owed service to the lord of the manor in return for protection
finial	the returned end of a hood moulding or string course
firebote	the right to collect firewood in a hunting forest
flagstone	a quarryman's term, originally, for thinly bedded sandstone. folding the process by which tectonic pressures cause rock beds to bend and buckle
frost shattering	the process by which extreme temperature changes cause water in the joints of rock to expand and contract repeatedly, thus leading to fracturing along the joints
gangue	mineral ores of no commercial value at the mine in question
geomorphology	the study of the processes that shape and modify the Earth's surface
Girvanella Band	a thin layer of algal concentrations, in nodules, that grew during a pause in the deposition of limestone
grange	an outpost of a monastery, the centre for local operations and farming
Green tourism	tourist developments that are in harmony with the environment
gritstone	a coarse sandstone with large particles of quartz
grough	an eroded gully on a peat moorland
gryke	the vertical cracks separating the blocks on a limestone pavement
hagg	raised sections of peat moorland, between groughs
henge	a circular enclosure, banked and ditched, of Neolithic or Bronze Age date
heriot	the fine payable to the lord on the death of a tenant, usually his best cow
hollin	a holly wood maintained as a source of stock feed
holloway	a sunken track worn by centuries of use
hood moulding	a decorative line of stonework over a window
in-bye	enclosed land near the farmstead
inverse relief	resistant rock, which "originally" may have formed low land,

	is left higher than surrounding land owing to erosion wearing away softer and less resistant rock
joints	vertical cracks within rock beds, opened up by dissolution or pressure release
kame	a large mound composed of drift from glacial meltwater
kettle hole	hollows between kames, which may sometimes be water-filled
kneeler	a decorative feature, like a step, at the lower end of coping stones
liesegang rings	coloured bands within rock beds arising from the effects of water having entered the deposits, oxidising them. The red bands have been more oxidised than the green ones
limestone	rock made up mainly of calcium carbonate derived from either skeletal or algal remains
limestone pavement	an area of limestone, representing one bedding plane, on which the joints have been opened up by dissolution, forming slabs
lintel	the horizontal piece of stone or wood over a door or window
Lobby-Entry plan	a housing style where the front door enters into a hallway
lodge	an outlying house or hamlet in a hunting forest, where forest officials were based
lynchets	narrow terraces that evolved through early medieval farming practices.
manor	the land and villages belonging to the local lord over which his authority held sway
marl	lime-rich mud
meltwater channel	a gully or gorge carved by meltwater from a glacier or ice sheet
midden	a domestic refuse dump within a settlement site
moraine	surface features made up of glacial till
mudstone	rock consisting of hardened clay with bedding thinner than shale
mullion	vertical stone division within a window. It could be wood also
Norse	incomers of Scandinavian origin, either directly or indirectly from Ireland. Popularly known as the Vikings
Occupation Road	a walled lane built through the in-bye to open or higher pastures
packhorse	a pony carrying panniers of trade goods.
pannage	the right to graze pigs in a hunting forest
percolation	the seeping of water through rock
permeable	the ability of rock to allow water to seep through joints and bedding planes
plates	thin sections of the crust, the Earth's outer layer
posser	a vessel used for doing the laundry
prehistory	the time before written records, ie before the Roman invasion for Britain
pressure release	the opening up of joints in rock beds owing to the removal of an overlying weight, such as a glacier
quoins	(pron. koin) dressed corner stones on a building to give a finished look to the edges

Ramsar site   a wetland site, deemed to be of international importance for breeding, passage or wintering birds, named after a convention held in Iran in 1971

sandstone   rock made up of compressed sand grains
sediments   material deposited in layers by water or wind
shakehole   a surface depression caused by the collapse of underlying limestone
shale   rock formed of thin beds of hardened clay
shatter belt   an intensely shattered zone along or between major faults
siltstone   rock made up of fine hardened silt grains
SSSI   Site of Special Scientific Importance : a small or large area, worthy of protection because of its flora, fauna or geology
spandrel   the space between the curve of a window arch and the squared moulding
strata   layers or beds of rock, each one representing a continuous period of uninterrupted deposition
string course   a hood moulding extending over more than one window
sustainable tourism   tourism which manages and promotes the environment without putting at risk its very beauty or attraction
swein   a free man in the medieval period
syncline   a downfold in rock beds

tectonic forces   the processes of folding, faulting and volcanic action that result from internal and heat-derived forces within the Earth
terracettes   minor, linear steps on a slope formed as soil creeps slowly down
till   see boulder clay
toft   the house site attached to a croft
transhumance   the seasonal movement of people and their stock
transom   a horizontal (stone) division within a window
tuff   rock made up of compacted and hardened volcanic ash
turbary   the right to dig and collect peat for home use
turnpike   a maintained road with toll gates at intervals

unconformity   a break in the sequence of rock deposits: one set of rock may have been eroded before the next was laid down, so today one set is "missing"

verderers   a forest officer in charge of the deer and the plants of the forest
vert   everything green in a forest; the right to cut green wood

woodward   a forest official responsible for the timber stock

yeoman   a freeholder farmer, of lesser status than a gentleman

CAFFEINE NIGHTS PUBLISHING

The Periwinkle Perspective

VOL 1

The Giant Step

Paul Eccentric

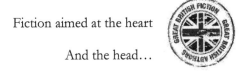

Fiction aimed at the heart

And the head…

Published by Caffeine Nights Publishing 2020

Published in Great Britain by
Caffeine Nights Publishing
4 Eton Close
Walderslade
Chatham
Kent
ME5 9AT

caffeinenights.com
caffeinenightsbooks.com

Also available as an eBook and audiobook

British Library Cataloguing in Publication Data.
A CIP catalogue record for this book is available from the British Library
ISBN: 978-1-913200-10-7

Everything else by
Default, Luck and Accident

To Mike,

This book is dedicated; as always, to Donna; without whom it would still be a series of texts on my Nokia 6500 Classic, where it would have stayed; forever unread, as I can neither type, spell nor use a computer. (Thanks, hon'!)

It's also dedicated to my fellow dyslexics and anyone else who finds it difficult doing things like 'the others'.

Paul Eccentric
November 2020

Adventure forth!

Leicester
Space Centre
Nov
22